THIS IS THE
SILKY TERRIER

by
Betty Young

OUR COVER DOG

CH. ARTARMON'S MAX is recognized by knowledgeable breeders and judges as having the richest possible coloring in Silky Terriers. His lovely reddish tan is in striking contrast to the beautiful deep, bright, very blue color of his body coat. Max also possesses excellent type, good movement, and marvelous temperament. He was selected by Mr. James T. Moss for the author and her husband from one of two litters produced at his Artarmon's Kennels in 1967, and has indeed been a joy to own and show.

FRONTISPIECE:

This portrait by photographer Cecil Davis shows the exquisite head and expression of CH. MAURIE TUPPENCE (by Ch. Wexford Pogo ex Ch. Maurie Lady Rita), owned by Mrs. Edward L. (Elinor) Morrison and bred by R. I. Navarro. Note that her ears are perfect in size, shape, and vertical carriage, adding much to her lovely and typical expression. Because of the Morrisons' love for "Tuppy," they made available for Specialty BOB wins the Ch. Wexford Pogo Memorial Trophy in honor of her sire.

Distributed in the U.S.A. by T.F.H. Publications, Inc., 211 West Sylvania Avenue, P.O. Box 27, Neptune City, N.J. 07753; in England by T.F.H. (Gt. Britain) Ltd., 13 Nutley Lane, Reigate, Surrey; in Canada by Clarke, Irwin & Company, Clarwin House, 791 St. Clair Avenue West, Toronto 10, Ontario; in Southeast Asia by Y. W. Ong, 9 Lorong 36 Geylang, Singapore 14; in Australia and the south Pacific by Pet Imports Pty. Ltd., 38-40 Chard Road, Brookvale 2100, N.S.W., Australia.
The U.S.A. book trade distributors are Crown Publishers, Inc., 419 Park Avenue South, New York, N.Y. 10016.

Published by T.F.H. Publications, Inc. Ltd., The British Crown Colony of Hong Kong.

Table of Contents

Foreword

"What a beautiful Silky!"—those words after about a decade of showing and breeding, especially here in the South and Southwest, are music to our ears, for they mean that the little fellows have "arrived." This is a marked change from the early question, "What a beautiful dog—what is he?"

Those old enough to remember when our men came back from World War II will recall the stories of "those fabulous Aussies" with whom our servicemen seemed to have such an affinity. And how our men loved the song that the Aussies created and shared with them—"Waltzing Matilda" —and how many reunions of American soldiers and sailors were enlivened by rousing renditions of that song! It seems fitting that this same land "Down Under" should have developed the wonderful little creatures known as Silky Terriers, for which Americans have displayed the same sort of affinity—and if there ever was a dog that lived up to the lively, lilting tune of "Waltzing Matilda," it is the Silky Terrier!

My husband, Jim, and I are eternally grateful to those Aussies for these most delightful, captivating, loving little dogs. The late Frank Longmore expressed it so well when he said: "The little dog that fits into our hearts and homes, no matter how large the former nor how small the latter; none fits better of all the breeds than the Australian Silky Terrier." Having lived with and cared for a goodly number of effervescent Silky Terriers, we can say that despite the anxiety and heartaches that all breeders must endure from time to time, our lives just wouldn't be the same without them. We hope that this book will serve in some measure to express our gratitude to the Silkys themselves and to those Silky breeders and others in the dog fancy who so freely extended their help and friendship to us in our early days in the breed. The writing of it has truly been a labor of love.

BETTY YOUNG

Little Rock, Arkansas
July 28, 1969

This fetching Silky puppy was bred by Col. and Mrs. J. J. Pavlas and was seven weeks old when the picture was taken. Size can be estimated by comparison with the Air Force boot in which BONDI'S SOUTHERN FLUFF fits so nicely.

CHAPTER 1

The Nature of the Silky Terrier

Although Silkys are Toy dogs in size and show classification, they are not lap dogs in the usual sense. While each enjoys sitting in your lap to be petted now and then, they are much too lively to stay there for long. Natural watch dogs, their courage is legendary. At times, in fact, they could do with a little more prudence! I well remember the day when I opened a motel door to find a very large Alaskan Malamute standing there—before I could register this and shut the door, a flash of silk went by me, as our Rainy attacked that enormous dog, thinking he was a threat to me. Ten pounds of fury, quick as lightning, he hit the Malamute almost at the jugular vein. Fortunately he was rescued from the consequences of his own bravery!

As one who has owned one or more dogs all my life, I can say that no other breed I have known can equal the Silky in intelligence and responsiveness. These qualities were demonstrated back in the days when we had only four, and one of our bitches was critically ill for nine days. Bonnie had to have absolute quiet, and somehow the other three Silkys understood this. They seemed to tiptoe around the house, and instead of going into the yard barking joyously as usual, they would go out and return in absolute silence. It took only a finger across my lips and a "shh" to convey this to them.

Silkys are fastidious in personal habits, the cleanest dogs I have ever known, and with their non-shedding coats and lack of doggy odor, make ideal house pets. But "sissies" they are not! I recall another day when all four had just been bathed and looked so very beautiful and glamorous as I let them out into the yard. After a few minutes, I looked out just in time to see Rainy break the back of a huge rat with one shake, after which he tossed it over to the three "girls" to finish off. They are said to kill snakes with equal dispatch.

Small but strong and vigorous, they are not subject to the ills of some of the smaller Toy dogs, and most Silky females are good natural whelpers.

Some of their mannerisms delight their owners. "Such a little character" is the theme running through their letters and conversations. Silkys have great facility with their front feet, and use their paws to grasp objects much like a squirrel or cat. They are great jumpers too—we call our little Sissy "the mountain goat" because there is no spot in the house so high that she cannot jump or climb to reach it. Then we have Dolly, who yodels very melodiously when especially pleased—everyone knows that Basenjis yodel but Silkys do not, but Dolly does not believe it. And we have the imperious Bonnie, who serves as spokesman for the group. When they want to go out, she stands in front of one of us and "talks" about it, and if we do not respond quickly, she stamps her foot! Their ears seem to serve as radar antennae, swiveling about to catch every noise; ears also express how they feel, fully up when well and happy, out to the sides when not well or displeased, and laid back in times of great excitement or preceding attack.

All Silky Terriers are very affectionate, but they express their affection in different ways. Our Suzie is a "kisser" and is pleased to clean your ear if permitted. Muffin is a "wagger"—not just her tail but all over. When company comes, she gets a chew stick in her mouth and wags till noticed; if necessary, she will go up and pat lightly on a knee to get attention. At about that point, everyone decides they must have one just like Muffin! Piper is a "nuzzler," and when extremely pleased, he grins at us. And Max is a "bubbler," perhaps the most effervescent of all. He is so happy he has "lead-trained" me to follow him around the show ring that he insists that everyone look at how well I am doing—what a pleasure to show such a little dog!

One of their most appealing characteristics is their zest for living, or as the French put it, their *joie de vivre*. When you have been away, even for a few minutes, they rush to greet you as if to say that they are sad when you are away, and so very happy to have you back. Silky Terriers acquire good manners upon reaching physical maturity, but they remain puppies at heart, never losing the joyous spirit, the gaiety of manner, the captivating personality that they have as puppies. Their "glad to be alive and happy to be with you" outlook will give your own spirits a lift!

CHAPTER 2

History in Australia

The Silky Terrier came to us from Australia, where it was developed around the turn of the century. Although many Australian breeds were found primarily in the bush country, it appears that the Silky was developed principally as a pet and home companion, and found greatest popularity among apartment and cottage dwellers. Nonetheless, they did prove their worth as ratters, and especially in killing the snakes with which Australia abounds. Whether the earliest breeders were attempting to develop a new breed, or whether the Silky Terrier was only a chance by-product, it seems clear that the breed developed mainly from crossing the Australian Terrier with the Yorkshire Terrier. The Australian Terrier, also a native breed in that country, is a harsh-coated, rugged, small terrier of heavier bone and weight than the Silky, while the Yorkshire is a toy breed, smaller over-all and more refined in bone than the Silky, and having a very long silky coat.

For many years, Silkys were called "Sydney Silky Terriers" in honor of the city where they originated, but in 1955 they became known as "Australian Silky Terriers," their official name today in Australia.

Australia is made up of six states, with each state having its own governing body on canine affairs. The largest numbers of the breed were in the states of Victoria and New South Wales, located in the more heavily populated southeastern coastal regions. The city of Sydney is in New South Wales. At the time the Silky Terrier was developed each state had its own standard for the breed. At the present time, the registering body in Victoria is known as the Kennel Control Council, and the Royal Agricultural Society Kennel Control (RASKC) handles breed registrations in New South Wales.

The breed was first exhibited in 1907, and in 1908 the Victorian Silky and Yorkshire Terrier Club was founded and a standard drawn up in Victoria in 1909. Also in the early 1900's, a standard was drawn up in the state of New South Wales. The two standards were similar in most points, both calling for a rather low-set dog with strong, wedge-shaped terrier head, and with front well set under a body which was long in proportion to height. They also agreed that the ears, muzzle, and feet should be free of long hair—in other words, the "clean-pointed" dog most desirable today. There were some differences that are of interest. On weight, for instance, the standard in Victoria provided for two classes, one under 6 pounds, the other 6 pounds and under 12 pounds. The New South Wales standard called for weight over 6 pounds and under 12 pounds. While the Victorian standard permitted ears either "falling to front or pricked," the New South Wales standard permitted only the pricked ear.

The late Frank Longmore of Balwyn, Victoria, was for many years one of the most loved and respected dog fanciers in all Australia—all-breed judge, long-time President of the Kennel Control Council of Victoria, and Editor of their monthly magazine. Before his death in 1969, Mr. Longmore had kindly given me permission to quote his paper written June 15, 1959 and titled *Brief History of the Silky Terrier.* He wrote as follows:

"Something over 100 years ago a harsh-coated sporting terrier, the Australian Terrier, developed from a mixture of short-legged terriers of all shapes and sizes. Further in the background was a small, sandy Scotch terrier, the progenitor of the bulk of this mixed force. A sandy, rough-coated Scotch terrier is not to be confused with the Scottish Terrier of today.

"The first Australian Rough-coated Terrier Club was formed in Victoria in 1889. The Club's first show was held in 1890. During this period and early in the present century, about twenty-five Yorkshire Terriers had been imported into Victoria from England, and probably a similar number into New South Wales. Several of these are recorded as weighing as little as four pounds; however, many of the later importations weighed considerably more.

"Australian Terrier breeders, always on the lookout to improve the color of the blue and tan of their breed, used these bigger, good-colored Yorkshire Terriers with their Australian Terrier bitches and produced heterogeneous mixtures in coat, color, size and shape. Interbreeding with these dogs continued—selection on the one side going to the Australian Terrier and on the other side to the Silky Terrier; a few very small specimens occasionally being exhibited as Yorkshire Terriers. It must be remembered that at this time, as now, the Australian Terrier was a Sporting Terrier, and that both the Silky Terrier and the Yorkshire Terrier were Toys.

"In 1905 an Australian Terrier Club was formed in Melbourne, Victoria; the breed also then being established in Sydney, New South Wales. In 1906 a standard for the Silky Terrier was drawn up in Sydney. A few short years saw the complete absorption of the true Yorkshire Terrier and in its place were left the three different types: the previously established harsh-coated Australian Terrier of from 10 to 14 pounds, some larger and some smaller, a silky-coated Australian Terrier of from 6 to 12 pounds, also both larger and smaller, and many tiny little fellows of less weight, mostly with half-length coats, having in many cases the appearance of poor type Yorkshire Terriers, few, if any, conforming to the requirements of the Yorkshire Terrier standard.

"Shortly prior to 1929, efforts were made to establish correct weight classifications for the three breeds and revised standards were published in 1926. In 1932 the Kennel Control Council of Victoria decided that the three breeds should be protected, and Canine Legislation was introduced prohibiting further cross-breeding. Australian Terriers were then well-established and in intervening years have consistently improved. Progress with the Silky Terrier was not as satisfactory. There were those who desired a silky-coated toy terrier of Australian Terrier type, weighing approximately 8 to 10 pounds, and others who preferred a much smaller dog. As the standard weight of Yorkshire Terriers in Australia was "up to 7 pounds" it became increasingly difficult to discriminate between the small Silky and the so-called Yorkie.

"Weight standardization in both the United States and Australia will, from now on, have a big influence on the improvement of the breed."

It is not entirely clear on what dates changes were made in the early standards of Victoria and New South Wales, but for a number of years prior to 1959, when the present Australian standard was adopted, standards in both states called for weight of 6 to 12 pounds, and both required that ears be pricked, the pendant ears having been mutually agreed upon as undesirable and damaging to the type and character of the breed.

In 1958, a goal long sought by many dedicated fanciers was achieved—the formation of the Australian National Kennel Council. Since the members of the Council were aware that the breed would soon be recognized by the American Kennel Club, one of their first projects was to revise and recommend the adoption of a National Standard for Silky Terriers in Australia. This standard narrowed required weight, the "6 to 12 pounds" being revised to read "The most desirable weights are from 8 to 10 pounds." The National Standard as revised in September 1958 was approved and adopted on March 30, 1959. A copy was rushed to the American Kennel Club in New York, where officials drew up the standard for Silky Terriers in the United States, which was approved on April 14, 1959.

The National Standard for the Australian Silky Terrier, as adopted in March 1959 and still in use today in that country is shown below.

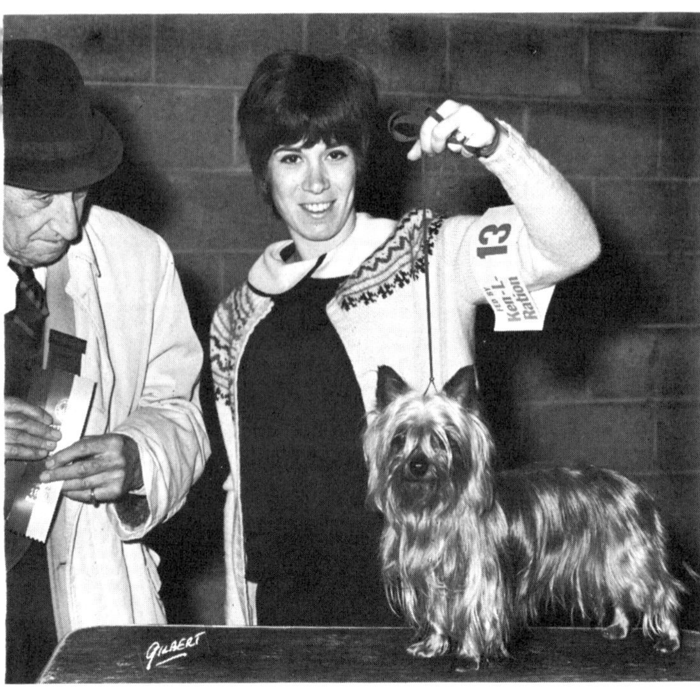

CH. RODLEEN ARUMA KARIE, lovely little imported bitch, is shown finishing under Judge Alva Rosenberg at Harford County (Md.) KC. She was handled by Arlene Byers (pictured) who co-owns her with husband Kenneth F. Byers. Breeders Mr. and Mrs. David Blewett. The Blewetts reside in East Keilor, Victoria, Australia.

AUSTRALIAN SILKY TERRIER

Standard of Points, revised on authority of Australian National Kennel Council, *September* 1958. *Approved and adopted by* Australian National Kennel Council, 30*th March,* 1959.

General Appearance—The dog is compact, moderately low set, of medium length with a refined structure, but of sufficient substance to suggest the ability to hunt and kill domestic rodents. It should display Terrier characteristics, embodying keen alertness, activity and soundness. The parted, straight silky hair presenting a well-groomed appearance.

Head—Of moderate length, slightly shorter in length from the tip of the nose to between the eyes than from the same position to the top rear of the occiput. It must be strong and of Terrier character, being moderately broad between the ears. The skull flat, without fullness between the eyes. Long fall of hair on fore-face and cheeks very objectionable. Fine silky topknot, not falling over the eyes.

Eyes—Should be small, round, dark as possible in color with a keen intelligent expression.

Ears—Should be small, V-shaped, leather fine, high on skull, and pricked, Entirely free from long hair.

Nose—Black.

Mouth—Strong jaws, teeth even and not cramped, the upper incisors fitting closely over the lower, lips tight and clean.

Neck—Medium length, refined and slightly crested. Well covered with long, silky hair.

Body—Should be moderately long in proportion to the dog's height. Level topline, well sprung ribs extending back to strong loins. Chest of moderate depth and breadth.

Forequarters—Shoulders fine and well laid back, fitting with well angulated upper-arms snugly to ribs, elbows turned neither in nor out, forelegs refined round bone, straight and set well under body with no weakness in pasterns.

Hindquarters—Thighs well developed. The stifles should be well turned and the hocks well bent. When viewed from behind the hocks should be well let down and parallel with each other.

Tail—Should be docked and carried erect, but not over-gay.

Feet—Small, well padded, cat-like, closely knit toes with black or very dark toenails.

Coat—Must be fine and glossy and of a silky texture; a length of coat of from 5 inches to 6 inches from behind the ears to the set-on of the tail is desirable. Legs from knees and hocks to feet free from long hair.

Color—Blue and tan or gray-blue and tan, the richer of these colors the better. Blue on tail to be very dark. The distribution of the blue and tan is as follows: Silver-blue topknot desirable, tan around the base of the ears, muzzle and on side of cheeks, blue from the base of skull to tip of tail running down the forelegs to near the knees and down the thighs to the hocks, tan line showing down the stifles and from the knees and hocks to the toes and around the vent.

Weight—The most desirable weights are from 8 to 10 pounds.

Height—Approximately 9 inches at the withers.

Movement—The movement should be free and straightforward without slackness at shoulders or elbows. There should be no turning of feet or pasterns. The hindquarters should have strong propelling power with ample flexibility at stifles and hocks. Viewed from behind the movement should be neither too close nor too wide.

Serious Defects—Nose: any color other than black. Coat: curly, woolly, wavy, short or harsh. Color: any color other than blue and tan or gray-blue and tan (puppies excepted). Mouth undershot or overshot. Weight under or over-weight. White toenails. Ewe neck. Weediness, coarseness, unsoundness. The blue body coat must be free from tan or bronze and the tan markings free from smut or dark shadings.

CHAPTER 3

History in the United States

As far as is known, Mrs. G. E. Thomas of San Diego, California, owned the first Silky Terriers to be imported into the United States. Her two Silkys, Beaconsfield Smart Tone and Dream Girl, were pictured in a dog feature of the *National Geographic Magazine* in February 1936. The caption under this picture read: "Australian Silky Terriers are rare in the United States. Smart Tone is long-haired and silvery gray, while Dream Girl is shorter-haired and colored black and tan, with just a little gray. He weighs but eight pounds and she even less. They were brought to this country by Mrs. G. E. Thomas of Washington, D.C., who says the breed contains some Skye Terrier blood. Recently this pair became proud parents and the single puppy is long-haired like his daddy." Mrs. Thomas also reported that the male was whelped July 12, 1933. His dam's line, Harrietville, still appears behind some U.S. Silkys. A puppy from the pair, Smart Tone of Hastings the Second, was owned by Mrs. George Walker of Manhasset, New York, for 15 years. In 1963 both Mrs. Thomas and Mrs. Walker still owned Silky Terriers, and had been members of the breed club since 1956.

As we might all imagine, in those days any Silky owner was delighted to find another Silky owner, and each must certainly have given some thought to having a national club for the breed some day. In the Summer and Fall of 1954, several Silky owners in the San Francisco Bay area learned of one another's interest in the breed, and they began to put their lists of names of Silky owners together with a view to developing a breed club. This early group included Mrs. Margarett Citrino, Mrs. Florence Dahlstrom, Mr. Thomas J. Fromm, Mr. Robert E. Garrett, and Mr. Howard A. Jensen. These founders of the Club sent out letters of introduction and application blanks to other Silky owners, with each assuming the title

"Board Representative" in sending them. The first official meeting of the Club, then called the "Sydney Silky Terrier Club of America," was held on March 25, 1955, at the home of the Roland Stegemans, Richmond, California. Officers elected were: Mrs. Margaret Citrino, President; Mrs. Betty Stegeman, Vice-President; Howard A. Jensen, Corresponding Secretary; Robert E. Garrett, Recording Secretary; Mrs. Florence Dahlstrom, Treasurer; T. J. Fromm, Librarian-Historian; and Roland Stegeman, Parliamentarian. Florence Dahlstrom held office as Treasurer of the Club from that date through 1966, a total of 12 years, the only officer to hold office continuously from the time the Club was founded. In July 1955, the members voted that the Club should be known as the "Silky Terrier Club of America," since it was felt that the American Kennel Club preferred the simpler designation of the breed as "Silky Terrier."

Charter Members who have continued their membership up to the present are:

Miss Phyllis Buchanan (Buchrich Kennels), Denver, Colorado.
Mrs. Florence Dahlstrom (Monte Mar Kennels), Sausalito, California.
Howard A. Jensen (D'Under Kennels), San Francisco, California.
Hugh E. Paine, New York, N.Y.
Mrs. Robert Seligman (Rogo Kennels), Crescent City, California.
Mrs. Merle E. Smith (Redway Kennels), Mill Valley, California.
Mr. and Mrs. Geoffrey H. Sutcliffe (Kanimbla Kennels), Charlotte, North Carolina.
Mrs. Elsa Vinisko (Elmike's Kennels), Middletown, New York.

A very appealing puppy picture of a Silky named Redway Blue Boy, taken by the famous photographer, Walter Chandoha, appeared November 28, 1954 on the cover of *This Week* magazine, a nationally syndicated newspaper supplement. It created such widespread interest in the breed that Mrs. M. E. Smith, breeder-owner of the puppy, and the publisher of the supplement were deluged with letters, telegrams, and long distance telephone calls. Partly as a result of this favorable publicity, and partly resulting from Silky Terriers being shown in Miscellaneous classes at dog shows, the Club had 34 members by May 1955.

In September 1955, the first American "Silky Symposium" was held at the home of Mr. and Mrs. R. J. Cooley in southern California, with almost 40 Silkys present, of which 13 had come from northern California. The late Fred David, Australian all-breed judge, discussed the history of the breed and the standard. At this informal showing, Mr. David chose Peggy Smith's Wexford Pogo as the most representative specimen. A summation of Mr. David's remarks was included in a booklet prepared in 1955 by Howard Jensen. (This booklet is now known simply as "the little blue brochure," and the author is grateful to Mrs. M. E. Smith for the

This is the picture which appeared on the cover of *This Week*, Sunday newspaper supplement, on November 28, 1954, and which created such widespread interest in the breed that it became a vital part of breed history. The photo was taken by the famous photographer, Walter Chandoha, and the puppy is REDWAY BLUE BOY, bred by Mrs. Merle E. Smith.

The seven puppies pictured were bred by Mrs. Dorothy Vanderhoof and were the last litter sired by Mrs. Merle E. Smith's Ch. Wexford Pogo. Few Silky litters contain as many as seven puppies, and these show more uniform type than is usually seen in a litter. Their dam is Canberra Cupie.

loan of her copy, and to Howard A. Jensen for sending a complete photocopy for permanent reference.) It must be remembered that this was in 1955, some 14 years before the writing of this book. In view of the lapse of time, it is surprising how appropriate many of Mr. David's comments are today. Some of his remarks are quoted for your interest.

"The head structure resembles the Australian Terrier more than the Yorkshire, being wedge-shaped with a terrier nose, free of long hair, whereas the Yorkshire has a profuse fall from the topknot and a long moustache from the muzzle. The topknot should be the lightest spot on the dog. The tan on the face must be a clear tan with no smutty marks, with the following exception. Although not stated in the Standard, there should be a blue smudge in front of the base of the ear and behind the corner of the eye (temple). The eyes should be dark in color and oval shaped for greater expression and character. The stop is the junction between the eyes and the top of skull and should not be absolutely flat or abrupt but be more a gradual slant. Teeth must be well aligned and strong and gums healthy.

"The ears should be carried high on skull, look like inverted 'V's' without long hair. Long hair may be plucked for showing in the ring by using the thumb and index finger to pull it out painlessly.

"The tail should be docked at the end of the tan on the underside. The adult dog carries his tail at a 90-degree angle or a little less, but it should not slant toward the head (over-gay).

"In viewing the profile, a Silky's forelegs should be set back from his chest line. He should walk on points (toes). Long nails will cause him to walk on pasterns (heels) and he will become splayfooted, a spreading of the feet. In viewing the fore-legs from the front, they should be straight and not too close together. A well-bent stifle (hind leg) means that the dog's rear legs, when standing, will be slightly slanted toward the back which results in show stance. Nails should be dark. There should be no long hair on the legs from the knees and hocks to feet."

Mr. David then expressed his personal preference for a silver blue body coat, as he felt it distinguished them from the Yorkshire which had steel blue coat, and the Australian Terrier, which he described as having even darker blue than the Yorkie. He continued: "The coat must be silky in texture, not harsh, wavy, or woolly, and is parted down the middle of the topline from the top of the head to the base of tail for show grooming. The richer the tan is in color, the better.

"A weight of 8 to 10 pounds is considered best, being average. Height at shoulder or topline should be at 10 inches. The topline should be straight, with a slight arch over the loins."

Mr. David's presence in this country resulted in columns about the breed in the California-based magazines, *Kennel Review* and *Western Kennel World*.

(Author's Note: The persons listed as breed pioneers in the paragraphs to follow are those who showed their Silky Terriers in the very early years, who showed consistently, and who have remained active in the breed. There were others who showed occasionally or who came into the breed shortly before recognition, many of whom are now devoted to the breed, but space would not permit our listing each and every Miscellaneous class entry.)

All Silky Terrier owners in this country owe a great debt to those early fanciers who showed their Silkys in Miscellaneous classes at dog shows. Without the dedication of these people, that lovable little dog beside you might never have been, and certainly none of us would have champions, since the A.K.C. would not have recognized our breed. In the Northern California area, we had a number of breed pioneers.

Howard Jensen of San Francisco began his D'Under Silky Terrier Kennels with Redway Lord Teasel, San Gate Lady Crumpets, and Waratah Winsome Winner, the latter having been pictured on the cover of *Dog World* magazine on the occasion of A.K.C. breed recognition. Mr. Jensen served from 1955 through 1959 as Corresponding Secretary and Newsletter Editor of STCA, and later again served as Secretary and as a Director. He showed his Silkys early and consistently in Miscellaneous and is still an enthusiastic supporter and breeder of Silky Terriers.

Henrietta and James T. Moss founded their breeding program with the imports, Prairie Joie and Janricka Mimi—both were among the early champions. When Mr. Moss retired from his work with a steamship company in 1962, they established their Artarmon's Kennels at Santa Rosa, California, about 65 miles north of San Francisco. They were among the first Miscellaneous class exhibitors, and both served as STCA Officers at one time or another. They still breed Silky Terriers and are among our most faithful breed supporters.

Mr. Howard Jensen of San Francisco is pictured at the first STCA Sanctioned Match in 1960, as he received a desk pen set from the Club in appreciation for his services for five years as Secretary and Newsletter Editor. The presentation was made by Mrs. Merle E. Smith, then President of the Club.

Florence Dahlstrom (Mrs. Ture Dahlstrom), mentioned earlier as STCA Treasurer for 12 years, acquired her first Silky Terrier, Chota Choy ("Gimlet)" in 1950, and supported the breed by showing regularly in Miscellaneous in the earliest days. Her breeding prefix is Monte Mar.

Betty Britt and Laurel Gilbertson, both of San Francisco, acquired their first co-owned Silky, Rojo Mister Winks, in 1956. They showed him in Miscellaneous and later acquired the import, Prairie Skipper, that later went on to become a Champion as well. Both have served the Club and breed long and faithfully—Miss Britt was Corresponding Secretary for five years, and Miss Gilbertson was President for two years, with both also serving in other capacities as well. Their breeding prefix is Kealoha.

Peggy Smith (Mrs. Merle E. Smith), now of Mill Valley, California, showed her Wexford Pogo in Miscellaneous in the early days, as well as her first female, Brenhill Splinters, imported in 1951. Pogo went on to become a Champion at the age of 7½ shortly after breed recognition, and with Splinters, founded the Redway line of Silky Terriers. Pogo became the sire of 14 Champions, and Splinters the dam of 4 Champions. A color picture of Pogo at the age of 2 years graced the cover of the first Silky book, "How to Raise and Train a Silky Terrier," by Betty Young. Mrs. Smith served as President and Recording Secretary of STCA for five years, and has been Recording or Corresponding Secretary for a number of terms since then.

In Southern California, Lucille Preston of Los Angeles was the only exhibitor in Miscellaneous in the very early days. She was also responsible for the formation of the Silky Terrier Club of Southern California; the

MAD MANOR TINY TIM (by Redway Senor Willie ex Rofter Susie) was the foundation stud for the Alcarla Kennels of Miss Suzanne J. Link of New Orleans, the second Silky breeder in the South. He was a very fine Silky Terrier, but was shown only a few times at point shows before his death in the early '60's.

KANIMBLA SIR POTCH, shown here as a five-month old puppy (that one tipped ear did go up a little later) born in 1951. He was one of the early homebred studs of the KANIMBLA KENNELS of Mr. & Mrs. Geoffrey H. Sutcliffe of Charlotte, N.C., who have been breeding Silky Terriers since 1948. Potch was the sire of one champion and grandsire of a large number of champions. He was by the import Wee Waa Aussie ex Kanimbla Tinker.

first meeting was at her home in 1957. Mrs. Preston was the first President of the Club and later Secretary-Treasurer. This Club had much to do with popularizing the breed in Southern California. Lucille and husband Julian Preston now live in Prescott, Arizona, where they still breed Silky Terriers bearing the prefix Fair Dinkum.

The first kennel established in this country which bred Silky Terriers exclusively was the Kanimbla Kennels founded in 1948 by Martha and Geoffrey Sutcliffe in Charlotte, North Carolina. During World War II, Mr. Sutcliffe was a prisoner of war in Shanghai, and while Mrs. Sutcliffe awaited his release in Australia, she learned to know and love the Australian Silky Terrier. They brought back with them the two males, Wee Waa Aussie and Kelso Dinkum, and a bitch, Glenbrae Sally. These Silkys were from the Australian lines Deandale, Glen Ayre, Sparking, and Sunclad. They are still breeding Silky Terriers at this writing.

CH. PRAIRIE SKIPPER (Smithfield Max ex Waswell Vixen) was imported, owned, and handled to his championship by Betty Britt and Laurel Gilbertson, early fanciers and Club workers in the San Francisco Bay area. A color snapshot of this Silky taken when he was nine years old reveals that even at that age, he still had beautiful, very rich blue and tan coloration. He was bred by T. Ridsdale.

CHOTA CHOY was the first Silky for Florence Dahlstrom (Mrs. Ture Dahlstrom), one of the founders of STCA. She showed him consistently in Miscellaneous classes. It is of interest that his registration number was Hong Kong Kennel Club 2191.

Mrs. Lucille Preston was the pioneer breeder-exhibitor in the Southern California area, having founded the STC of Southern California in 1957 which did much to advance the breed in that area. Few who were active in the 60's will ever forget the attractive Lucille as she appeared on the Art Linkletter show in a nationwide broadcast, holding two Silkys in her arms. She and husband Julian now live in Prescott, Arizona. Mrs. Preston is shown here with her FAIR DINKUM BRIGIT (by her foundation stud, Ch. Koolamina Aussie, ex her first bitch, Elysium Matilda).

REDWAY TINY TIM (Ch. Wexford Pogo ex Brenhill Splinters) is pictured winning Best in Miscellaneous at Oakland KC (California) in 1956. The judge was H. P. Saunders, owner-handler is Marion Bishop. He died in 1958 when only five years old, before Silkys could be shown in regular classes at shows.

Miss Nettie H. Simmons, our breed pioneer in New England, is pictured being interviewed in November 1962 by Mr. Jay Kroll of Television Station W.J.A.R. about her Silky Terriers. She has her Clavons Blue Shadow in her arms. Many breed enthusiasts had such interviews on their local stations in order to further popularize Silky Terriers.

KANIMBLA LADY PENELOPE (left), Silky Terrier foundation bitch for Miss Nettie Simmons' CLAVONS KENNELS (Reg.) and her daughter, CLAVONS BLUE SHADOW. Lady Penelope was by Kanimbla Sir Potch ex Kanimbla Fatima, and became the dam of two champions, including the author's first Silky, Ch. Clavons Blue Rain.

The author is pictured with her Ch. Clavons Blue Rain. She holds the ancient portable typewriter on which she typed the manuscript for the first exclusively Silky Terrier book in the world, published by T.F.H. in 1963.

Besides the Sutcliffes' Kanimbla Kennels, the first Silky breeder in the South was Suzanne J. Link of New Orleans, who bred under the name Alcarlou, later changed to Alcarla. She had obtained her first Silky from the Sutcliffes, Kanimbla Lady Jennifer, and another from Peggy Smith, Mad Manor Tiny Tim. The author was fortunate to obtain her first Silky bitch from Suzanne as a 9-week old puppy destined to become Ch. Alcarlou Lady Suzanne, having been named for her breeder.

In New England and the Northeast, Nettie Simmons of Newport, Rhode Island, was the first to exhibit a Silky in Miscellaneous. Her Clavons Kennels had been established in Pugs for many years. Her first Silky also came from the Sutcliffes, Kanimbla Lady Penelope, dam of the author's first Silky Terrier, Ch. Clavons Blue Rain. Miss Simmons recalled that she showed in Miscellaneous alone for "what seemed like a very long time."

Elsa Vinisko of Middletown, New York, showed her Redway Lord Michael in Miscellaneous, and he went on to become Ch. Redway Lord Michael, the first American-bred champion on the East Coast. He also became one of the top producers, with 11 Champions. Michael also sired the two lovely bitches, Ch. Elmike's Lady Elsa and Ch. Elmike's Lady Elfin Queen, who have distinguished themselves as the only Best-Brace-in-Show winners in the breed, with several other Brace Group placings.

Also in the Northeast, Mrs. N. Clarkson Earl, Jr., and the late Colonel Earl of Ridgefield, Connecticut, were among the breed pioneers. Their Iradell Kennels had been established many years before and were well known for their top-winning Skye Terriers. Their import, Ch. Milan Chips of Iradell, was the very first Silky Terrier to gain his U.S. championship, and was then campaigned to a splendid record of wins. He was also the first Silky to win a Toy Group, which he accomplished twice, along with a large number of other Group placements. The Earls also donated the Iradell Trophy from 1959 onward, presented to the Silky scoring the largest number of points based on breed wins. After Colonel Earl's death early in 1969, the Silky Terrier Club of America voted to present future Iradell Trophies in his memory.

Phyllis Buchanan and Suzanne Richardson, then of Upper Darby, Pennsylvania, began showing in 1955. Their first Silky was Redway Beau Brummell, who went on to become one of the early U.S. Champions and also sired 4 champions. Their first bitch, Mad Manor Blue Breeze, also became a Champion and was reported to be a very fine Silky. They used the prefix of Buchrich. These ladies moved to Denver several years ago with their Silkys, and Miss Richardson passed away there in 1968.

In the Midwest, Beverly and Bill Lehnig of Jeffersonville, Indiana, were the first to show Silky Terriers in Miscellaneous, having first shown

CH. MILAN CHIPS OF IRADELL, the first Silky Terrier to become a champion in the U.S., had a very fine record of wins. Shown only 88 times, he had 85 BOB wins, with 39 Toy Group placings including two firsts in Group. He was top-winning Silky in Phillips System in 1960 and 1961. Bred by A. G. V. Miles in Australia, he was imported by the Iradell Kennels of the late Colonel N. Clarkson Earl, Jr., and Mrs. Earl.

in 1956. Mrs. Lehnig recalls that in those days, many of the Midwestern shows did not offer Miscellaneous classes, so that the early fanciers had to request that the shows offer these classes. The Lehnigs' first Silky was D'Under Count Chequers, who became the sire of 4 champions. Their first bitch was the imported Ch. Aldoon Countess Candy; she went on to gain the enviable honor of the first Best of Breed win for a Silky at the Westminster Kennel Club show in 1960. Candy was the Iradell Trophy winner for breed wins in 1960, and her daughter, bred by the Lehnigs, Ch. Rebel Taffeta Ruffles, carried on to become Iradell Trophy winner in 1961. Candy also became a top producer, with 4 champions. Many present-day Champions carry the Lehnigs' Rebel prefix.

Mildred Pequignot of Fort Wayne, Indiana, was a pioneer Midwestern exhibitor. Her Austral Kennels began with Sarszegi Buttons, who became a Champion and also sire of 5 champions. Mildred's first bitch was Rebel Countess Myd, a daughter of the Lehnigs' Candy; she too became a Champion and dam of 2 champions. These two gave Mildred her first homebred Champion, Austral Prince Kirby, who had a fine record of wins,

Mildred Pequignot, pioneer breeder of Fort Wayne, Indiana is shown with the foundation pair for her Austral Kennels. On the right is CH. SARSZEGI BUTTONS, who also became a Top Producer. He was bred by Erica Baan. On the left is the future CH. REBEL COUNTESS MYD, then 8 months of age. She is by D'Under Count Chequers ex Ch. Aldoon Countess Candy and was bred by Mr. and Mrs. William Lehnig.

including two Toy Group firsts and numerous placings. Kirby is the sire of 10 Champions and winner of the Iradell Trophy in 1963 and 1964.

Also in the Midwest were Marjorie and Ralph G. Edwards (now of New Jersey), who began showing in Miscellaneous in 1957. Their home-bred Champion Mara's Silver Bob had one of the early Group placings (May 1960), handled by Mrs. Edwards. They had obtained their first Silky Terrier in 1956, and are still breed club members.

In reminiscing about those early days, Beverly Lehnig recalled the long distances they had to drive to win a ribbon for that Silky—no points, no BOB wins, with the sexes sometimes divided, sometimes not, and some people in recognized breeds telling them that Silkys would never be recognized, and finds it amazing that all of them "had so much heart."

Mr. and Mrs. Ralph G. Edwards were among our pioneer breeders in the Midwest area, having obtained their first Silky in September 1956. Mrs. Edwards is shown with her foundation bitch, ELLA PRINCESS VICTORIA, with two of her puppies, both of which became champions. On the left is the future CH. MARA'S TINY TUPPENCE, and on the right the future CH. MARA'S SILVER BOB. Their sire was the Lehnigs' D'Under Count Chequers.

I hope that all of us who love Silky Terriers, and who are so deeply involved with them now, will think of our early pioneers and realize how much they did for the breed. It should make all of us appreciate our dogs and our enjoyment of shows and our other Silky activities just a little bit more!

CH. ALDOON COUNTESS CANDY (by Glenboig Tim ex Aldoon Lassie) was the foundation bitch for the Rebel Kennels of Mr. and Mrs. William Lehnig. An import, she was bred by Mrs. J. Milne, and is shown wearing the rosette and ribbon awarded for her BOB win at The Westminster Kennel Club show in 1960, the first Westminster at which Silkys were able to compete in the regular classes.

And then came the day when each Silky owner was asked to fill out the green application forms for registration with the American Kennel Club. They were returned by the owners to the Silky Terrier Club of America, where Peggy Smith took on the mammoth task of checking the pedigrees, copying some of them once, some twice (for STCA as well as AKC records). Mrs. Smith recalled to the author that in those days and weeks, which must have seemed like years, that it took to do the work, she sometimes wondered which would happen first—would she get them all done, or have a nervous breakdown, or would husband Merle leave home? Fortunately for all of us, she did get them all done first, with 519 individual pedigrees sent initially to the AKC. How proud Mrs. Smith must have felt when they were acknowledged with compliments on their neatness and comprehensiveness.

From the April 1959 STCA Newsletter, in the colorful style of Howard Jensen, who was then Editor. With submission of these applications, "The first stage of dogdom's rocket, SILKY TERRIER, has successfully

Silky Terrier Club of America "Mascot." This is the picture used on the national breed club literature. Note the correctly V-shaped, small, erect ears, the keen expression of the eyes, the so-called "clean points" (no long hair on ears, face, feet, and lower legs). He also shows the ideal body conformation, with excellent topline, front legs well set under the body, rear legs moderately angulated, tail carriage erect, compact cat-like feet, as well as the characteristic breed gesture of raising one front foot while in show stance. (Of great importance, this photograph also illustrates correct coat length.)

fired and the rocket has begun its journey toward recognition as the 115th breed on the AKC roster. Happy? We are!," and from the May 1959 Newsletter: "WE'RE IN ORBIT!!" The account went on to say that the STCA members had received the registration certificates in April and that AKC had chosen "Silky Terrier" for the breed name, presumably to avoid confusion with the Australian Terrier, and that they would be in the Toy Group. Mr. Jensen also noted that the AKC Board of Directors had designated persons eligible to judge all breeds and those eligible to judge all Toy breeds as approved judges for Silky Terriers.

Approval was received from the American Kennel Club for the Silky Club's first sanctioned match to be held on August 13, 1960. Mrs. C. Bede Maxwell was selected as judge. The second sanctioned match was

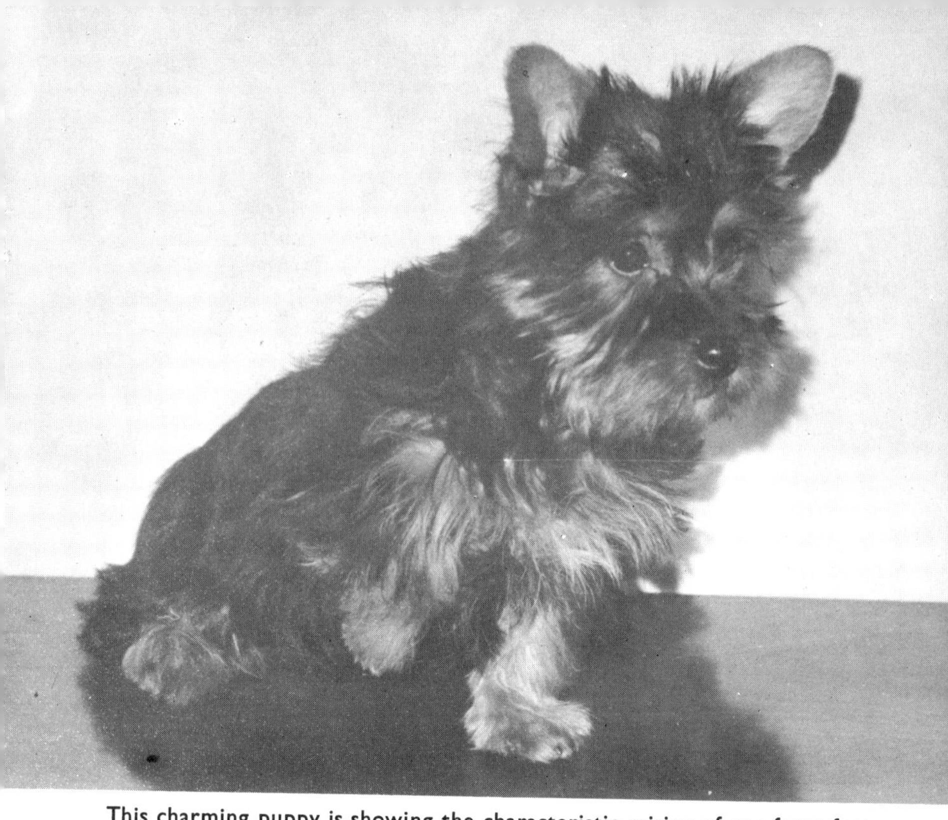

This charming puppy is showing the characteristic raising of one front foot even while sitting down! She was bred by Lester B. and Janet B. Cohen, and is now owned by Dr. and Mrs. Gordon Borkat of Alaska. Her name is SULE SKERRY CAT BALLOU; sire and dam are Ch. Silkallure Falstaff and Koonoona Pinafore.

held on April 23, 1961, with Thomas Witcher as judge. The first STCA Specialty was held with the San Mateo (Calif.) Kennel Club show on November 19, 1961, with Mrs. Virginia Keckler as judge. After that date, Specialty shows were held annually through 1967. The Board of Directors of the Club decided in 1967 that two Specialties would be held each year, one to be East of the Rocky Mountains and one to be West of the Rocky Mountains. Since the larger percentage of the breed population had been in California, it was thought that annual Specialties in the Eastern two-thirds of the country would help promote interest in the breed in that area.

Early in 1960, the first winner of the Iradell Trophy was announced by Mrs. Earl, this being for the latter portion of 1959 when Silkys could be shown at point shows. The winner was Ch. Coolaroo Sir Winston, owned by Susan and Fred Stern of Sepulveda, California. They initiated the

Silkallure prefix which is used by them and by others breeding from their stock. Sir Winston went on to become sire of the largest number of U.S. Champions, with 20 to his credit.

In 1961 a Silky Terrier column was added to the magazine *Pure-Bred Dogs—American Kennel Gazette.* The Board of Directors of STCA selected Beverly Lehnig to serve as columnist. She has done an excellent job with the column since the first in June 1961, and still serves in that capacity at this writing.

Popular Dogs magazine began a Silky Terrier column in 1962; the first column was written by Howard Jensen and appeared in October. Since then I have been the columnist.

CH. SILKALLURE FALSTAFF (Ch. Coolaroo Sir Winston ex Ch. Bowenvale Margie) was bred by Fred and Susan Stern and was the foundation stud for the Sule Skerry breeding of Lester B. and Janet B. Cohen.

In 1962, the STCA passed another milestone, having been incorporated in November of that year. In 1966, a goal long sought after was achieved as the American Kennel Club granted status as a member club to the Silky Terrier Club of America, Inc.

My book, *How To Raise and Train a Silky Terrier*, published in 1963 by T.F.H. Publications, Inc., was the first one on this breed. Although it is a small book (64 pages), it contains pictures of a great many of the 59 Silky Terriers which were at that time Champions in this country. It was one of the first of a series of books on rare breeds scheduled and later published by T.F.H. Publications.

Soon thereafter, in January 1964, *The Australian Terrier and the Australian Silky Terrier*, by the well-known Australian all-breed judge W. A. (Fred) Wheatland was published in Australia by Swales & Co. Pty. Ltd. This is also a small book, but has been valuable to both breeders and judges, written as it was from the judge's viewpoint. Some Silky Terrier breeders in this country have attempted to use Mr. Wheatland's book in an effort to justify over-size in the breed, since he emphasized that Silkys should not be frail, weedy creatures, which were at that time a problem in the show ring in Australia. Mr. Wheatland was in this country in 1966, at which time it was our pleasure to have him as a house guest, and he told the author a number of times that he had no intention of advocating over-size in the breed. But subsequently, he has written that he felt that an absolute top weight of 10 pounds should be put on the breed, and also the requirement that a 9-inch-tall Silky should weigh 9 pounds, the 10-inch Silky 10 pounds, and so on. Those of us who judge and also write do stress those points in which the breed seems weakest at the time, because those weak points threaten the welfare of the breed as a whole.

The Silky Terrier Club of Southern California which was mentioned earlier was the first area club for the breed. With the guidance of Lucille Preston, their first President, they became a very active and dedicated group. Mrs. Preston later became Secretary-Treasurer, and she mentions other early Presidents of this group as Dorothy Hicks and Dick LaBarre. Dorothy Hicks came into the breed very soon after recognition; her Cypress Kennels in Cypress, California, are well known, and it was there that all of the "action shots" were taken by a T.F.H. photographer to be used in the book, *How to Raise and Train a Silky Terrier*. Dick LaBarre and his wife, Ruth, acquired their first Silky in 1961 and have been dedicated workers in breed promotion in the Southern California area. As sometimes happens in any group, some differences of opinion arose within the Club late in 1965, with the result that one or two members withdrew and formed another Club in the area known as the Golden West Silky Terrier Club. Fred Stern was listed as founder of this latter group. For a

CH. REBEL KISSIN' ANGEL (by Ch. Redway Buster ex Rebel April Angel) is pictured on her way to her title, winning WB, BOW for five points at Chicago International show of 1966 under the noted Australian judge and author, Mr. W. A. (Fred) Wheatland. She was bred and is owned by Mrs. William (Beverly) Lehnig, who handles her. Mrs. Lehnig is herself licensed to judge Silky Terriers and several other Toy breeds.

time, there was considerable rivalry between the two groups, with both hoping to be recognized by the A.K.C. as the official area club. Early in 1968, after much work by members of both groups, the Clubs put aside their differences and merged to become one Club. This group is called the City of Los Angeles Silky Terrier Club, or C.O.A.S.T. for short. Mrs. Jan Cohen served as the first President of the new group.

The Silky Terrier Club of Central California was formed in March 1966 by Howard Jensen, one of the original founders of S.T.C.A., and Paul G. Hefner, who joined Mr. Jensen and his late father as a partner in D'Under Kennels in March of 1960.

CH. GARONA PRINCESS SUZANNE (by Aus. and Am. Ch. Koonoona Bo Bo ex Garona Blue Belle) is shown finishing for her title at the age of one year. She is owner-handled by Phyllis Cook of Hubertus, who was the founder of the Greater Milwaukee Silky Terrier Club. Phyllis is an enthusiastic supporter of the breed and has held numerous offices in the Wisconsin area club. Her import, Suzanne, was bred by Mrs. Helen Thornton, and was the first resident Silky Ch. in Wisconsin.

Early in 1968, through the efforts of Phyllis Cook of Hubertus, Wisconsin, another area Club was formed. The first name for the group was the Wis-Ill-Ind Silky Terrier Club, but it has been renamed the Greater Milwaukee Silky Terrier Club. This new Club is blessed with a number of very enthusiastic members, not the least of whom is Phyllis Cook, and they are making every effort toward breed promotion in their area. Information received from Diane and Richard Nachman of Alexandria, Virginia, reveals that the National Capital Silky Terrier Club with members from the Washington, D.C. area was formed at a meeting in their home on July 17, 1969.

The growth in popularity of the Silky Terrier in this country has been phenomenal. In 1960, the first year after A.K.C. recognition, 184 Silkys were registered. In 1968, the total for the year was 2,064. The rate of increase over the past three years has ranged from 30 to 35 per cent annually. With the undeniable, and perhaps unequalled, charm of the Silky Terrier, and the dedication of their fanciers, we can expect their popularity to continue to grow throughout the country.

CHAPTER 4

U.S. Breed Standard

The Silky Terrier is a lightly built, moderately low-set toy dog of pronounced terrier character and spirited action.

Head—The head is strong, wedge-shaped and moderately long. The skull is a trifle longer than the muzzle, in proportion about three-fifths for the skull, two-fifths for the muzzle.

Skull—Flat, and not too wide between the ears.

Stop—Shallow.

Ears—Small, V-shaped and pricked. They are set high and carried erect without any tendency to flare obliquely off the skull.

Eyes—Small, dark in color and piercingly keen in expression. Light eyes are a fault.

Teeth—Strong and well aligned. Scissors bite. A bite markedly undershot or overshot is a serious fault.

Nose—The nose is black.

Neck and Shoulders—The neck fits gracefully into sloping shoulders. It is medium long, fine and to some degree crested along its top line.

Body—Low-set, about one-fifth longer than the dog's height at the withers. A too short body is a fault. The back line is straight, with a just perceptible rounding over the loins. Brisket medium wide, and deep enough to extend down to the elbows.

Tail—The tail is set high and carried erect or semi-erect but not over gay. It is docked and well coated but devoid of plume.

Forequarters—Well laid back shoulders, together with good angulation at the upper arm, set the forelegs nicely under the body. Forelegs are strong, straight and rather fine boned.

Hindquarters—Thighs well muscled and strong, but not so developed as to appear heavy. Legs moderately angulated at stifles and hocks, with the hocks low and equidistant from the hock joints to the ground.

Feet—Small, cat-like, round, compact. Pads are thick and springy while the nails are strong and dark colored. White or flesh colored nails are a fault. The feet point straight ahead, with no turning in or out. Dewclaws, if any, are removed.

Coat—Flat, in texture fine, glossy, silky; on matured specimens the desired length of coat from behind the ears to the set-on of the tail is from five to six inches. On the top of the head the hair is so profuse as to form a topknot, but long hair on face and ears is objectionable. Legs from knee and hock joints to feet should be free from long hair. The hair is parted on the head and down over the back to the root of the tail.

Color—Blue and tan. The blue may be silver blue, pigeon blue or slate blue, the tan deep and rich. The blue extends from the base of the skull to the tip of the tail, down the forelegs to the pasterns, and down the thighs to the hocks. On the tail the blue should be very dark. Tan appears on muzzle and cheeks, around the base of the ears, below the pasterns and hocks, and around the vent. There is a tan spot over each eye. The topknot should be silver or fawn.

These Silky Terriers owned by Mrs. Merle E. Smith illustrate the dark center part so often shown in blue body coats. On the left is the import, BRENHILL SPLINTERS, Mrs. Smith's foundation bitch and a Top Producer, and on the right is her daughter, CH. REDWAY SPLINTERS, by Ch. Wexford Pogo. Both of these Silkys were also naturally clean-pointed and excellent inhead type.

The only BEST-BRACE-IN-SHOW winners in the breed are shown here. They scored this big win at Sussex Hills KC in 1964, had two seconds in Toy Brace Group at the prestigious Westminster KC show in 1963 and 1964, and several other Toy Group Brace placings. On the right is CH. ELMIKE'S LADY ELSA (by Ch. Redway Lord Michael ex Tee Pee Little Susie); on the left is her daughter, CH. ELMIKE'S LADY ELFIN QUEEN (also by Ch. Redway Lord Michael). Both were bred and are owner-handled by Mrs. Elsa Vinisko. Lady Elsa was also first in Veteran Bitch Class at the Devon Specialty in 1968 under Judge Mrs. A. E. Van Court.

Temperament—The keenly alert air of the terrier is characteristic, with shyness or excessive nervousness to be faulted. The manner is quick, friendly, responsive.

Movement—Should be free, light footed, lively and straightforward. Hindquarters should have strong propelling power. Toeing in or out is to be faulted.

Size—Weight ranges from eight to ten pounds. Shoulder height from nine to ten inches. Pronounced diminutiveness (such as a height of less than eight inches) is not desired; it accentuates the quality of toyishness as opposed to the breed's definite terrier character.

Approved April 14, 1959, by the American Kennel Club

CHAPTER 5

Judging the Silky Terrier

The ideal Silky Terrier combines the glamour and size of the Toy dog with the character and spirited action of the Terrier. He should proclaim himself a Silky Terrier when he steps into the ring, demonstrating a high degree of those characteristics required for correct breed type. He should be neither a short-coated Yorkshire Terrier, nor a soft-coated Australian Terrier—he is himself, distinct, with no infringement on the type of either of the two breeds that were his forebears.

For many years, it has been debated within the fancy whether type or soundness was more important in any given breed. "Type" is defined as "the characteristic qualities distinguishing a breed; the embodiment of a standard's essentials," while "soundness" is defined as "the state of mental and physical health when all organs and faculties are complete and functioning normally, each in its rightful relation to the other." Both definitions are from *The Complete Dog Book*, an official publication of the American Kennel Club. Basically, then, we see that "soundness" means only that a dog is healthy and free of disease, that he has the required number of legs, eyes, ears, and so on, and that all function in a normal manner. That is, he can walk or run on his four legs, he can see with his two eyes, and he can hear with his two ears. Since blindness, deafness, and monorchidism or cryptorchidism are all disqualifying defects in any breed, these extremes of unsoundness need not be considered here.

If judges were to base their assessments on soundness alone, they could as well have a ringfull of mongrels, for without breed type, you have just another dog. If only the soundness of the animals in the ring were to be judged, there would be no need for breed standards, written as they are for the purpose of setting forth what each individual breed should be in physical form, in movement, and in character. Type and soundness should not be considered as if they were traits that are in opposition to one another.

CH. HARGILL'S JOLLY JAMBOREE is the only Silky Terrier with two all-breed Best-in-Show wins. His outstanding record includes 9 group wins and 21 other placings in Group (Sept. 1969) and he is still being shown. He is pictured here winning Best of Breed at Westminster KC 1969 under Judge Alva Rosenberg, handled by Houston Clark. He was bred and is owned by Miss Harriett Gill. (Sire: Ch. Wilhaven's Wee Sweet William; Dam: Ch. Rebel Dancing Angel).

Given good health and the absence of physical handicaps, the Silky Terrier which fulfills the provisions of the standard will be sound as well as typical. The importance of correct breed type, the physical manifestation of those qualities which are described in words in the standard, must never be underestimated. Particularly in a relatively young-in-years breed like the Silky Terrier, it is imperative that those charged with the responsibility of judging should recognize and reward those dogs and bitches possessing the highest degree of correct type.

(There are, of course, some very serious faults manifested in movement that may properly be classed either as unsoundness or as conformation faults. Among these are the ribcage which does not extend far enough back and produces an up-and-down movement of the body when the dog is in

CH. BILLABONG TINY TIM is shown with his owner, Mr. Lee Shane. This fine dog had a "fairy tale" win at the 1962 Specialty when he won BOB under Judge Percy Roberts at his first show after Mr. and Mrs. Shane had been persuaded to enter him to support the STCA Specialty. This picture illustrates his excellent breed type, with the naturally clean points (ears, feet, and muzzle) that are most desirable in Silkys, and he had not been trimmed for the picture. He was bred by Mrs. Thora Sosinsky. His sire is Ch. Coolaroo Sir Winston, and his dam is Coolaroo Lady Penny.

CH. QUEEN'S OWN BLACK TRACKER is pictured in win of Best of Breed at Chicago International show in 1966 under the well-known Australian writer and judge W. A. Wheatland. His handler is E. E. Thorn, who has handled him to a very fine win record, with four Group Firsts and 150 BOB wins. He was in the Top 10 Phillips System for four years and runner-up for two years for the Iradell Trophy for breed wins. He is owned by Mildred Pequignot and was bred by Alice Hively.

motion, and the extremely serious fault called "weaving", in which either the front or the rear feet cross each other when the dog is in motion. The rear cross-over is especially bad, since Terriers must have good drive in rear, and should be faulted with the greatest severity.)

There is a characteristic gesture of the breed that delights owners but seems to puzzle some judges. When very intent on some object, a Silky Terrier will often raise one front foot in the air and hold it there, much like a bird-hunting dog when on point. Some Silkys will also do this when stopped during gaiting around the show ring. The gesture is so typical that the picture selected to illustrate national breed club literature shows a Silky in this pose. It should, of course, never be faulted in the show ring because it is characteristic of the breed.

General Appearance—We must have a dog small enough to fit comfortably within the Toy classification, but not by any means a weak, weedy specimen. Though of refined bone and small in stature, he has great physical strength for his size; pound for pound, it is doubtful if any other breed is equal to him in strength. Lightly built and moderately low-set—9 to 10 inches at shoulder and between 8 and 10 pounds—he has sufficient substance to let you know he is a real dog. On the other hand, he must not be a heavy-boned, coarse dog, heavy of foot, which plods around the ring

CH. BONNEEN'S ARUNTA CHIEFTAN is shown winning the Toy Group under Judge Mrs. Yan Paul at the Battle Creek KC (Michigan), handled by Lu Durocher. This Silky Terrier has an outstanding record of wins, including Best in Show (all breeds) at the Scarsborough KC in Toronto, Ontario on September 28, 1969. He is the only Silky to achieve this high honor in Canada; it was awarded by Judge Glenn Stephens. From January through September 1969, he also had nine Group wins and ten other placings in Canada, along with two Group wins and eleven other Group placings in the U.S. In 1968, he had a total of 46 Group placings in Canada and the U.S. He is by Tamworth Cal ex Bonneen Blue Mist bred by Darrel Jordon, and owned by Joseph Medina.

rather than moving in the lightfooted, lively manner of the ideal Silky. The plodders, the pounders, the cloddy dogs are not good Silky Terriers. Though he is a strong little dog, he should not have the rugged, rough-coated look of the Australian Terrier; neither should he give the more fragile impression of the Yorkshire Terrier. Bone must be refined but strong, neither as heavy as that of the Aussie nor as light as that of the Yorkie.

The "make and shape" of the dog are of the utmost importance. That is, the Silky must present the correct outline, or silhouette, as he comes into the show ring. Neither the long, very low-set dog, nor the tall, leggy dog is correct. The Silky that meets the standard's specifications of 10 inches at shoulder height and 12 inches in body length, with well-set-under front legs, is neither too low-set nor too leggy.

The Silky of correct size, ideal bone refinement, and correct conformation moves in a way that expresses his "joie de vivre," that zest for living that is so much a part of his character. Typically, he is almost never still, and whether moving forward, backward, or to the side, his movement is buoyant and four square, with never a foot placed wrong.

His straight silky coat, blue and tan in color, is parted from the nose to the root of the tail. Ideally, he is naturally clean-pointed, viz., he has no long

CAN. and AM. CH. CLAVONS BLUE COPY (by Ch. Kanimbla Wee Kelso Kelly ex Ch. Clavons Blue Gem) shown winning WB, BOW at the 1968 Eastern Specialty held with Devon DFA (Pa.) under Judge Mrs. A. E. Van Court. This win completed the title for this lovely bitch, bred, owned, and handled by Miss Nettie Simmons. Miss Simmons herself is licensed to judge Silky Terriers and several other Toy breeds, her Clavons Kennels (Reg.) being well known for their excellent Pugs as well as Silkys.

hair on muzzle, ears, and feet up to the hocks and knees. The coat should be of a fine texture which lies flat and shows the gleaming highlights of silk. Coat in mature specimens should be 5 to 6 inches in length, though there is variation in length over the body. The end of the coat should reach a point about midway from the bottom line of the dog's body (with brisket down to elbows) to the floor, and to some extent following the contour of the body. Puppies and young adults up to 18 months should not be faulted for somewhat less length of coat. Too much coat length is very objectionable, as it gives an over-all picture too much toward the Yorkshire. The tail is docked and carried erect or semi-erect.

Head and Expression—These are of great importance, not only of themselves, but because of their bearing on correct type. In the Silky, the alert, intelligent, somewhat quizzical expression demonstrates a degree of

CH. SILTI'S JOY BOY (Ch. Clavons Blue Rain ex Ch. Coolaroo Dame Wintiki) was bred and is owned by Mary T. Estrin, who handled him to his championship. Along the way, he had a placing in the Toy Group, was Winners Dog at the 1969 Eastern Specialty at Ann Arbor KC, and Reserve WD at the Western Specialty for 1969 at Santa Barbara KC.

BODY CONFORMATION

Note that the three dogs shown are the same height at shoulder, but are very different in general appearance. Their body weights will also differ widely.

RIGHT

The figure above shows the correct "make and shape" called for in the breed standard. This dog has the required moderately low-set body, and from withers to set-on of tail will measure one-fifth longer than his height at shoulder, as specified by the standard. The correctly built dog will weigh approximately one pound for each inch of height.

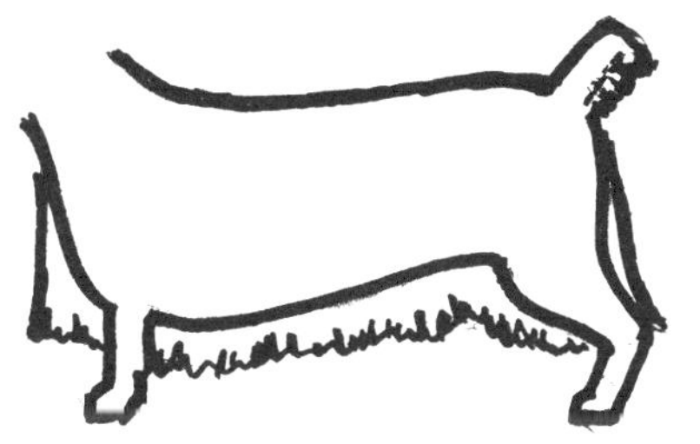

WRONG

This figure shows a very low-set dog, which will measure longer than the specified $1\frac{1}{5}$ times the height at shoulder. He will also be over the standard in weight.

WRONG

This figure shows the square-shaped dog, which will measure approximately the same from withers to set-on of tail as he does in shoulder height. A dog of this "make and shape" is more correct for the Yorkshire than for the Silky Terrier. He will also weigh too little for his height at shoulder.

AUS. and AM. CH. BOWENVALE CORALEE is pictured winning the 1968 Western Specialty of STCA. She was eight years old and finished her American title with this win. Judge is Keith Browne; handler Frank Albarta. She was only the second Silky bitch to win BOB at a Specialty show. Sire of this import was Bowenvale Blue Bill; dam was Dainty Girl. Owners are Mr. and Mrs. George Van Etten.

intelligence rarely encountered in any animal. With no loss of alertness, there is a sweetness to the best expressions that conveys some of the responsiveness of his nature. He looks at you inquisitively, as if to say, "I'm ready to make friends, how about you?" The head is wedge-shaped and strong, but never heavy; it is of moderate length. The skull is flat and a trifle longer than the muzzle (measuring from the center corner of the eyes to the base of the skull, and from the center of the eyes to the tip of the muzzle). The stop is definite but not too deep. A slight variation may be allowed in head proportions, with the dog being permitted somewhat more strength of foreface than the bitch. In no case should the muzzle be as heavy as that of the Australian Terrier, where skull and muzzle are equal in length, nor should it be as short as that of the Yorkshire Terrier. Snipey muzzles or weak underjaws are very undesirable. The ideal head is strong, but with no suggestion of coarseness.

Ears—The ears must be right, or the head is not right. They are small, V-shaped, and pricked, set high on the head. They should be carried entirely perpendicular to the plane of the head. Ears that are too large, set low on the head, or that flare out to the sides, completely spoil an otherwise correct head. Ears that are weak, or rounded at tips, are also very objectionable. Pendant or tipped-over ears are totally unacceptable; dogs with this serious fault should not be exhibited. Preferably, ears should be carried erect, but some do fold them back when in movement; the ears are very mobile, moving to catch every sound, resembling the action of a

CH. AUSTRAL VICTORIA REGINA, C.D., is shown winning the Toy Group under Judge M. L. Baker, handled by Mrs. Florise Hogan. Not only is she a dual champion, with both Conformation and Obedience titles, but also has two Group wins and a number of placings to her credit, and is the dam of two champions. She was bred by Miss Mildred Pequignot and is co-owned by her with Mrs. Arlene Lewis. Her sire is Ch. Austral Prince Kirby; her dam is Ch. Aldoon Lady Marrie.

radar antenna. When the judge commands the dog's attention, however, the ears must be turned well forward and held high and vertically from the plane of the head.

Eyes, Nose and Teeth—The eyes are also of great importance in making for a good head. They are small, dark in color, placed neither too far apart nor too close together, and showing a keen, intelligent expression. The beady black eyes required in some terriers are not correct for the Silky, as they do not denote the keen intelligence required. Eyes lighter than a dark shade of brown should be faulted according to degree, but the true yellow eye which is sometimes seen is an extremely serious fault of itself, and gives an entirely untypical expression. Although eye shape is not specified in the U.S. standard, "almost circular" or "almost round" probably best expresses the ideal shape. Eye rims should be black or dark

CH. ACKLINE'S GIN GIN KEG O'LUCK is shown here winning the Toy Group from the classes under Judge John Cuneo. She was handled by Tom Gately and had a very successful show career, with 35 Toy Group placings and four wins of the Group, giving her the most Group wins of all Silky bitches to date. During her show career she was owned by her breeder, Mrs. Edna F. Ackerman, but is now owned by Mrs. Elsa Vinisko. Her sire was Ch. Delalor Banjo Bluespec of Iradell; dam was Ch. Shaw's Sapphire.

CH. SILKALLURE REXANTHONY (Ch. Silkallure Rexandy ex Winston's Cinderella) is shown here in a win under Judge Derek Rayne. The handler is Corky Vroom. Rexanthony was bred by B. McFatridge and is owned by Mr. and Mrs. Fred Stern and Leonard J. Pilley. He had a fine win record, which included 36 placings in the Toy Group, including three firsts. He was top-winning Silky for 1968 (Phillips System) as well as winning the Iradell breed trophy for 1968. He was usually handled by E. R. Hastings.

brown. The nose must be black. In some specimens, the nose is slightly to seriously off-color, and should be faulted according to the degree of deviation from black. The partly pink, or butterfly nose, should be heavily faulted, but the nose that is only slightly off in color would be but a minor fault. The teeth should be strong, white, well-aligned, and meet in a perfect scissors bite. Marked undershot or overshot bites are very serious faults, but again the degree of the fault must be considered.

Neck, Shoulders, and Front Assembly—The neck must fit gracefully into sloping shoulders. It is somewhat long, fine, and crested along its top line. The dog with a truly good head atop correct length and crest of neck will display elegance and a degree of good breeding evident even to those not familiar with the breed. The short neck spoils correct balance, and imparts

EARS

RIGHT

Small, V-shaped, set high, carried erect, as specified in breed standard.

WRONG

Set too low, flaring obliquely off the skull.

WRONG

NOT small and V-shaped. Too large, and round at tips.

WRONG

NOT V-shaped, and too large. The so-called "leaf ear"

FRONT ASSEMBLIES

1 The shoulder slopes at an angle of 45 degrees (considered correct layback in many breeds). Shoulder and humerus (upper arm) are approximately same length; they meet each other at a right angle (90 degrees). The Silky with this front assembly meets the breed standard, which states: "Well laid back shoulders, together with good angulation at the upper arm, set the forelegs nicely under the body." The term "sloping shoulders" is also used in the standard.

2 The so-called "Fox Terrier front assembly" has the well laid back shoulder, but the short upper arm and overly wide angle (of shoulder to upper arm) prevent the forelegs from being set "nicely under the body."

3 The "straight" or "steep" shoulder, not well laid back and invariably accompanied by too-short neck. The very wide angle of upper arm to shoulder prevents the "well set under" forelegs. Also, if the upper arm is not shortened (it often is) with this straight shoulder, the dog will have excessive body depth for his over-all height. The correct ratio of body depth to leg length is approximately 1 to 1, while that shown here is about $1\frac{1}{2}$ to 1. This dog will also be over in weight for his shoulder height. The straight shoulder is also functionally inefficient.

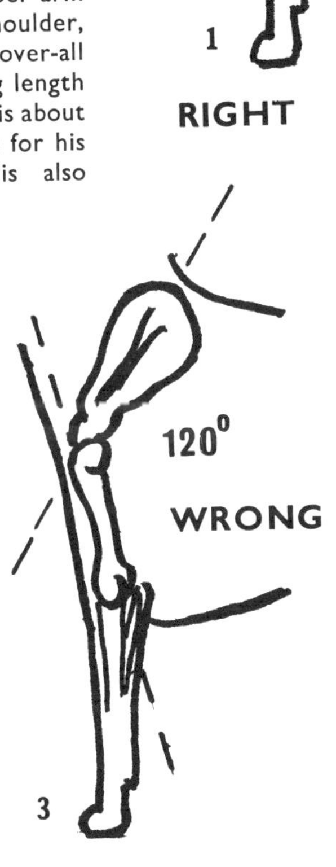

CH. BOWENVALE BLUE BOY winning BOB at the 1963 STCA Specialty under Judge Louis Murr. He was handled to this win (as customarily) by Miss Martha Frances Van Etten, one of the first members of "Silky Teens." Blue Boy is owned by Mrs. George Van Etten, who was President of STCA in 1963. Bred at Bowenvale Kennels in Australia; sire: Aus. Ch. Bo Bo; dam: Dainty Girl. The Van Ettens are the only ones who own two Specialty-winning Silkys.

a look of coarseness or commonness foreign to the Silky Terrier. It should be regarded as one of the most serious possible faults. Short necks, usually accompanied by incorrect front assembly, have become a prevalent and very damaging problem in the breed today.

In the recent past, we have begun to see several conformation faults of the utmost gravity, resulting as they do in Silky Terriers whose "make and shape" are far afield from the correct construction set forth in the breed standard. Although they carry over into bodies that are faulty over-all, they will be discussed here because the make of the front assembly of the dog is so much involved.

The correct front assembly itself is too little understood by both breeders and judges. The so-called "Fox-Terrier front," in which the face of the front leg comes down in a straight line from the neck, is totally wrong in the Silky Terrier, which should have a front well-set under the body. Where the front legs are set in under the shoulder blades, as they should be in the Silky, there is a distinct body overhang before them. Breeders with little or no understanding of anatomy and the correct structure required are generally unaware that the dog is incorrectly constructed, and judges often fail to check this feature at all.

Fox Terrier breeders developed their breed's special type front by breeding to shorten the upper arm to bring the front leg forward. The standard for that breed, though it calls for well laid back shoulders, also calls for forelegs to be straight "when viewed from any direction." It is understandable, therefore, that some judges with long experience in other terriers have put Silkys to high awards that actually have Fox Terrier fronts rather than the correct front assembly called for in the Silky standard. These Silky Terriers are not only wrong in "make and shape," they are frequently over the standard in weight because of extra length of the lower part of the body. Measuring from center-front point of the body to center-rear point of body at elbow level, the dog with

CH. SPARKLING BEAU RINGO shown winning WD from Bred-by-Exhibitor class at the 1968 Eastern STCA Specialty at Devon, Pa., under Judge Mrs. A. E. Van Court. His breeder-owner-handler is Helli A. Kiiveri.

Fox Terrier front assembly will measure several inches longer than will the one with the front correctly set under the body, though he may measure the same from withers to set-on of tail.

In the Silky Terrier, the length of the upper arm should be approximately the same as that of the shoulder blade, with the angle between the arm and shoulder blade being approximately 90 degrees. With such proportions and angulation, along with the well laid back shoulder blade of good length, the front is correctly set under the body, with the feet under the shoulder blade rather than under the neck or head. It should be noted too that when nature seeks to compensate for the shortening of the upper arm, the shoulder blade may also be shortened, resulting in a blade of inadequate length for the rest of the body.

Upright or steep shoulders are also seriously faulty but are more likely to be recognized by judges; they frequently accompany the too-short neck. The dog with straight shoulders will have faulty front movement, as he throws the front legs in a circular movement with each step or moves with a "hackney" gait.

Another form of seriously faulty construction, too often seen, is the Silky that is square in shape. These specimens are generally deficient in front assembly, and may or may not have too-short necks. These dogs measure about the same from withers to set-on of tail as their height at shoulder. The square shape is wrong of itself, being too reminiscent of the Yorkshire Terrier. Not only are these dogs too short in back for their height, they are often of a leggy build, with bodies too shallow for the length of leg. The brisket (lower point of chest) in leggy dogs will not extend down to the elbow as required in the Silky standard. They should be very severely faulted in the show ring.

The standard calls for forelegs to be "strong, straight, and rather fine boned," a very clear requirement. There are some who question whether the leg that is "rather fine boned" can also be strong, but medical authorities have pointed out that large bones are frequently less strong, being more porous, than those of smaller circumference. We do not, of course, want a thin bone of the "matchstick" variety; these are invariably seen on specimens that are weedy over-all, not even approaching the small but strong type required for the Silky Terrier. Such specimens are also likely to be deficient in rib spring (slab-sided) and to be under the minimum weight of the standard.

Body, Tail, and Hindquarters—The body should be moderately low-set, about one-fifth longer than the dog's height at withers, measuring from withers to set-on of tail. The topline can best be judged with the dog in movement; it is straight, with just perceptible rounding over the loins. Roached backs are a serious fault. The too-short body is specified as a fault in the standard, but the too-long back is also a fault. With a dog measuring 10 inches at shoulder, the length from withers to tail would be 12 inches for ideal proportions. The brisket should be medium wide and deep enough to extend down to the elbows.

The body should be well-ribbed back, the last rib farther back than the mid-point of the body. A rib cage shorter than this will produce the roached back, often with a peculiar up and down movement of the body when the dog is in motion. The ribs must be well sprung; there must be

CH. MIDLAND'S JAN'S WENDY ANNE at the Upper Potomac Valley KC show in 1967 under Judge Maxwell Riddle, was the first Silky to win a Best-in-Show, all breeds, in the U.S. She is shown here with breeder-owner-handler Carmen Cananzi. Sire: Aus. and Am. Ch. Koonoona Bo Bo. Dam: Ch. Lylac Jan.

no slab- or flat-sided ribcage. The ribs should not be rounded to the extent of producing the so-called "barrel chest," but this is probably less objectionable than the "fish-shaped" body. The thighs should be well-muscled and strong, but not so overdeveloped that they appear heavy. Angulation at stifles and hocks should be moderate but definite, with hocks low to the ground and parallel with each other.

The tail is set high and carried erect or semi-erect, but not farther forward than vertical. Whether erect or semi-erect is of no consequence; in fact, each dog in the ring will vary his tail carriage from time to time. The term "but not over-gay" used in the standard is sometimes not understood. This appears to be a carry-over from the Australian standard, and means simply that the tail is turned over the dog's back—it is farther forward than vertical. The tail is docked with feathering about $1\frac{1}{2}$ inches in length.

Feet—The feet should be small, round, compact, and cat-like. Good feet are lacking in most specimens today and represent a point of weakness in the breed in general. While feet may break down because of an improper exercising surface, it is also an inherited failing, and one to which breeders should turn their attention. The foot pads should be thick and springy, with nails strong and dark in color. Acceptable nail color may be either dark brown or black, and while white or flesh-colored nails are faulty, the presence of only one or two light nails should not be heavily penalized. Where one or more toenails are lighter than desirable, the degree of the fault should be taken into consideration. The feet must point straight ahead, with no toeing in or out, front or rear. Dewclaws should be removed, both on front and rear legs.

Movement—Characteristic movement is of the greatest importance, demonstrating as it does so much of the type, character, and physical structure of the true Silky Terrier. It must be that of a lightly built, moderately low-set toy dog of spirited action and happy nature. His movement is free, light-footed, lively, and buoyant. He should move true, coming or going, with good drive from the rear.

The dog which plods heavily around the ring, even if he moves true, must be severely faulted for incorrect movement, and for lack of the spirited action and lively nature of the typical Silky Terrier. Cowhocks or very close movement behind are serious faults; the rear cross-over sometimes seen is one of the worst possible faults. Neither should movement be too wide behind, as it is in the dog with over-developed hindquarters or slackness at hip joints. Weaving of the front feet in movement is also a serious fault; it is usually seen in specimens with the so-called "fiddle fronts."

The breeder or judge who has once seen and recognized correct move-

CH. TINKER BLUE BLAZES was campaigned to an outstanding record of wins by his owner, the late Mary V. Germany. After finishing for his Ch. title at the 1964 Specialty, he became top Silky Male in 1964, Phillips System ratings (based on Group wins and placings), Top Silky Terrier 1965 Phillips, and Best of Breed at the 1966 Specialty under Judge Forest Hall. He was the first Silky to win the Toy Group at a California show. He is pictured winning BOB under breeder-judge Mrs. Merle E. Smith at Harbor Cities KC (Calif.). He was handled by Mrs. Dorothea Metzger. Miss Germany took great pride in the fact that in six showings under four breeder-judges, Blue Blazes was never defeated. He is the sire of three champions to date, and was left to the author and husband when Mary died in September 1969. Mrs. Smith was the first Silky breeder licensed by AKC to judge the breed.

ment is not likely to settle for less. Agile, springy, and elastic, movement is also smooth and straightforward, the best movers often being described as "floating along."

Coat—The coat must be straight, of silky texture, glossy and gleaming with highlights; it should hang flat to the sides of the body. There is no undercoat—the single coat has bred true for many years, but a coat that is too profuse will not hang flat. On mature specimens the desired length from behind the ears to the set-on of the tail is from 5 to 6 inches. The coat of correct length will hang down from the lower line of the body to a point about halfway between that and the floor, assuming the correct depth of brisket down to the elbow. There is considerable variation in the age at which mature coat length is attained; judges should inquire as to age before dismissing an otherwise good specimen for less-than-ideal coat length. Some Silkys have full coat length at a year of age, but others not until they are two years old, and some continue to gain length until they are three years old or older. The clean-pointed dog usually gains mature coat more slowly than those with a profusion of hair on points, but naturally clean points are ideal for the breed and should be credited as a particular virtue. In these specimens, the tan hair on ears, muzzle, and feet up to first joints of legs is of somewhat firmer texture than the other hair on the body. Below the knees and hock joints, hair should be only about $\frac{1}{4}$ to $\frac{1}{2}$ inch in length, as should be the hair on ears and feet. It is allowable, and customary, to trim ears and feet as needed, but the muzzle should not be trimmed unless the fall is so long that it resembles that of the Yorkshire

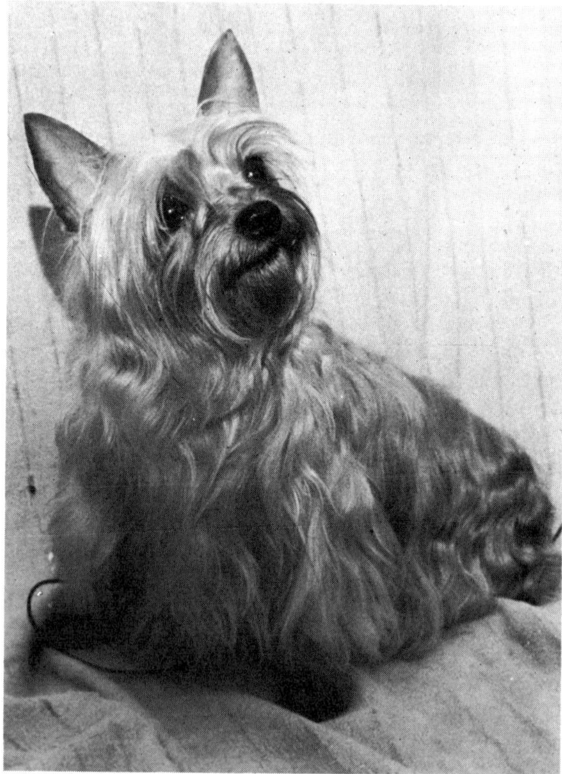

CH. LARRAKIN BLUEBERRY MUFFIN, owned by the author and her husband, James Young, Jr., has the rather wide-set eyes that give a Yorkie look to her head. Her excellent movement and body conformation enabled her to finish quickly, owner-handled, but the Yorkie-type head must be faulted. Such heads appear to be inherited quantitatively and recessively.

COAT LENGTH

CORRECT

The coat of the properly bred Silky will grow to this length and stop there. End of the coat is approximately half-way between lower line of body and floor, and to some extent following the contour of the body.

TOO SHORT

except for puppy or young adult, but far less objectionable than the too-long coats shown in Figures 3 and 4.

WRONG

But proper trimming can improve this coat. The tail feathering should be shortened to 1 to 1½ inches length, and feathering up to wrists and hocks should be shortened to about ¼ inch in length. No long hair should fall below these first joints; feet should always be visible.

TOTALLY WRONG

OFF-TYPE for the Silky Terrier. The dog with this over-long coat will, depending on his "make and shape," resemble either the Yorkshire or the Skye Terrier more than he will his own breed. Those with such excessive coat should be out of contention in the judging ring, as they are completely untypical of the breed.

These young bitches owned by the author show correct head proportions as viewed here. Left is the future Ch. Redway Bonnie Lass at sixteen months; right is future Ch. Larrakin Blueberry Muffin, then eleven months old.

Terrier. Muzzle fall of only two to three inches can be brushed back under the jaw into the coat on the neck. On the head, the hair should be so profuse as to form a topknot, but with the parting of the coat from the nose over the head, the eyes of the dog must always be clearly visible. The coat is parted from the nose to the set-on of the tail. The tail should be well-coated, with feathering about $1\frac{1}{2}$ inches in length, to balance with the size of the dog. Feathering exceeding this amount should be trimmed, but the tail should never be stripped of all feathering. The word "plume" used in the current U.S. standard has caused considerable confusion and will probably be deleted in future revisions of the standard.

Too much coat is seriously faulty, as the Silky with excessive coat will have too much resemblance to the Yorkshire Terrier. While a short coat may grow long, the overlong coat will never improve.

Color—The distribution of color is described clearly in the standard, where it is stated: "The blue extends from the base of the skull to the tip of the tail, down the forelegs to the pasterns (knees), and down the thighs to the hocks. On the tail the blue should be very dark. Tan appears on muzzle and cheeks, around the base of the ears, below the pasterns (knees)

CH. MILAN MISS SANDRA OF IRADELL was top-winning Silky in both 1963 and 1964 Phillips System. Her fine show record included winning the Toy Group at Westchester KC in 1963 under Judge Miss Anna K. Nicholas, and she was the first Silky Terrier to place in the Toy Group at Westminster, which she achieved in 1964. She won three Toy Groups during her show career. Owned by Mrs. N. Clarkson Earl Jr., Sandra was bred by A. G. V. Miles (Australia). Her sire was Aus. Ch. Milan Tony; dam Milan Lindy Lou.

CH. PRINCESS SUE OF IRADELL, home-bred winner for Mrs. N. Clarkson Earl, Jr. She finished at barely eight months of age and was top winner in U.S. for 1966 (Phillips System). Her sire was Ch. Lucky Prince of Iradell; dam was Ch. Milan Susanna of Iradell.

and hocks, and around the vent. There is a tan spot over each eye. The topknot should be silver or fawn." Although not specified in the standard itself, the blue on the tail is usually darker only at the tip. Although tan at the base of the ears only is mentioned, the tan should also appear on the backs of the ears, where it may also be shaded with black. In mature specimens, the tan spot over the eyes has usually become a rather narrow strip of darker tan between the top of the eyes and the lighter color of the topknot. The Australian standard gives preference to silver topknots, in specifying "silver-blue topknot desirable," but in actual practice, topknots described as "fawn" in this country are frequently called "silver" in Australia.

There has been a great deal of confusion as to what shades of blue are correct. The standard calls for "silver blue, pigeon blue, or slate blue," but the various shades of each of these colors actually overlap, so that any shade of blue is correct. The almost-white body coat is not correct, and too many of these are seen in the show ring. One of the tests of whether the blue color is correct is that it should have a blue cast. Some dogs have body coat tending more toward gray than blue, but since gray-blue is a shade of the color blue, the gray-blue should not be faulted. In close decisions, however, the dog nearest to a true blue color, whether rich silver or deep pigeon blue, should be credited with an important virtue which should weigh heavily in his favor. Another test, especially with lighter blue shades, is whether the coat is dark at the part and next to the body. If it is, this should be considered a correct blue. Some specimens have the blue part, however, with most of the rest of the coat being blondish or gold in color, and this is not correct. Ideally, the blue would be fairly even through the body coat, but given a good over-all blue, some variation of shade in the individual coat should not be penalized. There should be no bronze or gold running through the body coat; where it is present, it should be faulted according to degree. The dog with body coat that is solid bronze, or nearly so, becomes a brown dog rather than a blue-and-tan one, and as such, should be out of contention as a completely untypical specimen. In those dogs in which only a few bronze hairs are found in the blue, there should be little or no fault assessed, since the coat would still be blue. Those between the two should be faulted according to the amount of gold present in what should be a blue body coat.

There should be no confusion in the standard requirement for tan, as it states: "the tan deep and rich." Almost-white, or light beige, in areas which should be tan, is one of the most serious possible faults, and should be faulted very severely. There is considerable variation in shade of tan in the individual dog, but there must be deep, rich tan on muzzle and cheeks, backs of ears, and on the legs below the knees and hocks. The tan may be of either reddish or brownish hue. The leg tan should be free of black or blue hairs, as should muzzle and cheeks, but black shading is permitted on backs of ears (and often seen on richly colored specimens), and blue temple marks just in front of the ears are characteristic in many, especially puppies and young adults. Many specimens which show no blue hairs in the topknot will still show the blue temple mark at the skin. Occasionally, full black masks are seen, and Silkys showing this trait should be out of contention as totally untypical of the breed, with the exception of very young puppies, in which the black may clear with maturity. The fall from the neck is a blending of blue and tan hairs.

In puppies and young adults, the body coat may be mostly black, but if there is no breaking to blue in a dog two years or over, he would have to be faulted for lack of correct color. In the case of black body coats in adult

The first Silky Terrier litter at the author's Larrakin Kennels. The day-old puppies are inspected by their sire, Ch. Clavons Blue Rain (left), and their dam, Ch. Alcarlou Lady Suzanne. At this age, puppies are jet black with tan markings on heads, feet, and legs, and around vent and underside of tail. The sheen of the coats is an indication of good healthy puppies.

The Silky on the left illustrates the lovely neck and proud head carriage that are ideal for the breed. He is the author's CH. CLAVON S BLUE RAIN, pictured at the age of seven months. On the right is MAURIE LADY BONNIE (Ch. Wexford Pogo ex Mitry Lady Mandy), owned by Mr. and Mrs. Joe Burlingame and bred by R. I. Navarro.

classes, judges should inquire as to the age of the dog. Many specimens show the first break to blue on the back of the neck, others along the center part, and others from the lower sides of the body up through the coat, or at the shoulders.

The lightest spot on the Silky should be the topknot, which may be silver or fawn. Some dogs with very deep tans have topknots that are more tan than fawn. They should be faulted for incorrect topknot color, as well as for the detrimental effect this trait has on good expression. Those specimens which have the very deep tan on muzzle, cheeks, and ears, with very light fawn or silver topknots, not only present a beautiful appearance,

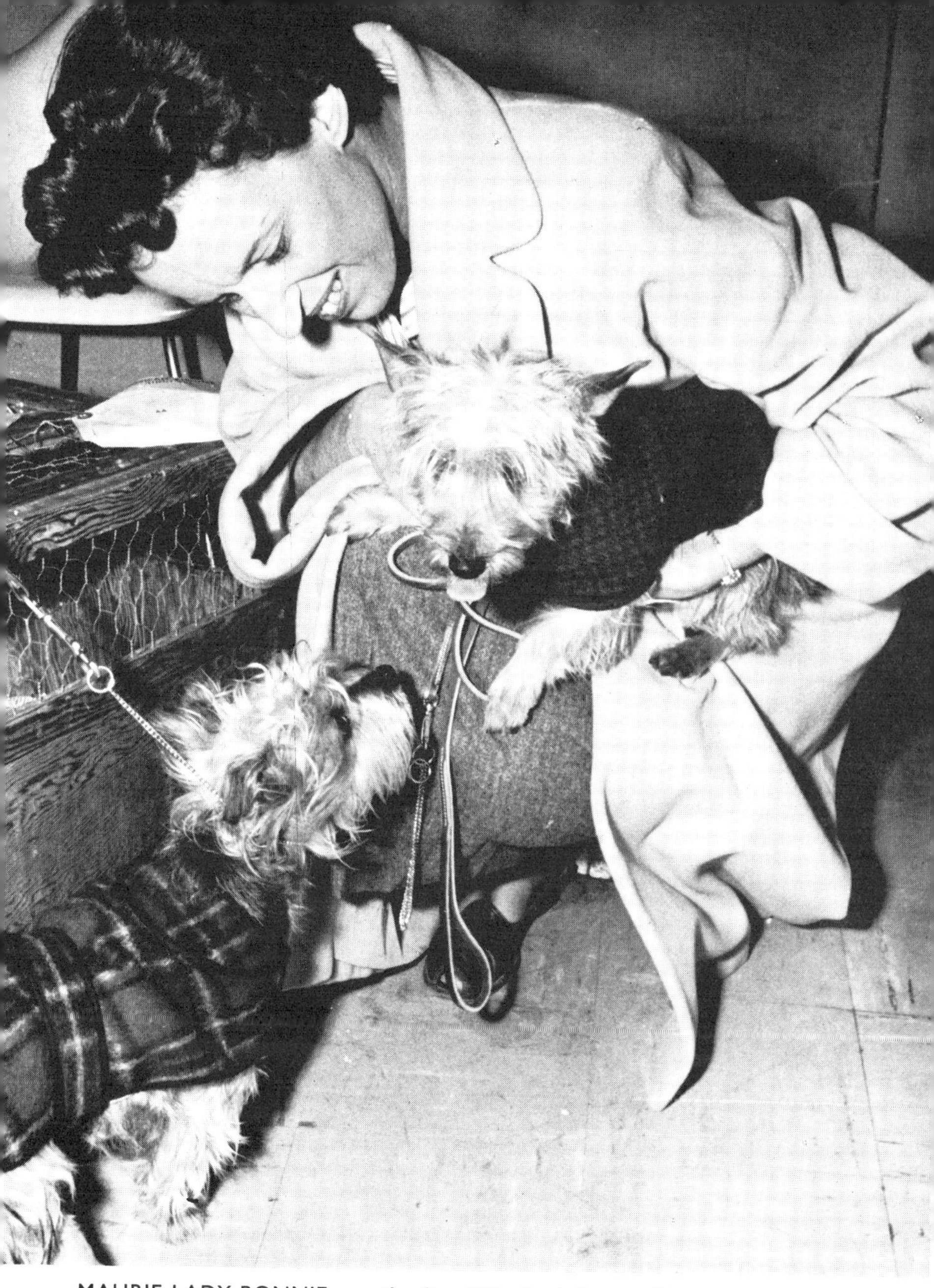

MAURIE LADY BONNIE was the first Silky in Arkansas. Here she greets Arkansas' second Silky, CH. CLAVON S BLUE RAIN, held by Betty Young. Rainy indicates his displeasure at delayed arrival in typical manner, the folding out of his ears. The woolen coats shown are best for Silkys in extreme cold, as knitted sweaters tend to cause matting of the body coat.

but the striking color contrast aids in producing a lovely and typical expression.

Temperament—The standard calls for the keenly alert air of the terrier, with quick, friendly, responsive manner. Temperament is of the greatest importance in any breed, but especially in Silky Terriers, created as they were primarily as the pet and companion of man. The Silky which displays snappishness toward any person, whether his handler or the judge, should be severely faulted or dismissed from the ring. Aggressiveness toward other dogs should never go beyond the point where the handler loses control. The dog that is snapping and snarling and straining at lead is a sorry spectacle, but the dog which simply spars up to another, as if to say that he is ready to do battle if challenged, is another matter and is quite characteristic of the breed. Because of their tendency to be aggressive toward other dogs, Silkys (especially males) should never be crowded together when placed on the table for examination. With a small table, one at a time should be the rule; with a long table, one may be placed on either end.

Ideal temperament is displayed by the Silky which is friendly and responsive toward the judge in the show ring. When approached by the judge, he should never shy away or display nervousness or fear, nor should he show any hostile tendencies toward him. Ideally, he will stand with his ears up, head cocked to one side, with the typical quizzical, waiting-to-make-friends expression. If he also wags his tail and sniffs the judge's hand extended toward him, you may be sure it will take a very good dog to beat him! When judging, I think of these dogs as "sparkling" at me, and credit them for having one of the most important virtues in any breed, good temperament.

Size—In this tenth year after breed recognition by the American Kennel Club, over-size, either in height or weight or both, is probably the most serious problem in Silky Terriers (along with deficient front assemblies). Some four to five years ago, under-size threatened the breed, but as this was corrected, the pendulum swung too far the other way. We see too many exhibits that are over correct weight, even to the extent of being over 12 pounds, with others well over 10 inches at shoulder, some even exceeding 11 inches at shoulder. The standard is quite specific on this point, and states: "Weight ranges from 8 to 10 pounds. Shoulder height from 9 to 10 inches." While a leeway of one pound might be given either way, anything under 7 pounds (puppies excepted) or over 11 pounds should be clearly out of contention for any top award. Likewise, height at shoulder that is under 8 inches or over 11 inches should be virtually disqualifying.

Size is indeed a difficult matter for a judge to deal with, since he is not permitted to ask for measurements of height and weight in the absence of a disqualification clause on size. Many judges concerned about our breed have suggested that we should adopt height and weight disqualifications in the breed standard so that they would be able to assess height and weight precisely. Whether Silky breeders as a whole would vote for such disqualifications for the sake of the breed is not known. Some judges have adopted a practice of "hefting" those dogs that seem overly large, which may be helpful. Conscientious judges are interested in the welfare of the breeds they judge, and those who are aware of the problem are trying to help by severely penalizing those dogs that are over the standard height and weight.

Ideally, serious breeders and exhibitors would correct this situation themselves by not showing or breeding from over-size specimens of the breed. However, human nature being what it is, with deep emotional attachments to their dogs, many are able to rationalize to the extent of justifying (at least to themselves) the use of such undesirable Silky Terriers in breeding and showing. If such dogs are able to win, either because of the absence of Silkys of correct size in the entry or because some judges may be unable to assess height and weight correctly, their owners are likely to conclude that the wins justify the dog, and thus the problem compounds itself.

Judging the Silky Terrier Puppy—One of the most puzzling aspects of the breed, both to new breeders and to judges who lack experience in the breed, is the variation in type in puppies. Some resemble Australian Terrier puppies; these have little or no headfall, short coats, often somewhat coarse in texture, and are generally dark in color. Others look very much like Yorkshire Terrier puppies, with softer, more profuse coats, considerable headfall and long hair on points, and may be either light or dark in color. Others are between the two extremes. For the most part, the puppies intermediate in type or resembling the Aussie puppy can be expected to mature as better Silky Terriers than those resembling the Yorkie, but this is not always the case. The puppy which breaks very light at the skin at an early age is likely to be too light in body coat at maturity, but there are exceptions. Puppies should not be faulted for black body coats.

Judges faced with this sort of variation in the ring can only make their placings as the entries look on that particular day. Breeders learn with experience that they may obtain puppies of varying type in the same litter, but that at maturity, these Silkys may resemble each other more than they did as puppies.

CH. WILHAVEN WEE BONNIE BLUE BELL (by Ch. Koonoona Bo Bo ex Wilhaven's Wee Daffodil) was bred and is owned by Edith and Bill Williams (Wilhaven's Silky Terriers) and was handled to her title by Mrs. Williams.

CHAPTER 6

Your First Dog Show

To enter your Silky Terrier at a regular conformation show where championship points are awarded, you must first obtain a premium list, either from the Show Superintendent or from someone in the local kennel club who has available forms. These contain entry blanks and directions as to the amount of the entry fee at that show and where the entry and fee should be sent. A puppy must be six months old before he can be entered at a point show. For information on dog show classes, please refer to the next chapter.

There is a closing date for entries for each show, after which the Show Superintendent cannot accept further entries, so be sure to mail the completed entry form and check for entry fee in plenty of time. Some shows have a closing date about three weeks before the show (especially shows in the northeast U.S. and California), while others have closing dates just 12 days before the show is to be held. Entries will close at noon of the day specified in the premium list. Some shows accept only a limited number of entries, and with these, entries close with the mail delivery containing the 400th entry or the 2,000th entry, whatever the limit is for that particular show. Other entries received in the same mail with the one reaching the limit are also accepted, so that a show with a limit of 400 dogs might actually have 429 entries. Probably the best known of the limited-entry shows is the famous Westminster Kennel Club show held each February at Madison Square Garden in New York City.

It usually takes the office of the Show Superintendent about a week to compile a list of entries for a particular show. After this is done, they mail to each exhibitor a schedule of the show, setting certain hours of the day for judging the different breeds. If the show is benched, dogs must be on the benches during certain hours of the show (which will be specified in the premium list), and you should plan to stay there with your dog for the duration of the benching hours. The majority of shows today are not benched, and in such cases the premium list will state that it is an unbenched show and that dogs need not be present except at their scheduled time of judging. If your Silky's first show is unbenched, you should plan to be there at least an hour before breed judging. This will help your Silky, as he can become accustomed to the noise and presence of many dogs before the time he must go into the show ring.

Mrs. Elsa Vinisko is pictured with her CH. LARRAKIN TINY TRINKET, then a puppy, as she won Best Puppy in Toy Group at Brookhaven KC ail-breed match show. Mrs. Vinisko also handled Trinket to her title. Her sire is Maryanne Sir Charles; her dam is Ch. Redway Bonnie Lass. She was bred by Mrs. Jim Young.

Mrs. George (Mary) Stahl is pictured with her two foundation bitches. Left is KOONOONA ROSLYN TOO (by Aus. Ch. Bowenvale Sir Rex ex Koonoona Karlee) who is well on her way to championship, and her year-old bitch, LARRAKIN LI'L ABBIE (by Ch. Artarmon's Max ex Rebel Little Bo Peep). Roslyn is an import bred by P. Brown and Abbie was bred by Mr. and Mrs. James Young, Jr.

Most puppies or adult dogs will be somewhat nervous at their first show unless they have had the advantage of attending a number of match shows. If there are outdoor shows in your area, one of them would be best for the first show, since the noise and confusion are less noticeable outdoors than inside a building. You must also try to be calm yourself, as your nervousness will transmit itself to the puppy. If this is the first show for you as well as your puppy, just remember that every exhibitor, handler, and judge present once had his or her first show, and no one will expect a puppy to perform perfectly the first time he is shown. He will gradually get used to the noise and odors of a show, and in time will learn to enjoy being there.

Before you put your Silky down to walk in the building or on the grounds of a dog show, be careful to check to see if there are other dogs near, especially of much larger breeds that might frighten or harm him. Silky Terriers frequently have more courage than prudence, and will challenge a much larger dog to fight, which could be disastrous to the Silky if the larger dog accepts the challenge.

CH. STARLINE TUTUBLU BOY (by Mex. and Am. Ch. Silkallure Starbright ex Coolaroo Miss K. C.) is shown with handler, Dick Webb. He was bred by Jerry Rose, and is owned by Howard and Betty Thomas

You should bathe your puppy the day before the show, and if time permits go over him with a comb before you leave home on the morning of the show, to be sure he has no snarls or tangles. You will still have to give him the finishing touches at the show, but it will be easier to have as much as possible done before you leave. You should take to the show whatever grooming supplies you will need for that last-minute grooming, usually his comb or brush and some type of non-oily coat dressing. Most exhibitors use various brands of hair spray to keep the coat in place, but you should never use any preparation containing oil, or anything containing a coloring agent. Oil makes the silky coat look dirty, and use of artificial coloring is grounds for disqualification of the dog under American Kennel Club rules and regulations.

You should also take a water bowl for the puppy, so that you can offer him water, especially if the show is too warm, as crowded show buildings

CH. ELMVALE MARGARET ANN is shown with handler Houston Clark as she finished with five majors at the age of thirteen months. She is by Ch. Cypress Aristo ex Elmvale Margaret and was bred by Mrs. E. L. (Vickie) Macy and represents the fourth generation at Mr. and Mrs. Macy's Elmvale Kennels.

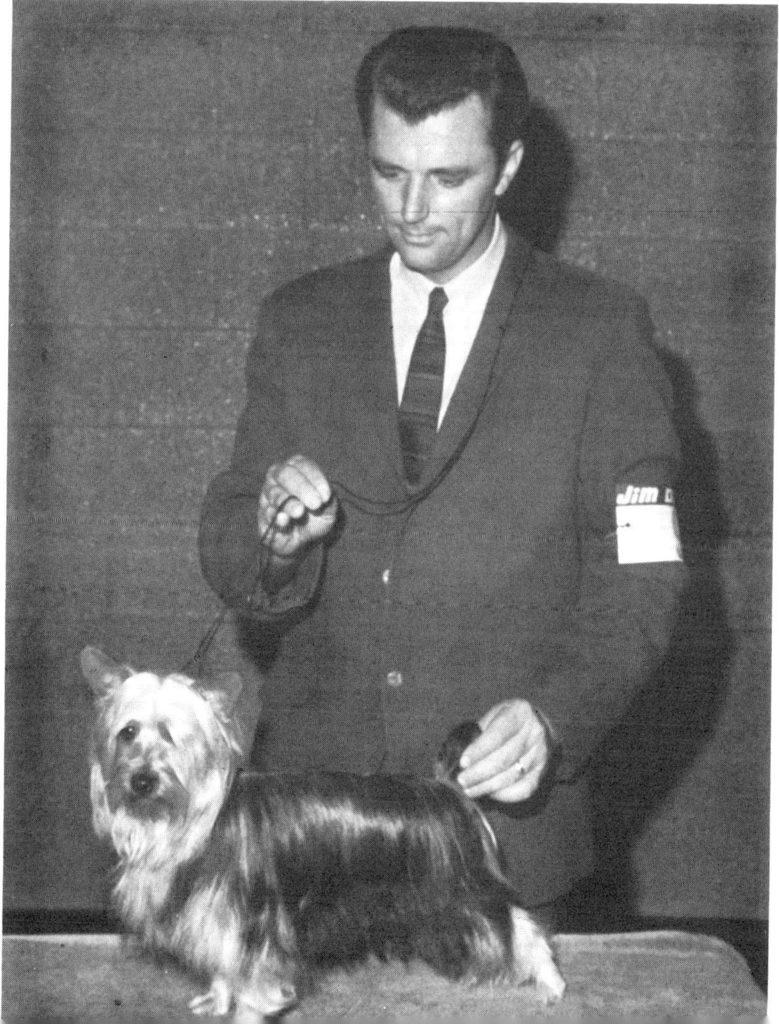

often are. You will also take his show lead, of course, though you may wish to use his leather collar and leash until ready to take him into the ring. I usually take a spare show lead, in case one should break. Exercise the puppy about 30 minutes before he is due in the ring. Some shows have exercise pens inside the show building, while others will request that only certain areas outside be used for this purpose. Obtain a supply of glycerin suppositories, infant size, so that if your puppy has not had a bowel movement that morning, you can use one of the suppositories to induce him to have one. Otherwise he will almost certainly empty in the ring because of the excitement! The last-minute exercising is a necessary precaution with adult Silkys as well as puppies.

CH. BLUE ROGUE OF THE BRYN is shown completing his title requirements winning WD, BOW at the Westchester Kennel Club under Judge Langdon Skarda, handled by Mr. Edwards. He was bred, owned, and handled by Bob and Paulette Edwards. This fine little showman also won a Toy Group second under Judge Maxwell Riddle from the classes, while on the way to his title. He is by Ch. Tinker Blue Blazes ex Ch. Silk Oaks Amy. Note that he displays the correctly well-set-under front legs as required by the standard.

CH. KOONOONA COLEEN (by Aus. Ch. Bowenvale Sir Rex ex Koonoona Karlee) is pictured in win of WB, BOW and BOS under breeder judge Mrs. Edna Ackerman at the Santa Barbara KC show. This import was bred by P. Brown and is owned by Mrs. Jacqueline B. Abarta and handled by Mr. Abarta.

To review, the supplies your kit or small bag should contain when you take your puppy to a show are: Comb and/or brush, coat dressing (usually in a spray bottle), show lead and a spare lead if you feel it might be needed, water bowl, and glycerine suppositories. If you plan to use some sort of treat to encourage your Silky to perform in the ring, this should be packed at the last minute if meat or anything that might spoil is used. Some exhibitors object to the use of treats in the ring, but all professional handlers that I know of and the vast majority of experienced owner-

CH. ARTARMON'S MAX, owned by Mr. and Mrs. James Young, Jr., is shown winning fourth in the Toy Group under Judge Mrs. A. E. Van Court. Mrs. Young handled him to his title and he took four major wins, the first from Puppy Class, in only eight shows. He is by Ch. Artarmon's Jonbon Boy ex Artarmon's Raggedy Ann and was bred by H. Norman and Jo Ann Charles.

These littermates were bred by Mr. Ronald Hartright-Leighton, and are by Ch. Koonoona Bo Bo ex Ch. Ellwyn Princess Anne Marie. On the left is CH. RONNSOWN BEAU KAYE O'RONHOFF, handled by R. C. Wanzer, finishing with WB, BOW under Judge Kenneth Given. She is breeder-owned and also won 4 points WB, BOW at Westminster, 1968, largest number of points awarded in Silkys to date at that show. Right is CH. MIDLAND'S BEAU O'RONHOFF, handled by Carmen Cananzi; he is also a Group winner.

handlers do use this handling aid. The treat most generally used is cooked liver, either purchased in cans or prepared as described in the chapter "Training the Puppy for Conformation." Whatever kind of treat you decide to use, be careful not to drop it on the floor or the ground within the ring, as it will tempt some dogs to break their gait to pick it up. Some handlers are careless about this, and it is very inconsiderate of other exhibitors.

The new exhibitor is not likely to have a carrying case or crate in which to take his dog or dogs to shows, but most experienced exhibitors do purchase this equipment and find it of great value. When you do not have a carrier, you must hold your Silky until time for him to go into the ring, which is more tiring to the dog than being placed in a crate where he can rest. I say that you must hold him advisedly, for with shows as crowded as they are today, it is generally unsafe to put a small dog on the floor near the ring, unless you are fortunate enough to find a sizeable space clear of spectators and other dogs, especially large ones. Some shows make a practice of having aisles between rings, with no one but actual exhibitors permitted in the aisles, which is very helpful in a crowded show. Since these cleared aisles are not always available, however, it is best not to count on them. In addition, the crate affords your Silky some protection from the noise and distractions of a show. Also, should you finish grooming him before time for him to go into the ring, keeping him in his crate will keep him from getting mussed.

The carrier we have found most satisfactory for our Silky Terriers at shows is a wooden one which is 20 inches in length, 12½ inches in width and 14 inches in height. This is large enough to provide adequate room for an adult Silky, but small enough not to be too heavy to carry—the ones we

CH. COOLAROO SIR NOBLE (Ch. Coolaroo Gantine's Yen ex Coolaroo Miss Comet) is shown winning BOW under Judge Mrs. Carl B. Cass, handled by owner Noble M. Moss. Mr. and Mrs. Moss are working to form an area club for Silky Terriers in the Dallas, Texas area.

Mrs. Raymond Ellis is pictured with her first two Silky Terriers. LARRAKIN CONFEDERATE YANKEE (Ch. Larrakin Lucky Lochinvar ex Ch. Baby Doe's Delilah), is flanked on the right by CH. LARRAKIN LITTLE MISS TASSY (Ch. Clavons Blue Rain ex Koonoona Roslyn Too). Yankee was bred by Mrs. Myrtle Puett, and Tassy by W. S. Guess and Mrs. Jim Young. Tassy was handled to her championship by Mrs. Ellis.

Pictured is AKC's first Alaskan-born Silky Terrier champion, CH. D'UNDER CAVALIER ENLU O' DIMITY by D'Under Lilibet O' Lover Boy ex Blue Chantilly. She finished under Judge Roy Cowan at Klamath Falls, Oregon, August 31, 1968, with Howard A. Jensen handling. She was bred by Billie Grace and Mrs. Arthur L. Waldron. Jensen and Paul G. Hefner are her co-owners.

CH. GEM-G'S KOOL HAND LUKE (by Hayes' Junior de la Ek ex Hayes' Lady Tina de la Kreaux) is shown winning BOB at Golden Gate KC under Judge Mrs. B. H. Ackerman. This glamorous young dog has a Group win to his credit at Peninsula DFA, Judge Rutledge Gilliland, and is being campaigned by his owner-handler James W. Green. He was bred by Joe A. Hayes.

have weigh about 10 pounds without the dog. They have a solid panel of wood at the back, but provide adequate ventilation through air holes set high in the side panels and a larger air panel in the door. The solid back panel can be an advantage if you find yourself in a location where there is rain, cold, or wind coming from one direction, as you can place the solid side of the carrier so that it will protect the dog from the elements.

If you find that you and your Silky Terrier enjoy the shows, and expect to show regularly, there is another piece of equipment that is well worth the purchase price. This is the portable exercise pen which you can take to the show. They are folded for ease of transport (do get one with carrying handles) and then set up at the show, after covering the space that will be inside the pen with layers of newspaper. Our exercise pen is 30 inches in height when set up, and has eight panels; these panels are like fencing panels except for being lighter in weight. Whatever height pen you purchase, do not leave your dogs in the pen unattended, as some Silkys

MEX. and AM. CH. HEATHER'S MISTY C.D. is pictured finishing for her Mexican championship under Judge Virginia Miller at Ensenada, Mexico. Her owner-handler is Mrs. C. M. Needham. This excellent bitch was sired by Ch. Cypress Aristo; her dam was Swaledale Ballook; and she was bred by Nancy Purves.

can and will climb out of anything. Occasionally a show building is so small that the premium list will state that exercise pens will not be allowed inside the building, but in those cases you can usually find a spot outside to set it up, again on newspapers, unless the weather is very bad. By using your own exercise pen, you give your dog a safeguard against picking up worms of some kind from walking through stools of infested dogs. The newspapers in your pen should be taken up as soon as they are soiled and deposited in one of the containers provided for waste disposal at every show. If you show several dogs at each show, the exercise pen will be almost indispensable.

Many exhibitors, and all professional handlers, take grooming tables to each show. These tables are fitted with a neck loop through which you put the dog's head while you groom him. It should go without saying that your Silky should never be left alone on the grooming table with the loop around his neck, since he could jump off and hang himself. If you are

PEPI OF AVONWYCK (by Cavalier Mighty of Avonwyck ex Silkallure Rexabigail) is shown winning WD and BOW from Puppy Class at San Fernando KC show. He is owned by Mr. and Mrs. A. Hochman and is handled by his breeder, Janean S. Wylie. Soon after this show he was awarded Best Puppy and BOS at C.O.A.S.T. match. Note his lovely head and expression. At the same show (below) Judge Mrs. Jim Young chose CH. CHATHAM'S CHINITA'S OBERON (by Ch. Silkallure Casanova ex Casa de Casey Chinita) winner of BOB. Bred and owned by Dr. and Mrs. Dennis Harrison, the dog is handled by Dr. Harrison.

showing only one dog, you probably would not need a table, but when showing several, it does speed up your last-minute grooming of three or four Silkys.

If you must travel some distance to the dog show, be sure to leave in ample time so that you will not be rushed. In addition to highway time, you should allow an extra hour or more to find the site of the show building, especially in one of the large cities. If you are travelling as far as 350 to 400 miles for one or two shows, you will have a more enjoyable trip if you travel the day before the show and stay at a motel during the night. Your dog or dogs will also be less tired at the show than they would be if you made a very long drive and then took them immediately to be shown. If the city is unfamiliar to you, and especially if you have an early-morning time to show, make a trial run to the show building the afternoon before the show, both to be sure how to find it and to know how long it will take you to get there from your motel.

CH. D'UNDER SIR N. DIPITY (by Ch. Wexford Pogo ex Ch. D'Under Cavalier Enlu O'Dimity) is shown in a win under Judge Miss Iris de la Torre Bueno, with Paul G. Hefner handling. He was bred and is owned by Mr. Hefner and Mr. Howard A. Jensen.

CH. MARA'S SILVER BEGGAR BOY (by Ch. Redway Beau Brummell ex Ch. Mara's Tiny Tuppence). Owner, Miss Bobbie Jean Davis, handled him to his championship, and he was the first Silky for the SOBLU KENNELS of her parents, Edna and Bob Davis. He strutted his way from first in Veterans Class to BOS at the 1967 Specialty under Judge Nettie Simmons, first breeder-judge to officiate at a Silky Specialty. He was bred by Marjorie P. Edwards and was nine and a half years old when this photograph was taken.

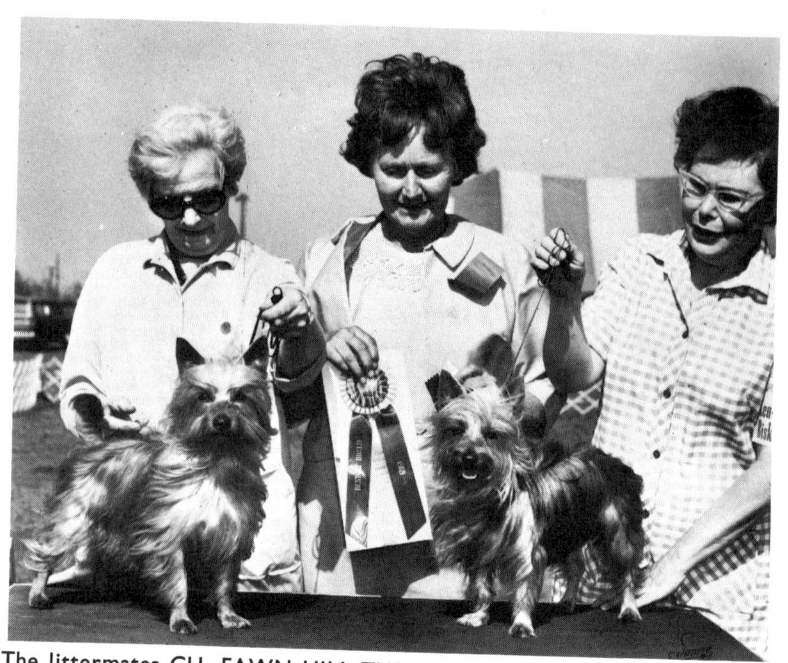

The littermates CH. FAWN HILL THE SOROBAN (left) and CH. FAWN HILL THE ABACUS are shown winning BOB and BOS at Penn Treaty KC under Judge Mrs. Anna Cowie. Soroban is handled by Verna Tucker, breeder-owner, while Abacus is handled by Elinor Norton. Soroban is the only Silky to this time to have won BOB at two STCA Specialty Shows, which he did at Devon D.F.A. in 1968 under Judge Mrs. A. E. Van Court and at Ann Arbor KC in 1969 under Judge Mrs. Georgina Lane. Ch. Larrakin Gorgeous George and Larrakin Young Betty were sire and dam.

If you wish to show at a number of shows, you should obtain a list of licensed Show Superintendents and write to each with the request that they send you premium lists for all shows to be held in your area. When you make your request, be sure to give your full address including zip code, since the premium lists are not sent by first class mail, and will not be delivered without your zip code number. In some areas, you may have your choice of several shows each week–end, while in other areas, considerable driving will be necessary to attend the nearest show. Shows are usually held in pairs, with one kennel club having theirs on Saturday and the other on Sunday. In other cases, there are "show circuits" in which shows are held through the week as well as Saturday and Sunday. Some of the circuits cover a period as long as three weeks. The list of Show Superintendents with their addresses will be found in the dog magazines, or you can write the American Kennel Club to request this information.

CHAPTER 7

Dog Show Classes, Ring Procedure, and Championship Points

New exhibitors find it strange at first that female dogs are called "bitches." However, this is the correct word for female canines, just as the word "vixen" is the correct term for the female fox. Males are classed at shows simply as "dogs." There are five classes in each sex in which you may enter your Silky Terrier to compete for championship points. The winners of each of these five classes in dogs come into the Winners Class for selection of the Winners Dog, and the winners of the five classes in bitches come into another Winners Class for the selection of Winners Bitch. The final class of judging in each breed is called "Best of Breed Competition." The classes are listed below:

Class	*Eligibility Requirements*
PUPPY	Must be 6 months of age but under 12 months. Must be born in the United States or Canada, and may not be a champion. To calculate age, the puppy born on January 1 is eligible to be shown at a show on July 1 of the same year and at shows held through December 31 of the year. He is not eligible for puppy class on January 1 of the next year, but must be shown in one of the adult classes.
NOVICE	Must be 6 months of age or over and born in the U.S. or Canada. May not have won one or more points toward his or her championship. May not have, prior to closing date of entries, won a first prize in Bred-by-Exhibitor, American-Bred, or Open Class, and may not have won more than two

first-prize awards in Novice Class. May not again be shown in this class after winning three first place awards in Novice Class.

BRED-BY-EXHIBITOR Must be 6 months or over, born in the U.S., and not a champion. Also must be owned wholly or in part by the person or by the spouse of the person who was the breeder or one of the breeders of record. Entries

This two-month-old puppy, bred by Mrs. Merle E. Smith and later co-owned with Mrs. Wm. Lehnig, grew up to become CH. REDWAY BUSTER, a very fine Silky and a Top-Producing sire, He is by Ch. Wexford Pogo ex Redway Smith's Gamble, and is now fully owned by Mrs. Lehnig.

ABOU BEN ADHEM, C.D.X. (by Ch. Tinker Blue Blazes ex Totham Miss Ginny-Jo) is a happy and very successful worker in Obedience Trials. He was trained in Obedience work by his breeder-owner, Mr. Harry Wallach, an authority on Obedience training who stresses that "A happy dog is a good-working dog." Mr. Wallach is Vice President of STCA.

in this class must be handled in the class by an owner, or by a member of the immediate family of the owner (husband, wife, father, mother, son, daughter, brother, or sister.)

AMERICAN-BRED — Must be 6 months or over, not a champion, and whelped in the U.S. by reason of a mating which took place in the U.S.

OPEN — Must be 6 months or over. All imported dogs and bitches must be shown in this class, even if they are puppies. Champions may also be shown in this class, but it is not customary to show them here.

You will enter your non-champion dog or bitch in one of the above classes in the appropriate sex. A male puppy would be entered in Puppy, Dogs, a female puppy in Puppy, Bitches, and so on for each class.

CH. REDWAY BONNIE LASS (by Ch. Wexford Pogo ex a double-granddaughter, Redway Rebecca) was one of the foundation bitches of the author's Larrakin Kennels. Bonnie became the dam of five champions and was the first Silky bitch to win BOB at a national Specialty. She is with Jim Young above and is being handled by Mrs. Young (opposite) to a BOB win at the STCA Specialty, Louisville KC, September 4, 1967. Judge is Miss Nettie Simmons and she is holding one of the Australian trophy sashes (customarily given in Australia) presented to top four winners in all Silky Specialties.

WINNERS CLASS

Following judging of all dogs entered in the classes above, the 1st-place winners come into the Winners' Dog Class for selection of the Winners Dog. The 1st-place winners in the classes for bitches come into the Winners Bitch Class for selection of Winners Bitch. Points toward championship are awarded to the Winners Dog and Winners Bitch, depending on the number of entries in each sex, and the area in which the show is being held.

BEST OF BREED COMPETITION Winners Dog, Winners Bitch, and A.K.C. Champions of both sexes are shown in this class. (Imported dogs and bitches which are champions in their country of origin may NOT be shown in this class unless they have also completed the requirements for American Championship.)

The classes for dogs are always judged first, starting with "Puppy, Dogs" (if this class has entries), or the first class for dogs which does have entries. They are shown in judging order in the show catalog. Where large entries are expected, the puppy classes may be divided, so that in each sex there will be classes for "Puppies, 6–9 months" and "Puppies, 9–12 months." In some breeds, Open classes may be divided by color, but this does not apply to Silky Terriers. Some breeds are also divided as if they were two separate breeds, such as "Chihuahuas, Long Coat" and "Chihuahuas, Smooth Coat," and rather than having Best of Breed winners, they will have Best of Variety winners. There is no such division in Silky Terrier judging.

CAN. and AM. CH. WYM-WEY WITH A WAG (Kiku) is by Ch. Mavrob Smokee ex Ch. Kadina of Carriewerloo. Owned by Jon and Kay Magnussen, KIKU Kennels.

You should purchase a show catalog as soon after you arrive at the show as possible. They are available near the entrance to the show building or grounds. The name of each dog and bitch entered will be printed in the catalog, with those in the same classes listed together; the number assigned to each dog or bitch will also be shown. There will not always be entries in every class, and by following the catalog, you can not only follow the judging better, you can see how many dogs or bitches are to be judged before the class in which your Silky is entered, and how many are in the class with your dog.

Each show ring has one and frequently two ring stewards. It is their duty to assist the judge in every way they can to expedite judging; they do not have any part in actual judging of the dogs, nor are they permitted to discuss anything in the show catalog with the judge. The judge's book contains only the number of each entry, listed by the classes in which they are entered. Most shows have public address systems, and when the ring steward sees that the judge will soon be ready for Silky Terriers, he or

CH. KANIMBLA MR. MURDOCH (by Kanimbla Cloncurry Gold ex Kanimbla Blue Heather) is a fifth-generation homebred champion for Mr. and Mrs. Geoffrey H. Sutcliffe. He is pictured finishing for his championship under Judge Mrs. Marie Meyer and handled by E. E. Thorn.

she will have the announcement made, "Silky Terriers, come to Ring (specifying the appropriate ring number) for your arm bands." If this announcement is not made before judging or if you do not hear the announcement, you should go to the ring steward and ask for your arm band specifying the entry number assigned to your Silky. The arm band is worn on your left arm and shows the catalog number of your dog. The judge records his placings in the judge's book from the numbers shown on the arm band worn by the handlers.

Although there may be slight variations in the order of procedure used by different judges, they are essentially the same. As the exhibitors come

BABY DOE'S MOONFIRE by (Ch Artarmon's Max ex Ch. Baby Doe's Delilah) is shown in a major win under Judge Robert Waters at Big Spring KC (Tex.) show. Her breeder-owner-handler is Mrs. Myrtle Puett.

CH SILK OAKS AMY (by Ch. Clarkdale Swagie ex Clarkdale Mary Weldon) is owned by Robert and Paulette Edwards and was handled to her championship by Mr. Edwards. She was bred by Dr. R. T. Gardner.

into the ring with their dogs, they should show the judge the number on their arm bands so that he can note the entry as present. As soon as the first class is assembled in the ring, with absentees noted in his book by the judge, he will direct the handlers on the procedure he uses. For the most part, he (or she, if it is a woman judge) will first have the handlers move their dogs around the ring, with all dogs in the class moving around at the same time. The rings are square or rectangular in shape, and at indoor shows, there is usually a strip of carpeting or rubber matting put down in the same square shape as the ring. Handlers will be directed to move their dogs counter-clockwise around the ring. After watching all dogs move around the ring together, usually two or three times, he will signify to the handlers that they should stop moving. He will then proceed with individual judging of the dog at the head of the line. He may request that the dog be "gaited," that is, moved away from him and back in a straight line, or he may first have the dog put on the table for that examination. Starting with the front of the dog on the table, he will check eye shape, whether the dog's bite is correct, front legs and feet, depth of chest, and proceed through the examination of the dog from front to rear. The judge is also required to check each male for the presence of both testicles

CH. KEALOHA SKIP'S MISS PENNY (by Ch. Prairie Skipper ex Miss Tish) is shown winning BOS from Puppy Class at the Oakland KC show under Judge Mrs. Anna Young. Penny was bred by James and Kathleen Fruit and was owner-handled to her title by Betty Britt and Laurel Gilbertson. Miss Britt is shown in this picture.

normally located in the scrotum. Absence of one or both testicles from the scrotum requires disqualification of the dog, whatever his breed. After the table examination, he will ask that the handler move the dog away from him and back in a straight line. This is called "gaiting" the dog, and he may be moved down and back on one side of the ring, or down and back on a diagonal strip of matting laid down in some rings for this purpose. Some judges ask that the dog be moved away from them and then make a turn to the left, in an inverted "L" shape, so that he can again check the side view, as well as assessing movement from both front and rear. With the exception of the movement into the "L" shape with your Silky, you should always keep him on your left. When you turn to go back from the "L," however, you must switch the dog to your right side, as otherwise you will be between the judge and your dog. When you get back to the long side of the L, you may either switch again to place your dog on your left, or you may come back toward the judge with the dog on your right side. After finishing with the first dog, the judge will proceed to his examination of the second dog, and so on down the line until all dogs in the class have been judged. Many judges will again move all the dogs in the class around the ring together, especially if they have some close decisions to make. When he has decided on his placements in that class, he will direct the dogs to the ring markers in the order of his placings. There are four of these, marked 1, 2, 3, and 4. If there are fewer than four dogs in the class, of course, only the number in the class will be sent to the ring markers. If there are more than four dogs in the class, the

CH. SOBLU PEPITA BONITA, bred and owned by Edna H. Davis and handled by her husband Bob, is shown completing her championship under judging of Mrs. Jim Young. This very typey bitch was sired by Ch. Redway Buster; her dam is Davises' Ch. Redway Rebel Rozalind.

CH. KOONOONA CO LODI is shown winning BOB at Yakima Valley KC under Judge L. E. Piper. The handler is Eugene Hahnlen and owner is Mrs. Connie Alber. This lovely bitch also won BOS at the 1969 Eastern Specialty at Ann Arbor, Michigan, under Judge Mrs. Georgina Lane. She was bred by P. Brown of Australia.

dogs which are not placed are excused from the ring. If you are directed to one of the place markers by the judge, you stand there with your dog, turning your arm band to the judge so that he can mark the number of your dog in his book according to the placement awarded. He will then award the appropriate place ribbons to each dog, along with trophies if any are given in the class. After the ribbons and trophies (if any) are awarded, you will be excused from the ring with your dog. The judge will then proceed to his next class, where the same procedure will be followed.

After going through all of the dog classes in order (provided each contains entries), he will call for the 1st-place winners in each class to come back into the ring for competition for the Winners Dog award. If your dog has won 1st or 2nd place in his class, stay close to ringside for further competition. In the Winners Class, the judge may go through the same detailed procedure he did in the earlier classes, or he may shorten his individual examination of each dog, since he has already examined each dog in his class. This is left to the discretion of the judge. At times, the judge may request that two of the dogs be gaited down and back toward him at the same time; this is usually done when the judge feels he has a close decision to make on certain points. Every dog has some virtues and some faults, and judges must weigh those virtues and faults against each other in the individual dog, and also compare each dog to the others with which the dog is competing. After satisfying himself that he has evaluated each dog thoroughly, he will select one of these 1st place winners as the Winners Dog. This is one of the most coveted awards, as the dog chosen as Winners will receive points toward his championship, in accordance with the Schedule of Points set up by the American Kennel Club.

CH. MIDLAND'S FANCY FRANKIE (by Ch. Koonoona Bo Bo ex Ch. Lylac Jan) is shown winning BOB under Judge Dr. H. L. Huggins. He was bred by Carmen Cananzi and is owned by George Nave and handled by Mrs. Nave. He has also had a number of placings in the Toy Group.

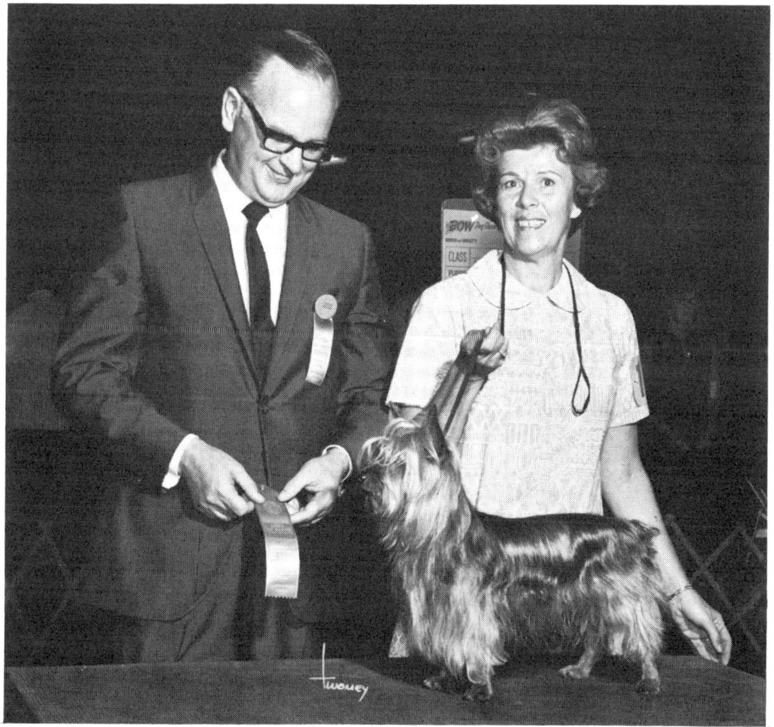

After selecting his Winners Dog, the judge then selects the dog he thinks next best as the Reserve Winners Dog. The procedure connected with this award frequently confuses new exhibitors, so we will explain it in some detail. Let us assume that the judge has designated the 1st Open Dog as his Winners Dog. Having already gone Winners, the 1st Open Dog will not compete for Reserve Winners, but the dog that placed 2nd in Open Dog Class is eligible to compete for Reserve Winners Dog (R.W.D.), so he will come back into the ring to compete against the 1st place winners in all classes: in Puppy, Novice, Bred-by-Exhibitor, and American-Bred classes for Reserve Winners. Should the 1st American-Bred Dog be selected as Winners Dog, the second place winner in the American-Bred class will come back into the ring to compete against the 1st place

CH. MAVROB DINKY DI PANDORA is shown winning under Judge Mrs. Byron Hofman and handled by Miss Faith Medina. She was owned by Mrs. Doris Coburn and bred by Mr. and Mrs. R. G. LaBarre. Her sire was Ch. Fair Dinkum Maverick C.D. and her dam Ch. Mavrob Dorable.

CH. ALLUNGA GALMAHRA, an import owned by Mrs. Bertha Landers, is shown taking Winners Dog award at the 1969 Westminster KC show under Judge Alva Rosenberg. The handler is Jim Henderson.

winners in Puppy, Novice, Bred-by-Exhibitor, and Open Dog classes for Reserve. The award of Reserve Winners does not carry any points, but if for any reason the Winners Dog should be found ineligible for his win, such as being entered in the wrong class, the points he won would be cancelled for that dog, and would instead be awarded to the Reserve Winners Dog. This is the reason you should stay at ringside with your dog if he took 2nd place in his class, at least until you see whether the dog which was 1st in the same class is selected as Winners Dog (W.D.). If the Winners Dog was 1st in a different class from your 2nd-place dog, your dog would not compete for the Reserve Winners award.

The same order of judging will then be followed for the bitch classes, with a Winners Bitch and Reserve Winners Bitch selected. The Winners Bitch will receive points toward her championship according to the number of bitches competing in the classes and the Schedule of Points set up by the A.K.C.

After the bitch classes have been judged, the Best of Breed competition is held. Dogs eligible for this class are American Champions (both male and female) and Winners Dog and Winners Bitch from the class judging. While there is no official separation by sex in this competition, most judges do line up the entries according to sex, especially if the class is large. This is for the purpose of keeping clear in the judge's mind which are dogs and which are bitches, since the sex of the animal is a factor in evaluation of his or her quality. In some breeds, the standard sets out different attributes for each sex; our Silky Terrier standard does not make such specifications, but most judges prefer that a dog appear masculine and a bitch feminine.

In the competition for Best of Breed, the judge will follow the same procedure in judging as he did in the dog and bitch classes. The ring markers in this case are for Best of Breed, Best of Winners, and Best Opposite Sex. Most judges select all three of these at the same time, but if he wishes, he may select the Best of Breed winner, and then call for further examination before deciding on his Best of Winners (only two entries, the Winners Dog and Winners Bitch, compete for this award), and then select the Best Opposite Sex Winner. Should either the Winners Dog or Winners Bitch be selected as Best of Breed, he or she is automatically Best of Winners. The Best Opposite Sex winner will be a bitch if the Best of Breed is a dog, or a dog if the Best of Breed is a bitch. No points are awarded for the Best of Breed and Best Opposite Sex awards, but the Best of Winners award may at times carry points, as will be explained in the next paragraph. It should be noted here that if the Winners Dog or Winners Bitch should win Best of Breed or Best Opposite Sex, defeating one or more champions in doing so, he or she would receive no additional points for the champions defeated.

The dog or bitch which is awarded Best of Winners may receive additional points for that award, but only if the points awarded in the defeated sex should be higher than those in his or her own sex. To illustrate, if there were three points in dogs and three points in bitches, the Best of Winners award would not change the number of points won. If there was only one point available in dogs, however, and three points in bitches, and the Winners Dog won Best of Winners over the Winners Bitch, he would then receive three points instead of the one point awarded him as Winners Dog. The Best of Winners is entitled to the same number of points as awarded in the defeated sex, *not in addition to* those won in his own sex, *but instead of* those already won if they are lower. Thus, the W.D. in the illustration which went Best of Winners would be awarded three points instead of one point, but would not get four points for B.O.W.

There is one other way in which a class dog or bitch (a non-champion)

CH. AVONWYCK MAIRI STUART in win of WB, BOS to finish at Lizard Butte KC under Judge H. Tyler, handled by Bob Hastings. Bred and owned by Miss Janean Wylie. Sire is Ch. Silkallure Casanova; dam Mavrob Fair Trina C.D.

may gain points toward the championship title. After the individual breeds have been judged, the Best of Breed winners then compete in their respective Variety Groups. There are six Groups: Sporting Dogs, Hounds, Working Dogs, Terriers, Toys, and Non-Sporting Dogs. Silky Terriers are assigned to the Toy Group. Should either the Winners' Dog or the Winners Bitch from the class judging go on to win Best of Breed, then he or she would go into the Toy Group as the representative of Silky Terriers. If he should win 1st place in the Toy Group, he would be entitled to the highest number of points awarded in the class judging in any breed that is a member of the Toy Group, with five points the maximum number possible in any one show. The competition in the Groups is very keen, so this does not occur very often, but a few Silky Terriers have won the Group before having obtained their championships.

CH. ARTARMON'S TRITON JODY (Ch. Artarmon's Jonbon Boy ex Artarmon's Raggedy Ann) shown winning under Judge Mrs. Irene C. Khatoonian and handled by Frank Abarta. At right is Miss Julie Poimiroo, daughter of Jody's owners, Mr. & Mrs. Maurice Poimiroo. Mr. Poimiroo was President of STCA in 1967 and 1968 and it was he who proposed having two annual STCA Specialties, one east and one west of the Rockies, proved a great success with the membership. Jody was bred by Mr. and Mrs. H. Norman Charles.

After each of the six Variety Groups has been judged, the winner of each Group goes back into the ring for the final judging of the day, the selection of the Best In Show.

Championship Points—To become a Champion of Record under American Kennel Club rules, a dog or bitch must win 15 points. At least six of these points must be won at two shows with a rating of three or more points per show and under two different judges. One or more of the remaining nine points must have been won under a third judge. The number of points awarded in each sex of each breed are determined by a Schedule of Points established by the Board of Directors of the American Kennel Club. There may be 1, 2, 3, 4, or 5 points awarded in each sex of each breed or variety, but no more than five points are awarded at any one show. Where competition is sufficient for the dog or bitch to win 3, 4, or 5 points at one show, he or she is credited with a "major" win. The requirements for the title of Champion are generally stated simply as "15 points and two majors, under at least three different judges." Occasionally, especially in rare breeds, the sexes may be combined in the classes, and in this case, there is only one point winner, whichever dog or bitch is named as Winners. We rarely see this now in Silky Terriers, with their tremendous growth in popularity in recent years.

MABROUKA EAMONN, U.D., was the first Silky to complete the Utility degree in obedience training. An import, he is owned by Mrs. Ernest (Alicia) Hanschman and was trained by her and shown by her and Mr. Hanschman, completing his U.D. requirements in November 1962. Not until seven years later, when Lady Brandewyne, U.D., owned by the Gordon Schulte family, earned this advanced degree (September 1969) was there another Silky with this title.

The Schedule of Points is based on the number of show entries in each sex and breed during the preceding year, and further broken down by geographical divisions of the country. Champions shown are not considered in arriving at the point scales. The Schedule is revised annually and becomes effective on May 15 of the year.

The point scale applicable at a particular show is given in the front of every show catalog, before the listing of the individual entries at the show. If you have any question as to how many points are to be awarded in any breed, you can refer to the Schedule in the catalog, which applies to the geographical area in which that particular show is held.

CH. REBEL COUNTESS MYD (D'Under Count Chequers ex Ch. Aldoon Countess Candy) is shown finishing her championship under Judge E. D. McQuown. She is handled by E. E. Thorn. Owned by Miss Mildred Pequignot, she was bred by Mrs. Wm. Lehnig.

The minimum point scale for any breed requires 2 dogs or 2 bitches for one point. In other words, if you have a dog entered, he must defeat one other dog to win one point; if your entry is a bitch, she must defeat one other bitch to win one point; the dog or bitch could also win one point by winning Best of Winners over the other sex winner, as explained previously. To continue with the minimum point scale, 3 dogs or 3 bitches are required for two points, 4 dogs or 4 bitches for three points (a major win), 5 dogs or 5 bitches for four points (major), and 6 dogs or 6 bitches for five points, the latter a major and the maximum points allowed for one show. The minimum scale is no longer applicable to Silky Terriers except in Alaska, Hawaii, and Puerto Rico, each of which is calculated as a separate area.

CH. FAWN HILL THE SOROBAN (by Ch. Larrakin Gorgeous George ex Larrakin Young Betty) is shown winning BOB at the 1968 STCA Specialty at Devon DFA show under Judge Mrs. A. E. Van Court. His breeder-owner-handler is Mrs. Verna Tucker. Mrs. Elinor Morrison is shown presenting the Ch. Wexford Pogo Memorial Trophy which she and her husband Ed Morrison donate to Specialty winners in memory of Pogo. Soroban is the only Silky Terrier to have won two STCA Specialties.

Continental United States is divided into four geographical divisions, consisting of from one to 21 states each. The State of California, where show entries are large in most breeds, makes up Division 3 by itself. Division 1 consists generally of the 17 states in New England, the Northeast, and part of the Midwest, with the District of Columbia also included. Division 2, with 21 states, includes southern states extending from Florida to Arizona, also Colorado, Iowa, Kansas, Nebraska, Minnesota, Tennessee, Kentucky, and West Virginia. The 9 states of Division 4 are the Dakotas, Montana, Wyoming, Utah, Nevada, Idaho, Oregon, and Washington.

The formula used in calculating the point scale is complex and need not concern us here. The reasons for use of this method are soundly based,

Children and Silky Terriers get along very well, as many owners have discovered, but children must be mature enough to accept responsibility before being given complete charge of their dog's development. The two lovely girls shown are Yvonne and Gwendolyn Lattin, twin granddaughters of Mrs. Dorothy Hicks. The picture was taken in 1962, when the girls were seven years old.

as are most of the regulations of the American Kennel Club. The Schedules are set up in such a way that enough points are available in competition in different breeds to continue the exhibitor's interest in showing his dog, but not so freely available that large numbers of unworthy dogs could become Champions.

In Silky Terriers, the highest requirements for points are in the state of California because the largest entries in the breed are found there. With the year effective May 15, 1969, a 3-point major win in California requires 13 class dogs or 12 class bitches. For the maximum 5-point major win, 17 dogs or 19 bitches are required.

CHAPTER 8

Handler—Owner or Professional?

The new exhibitor is often unaware of the existence of professional dog handlers until he has attended some shows. After he discovers their existence, he wonders if he should go ahead and handle his own dog, or if he should engage the services of a professional. If he decides to handle his own Silky, he wonders if his dog can defeat the dog handled by a professional. The answer to the last question is yes, but the owner-handler will have to work hard to train his dog properly if he hopes to be successful with him in competition. I was not fully aware of how bad a poor handler can make a good Silky Terrier look until after I began judging in the show ring. If you cannot train your dog to gait properly in the ring, and to show himself to advantage otherwise, you cannot expect him to do well at shows.

The matter of whether or not to hire a professional handler depends on the individual circumstances. We have always handled our own Silkys because we enjoyed travelling with them, we loved attending dog shows, and we enjoyed visiting with fanciers of Silky Terriers and other breeds as well. There is certainly more satisfaction in handling your own dog to his championship than there is in having someone else accomplish this, and by attending dog shows in person, you will learn a great deal more about dogs than you could by staying at home while you send your dog to the show. In any event, it is probably wise for an owner, especially with one or two dogs, to handle the Silky himself at least in puppy classes. In that way, the puppy will learn that going to dog shows with his beloved owner is a very pleasant experience, and he may well adapt more readily to going with a handler than if both the handler and the shows are strange to him when he starts out.

If you feel that you are too nervous to handle your Silky well, or if circumstances at home are such that you have difficulty in getting away for the shows, then by all means employ the services of a professional handler. As in any occupation, different handlers possess different degrees of skill, and you should check thoroughly into various handlers in your area. Many of the women handlers specialize in handling small breeds, and if the Silky's owner is a woman, he or she may well do better with a woman handler. You will want to know how well a particular handler cares for the dogs he handles, how skilful he is at training and handling, and in the case of the most successful handlers, whether or not he or she considers your Silky Terrier a good specimen of the breed that he or she would like to show. The better handlers should, and do, turn down dogs which they consider unworthy of being shown, thereby maintaining their reputation as handlers of dogs of excellent quality.

Mr. and Mrs. William Lehnig were our first breeders in the Midwest, and are shown with two of their early homebred Champions in BOS and BOB wins under Judge Earle Adair. Beverly Lehnig is on the left with CH. REBEL MR. WONDERFUL (by D'Under Count Chequers ex Ch. Aldoon Countess Candy) and Bill, on the right, is handling CH. REBEL TAFFETA RUFFLES (by Mr. Wonderful ex Ch. Aldoon Countess Candy). Ruffles won the 1961 Iradell Trophy for breed wins and also had several Group placings.

CH. BRINKERHOFF'S CECIL BEAT 'EM (by Ch. Midland's Beau O'Ronhoff ex Ch. Midland's Sparkling Dolly) is shown at the age of ten months with his handler, Terry Correll. Cecil was bred and is owned by Lillian Brinkerhoff.

If you enjoy the shows, the other people, and getting to see Silky Terriers owned by others, by all means do train and handle your dog yourself. If you do handle your Silky, you must learn to be a good loser when necessary and a gracious winner when such is your lot. Owners who are so emotionally involved with their dogs that they feel it is a disaster if the dog is defeated, and who find fault with every dog which defeats their own, should NEVER handle their Silky Terriers. This type of exhibitor not only spoils his own possible enjoyment of dog shows, he usually manages to spoil the shows for the other exhibitors as well. Individual judges will

Top of facing page is CH. GIMMY-DEN TEE CEE (by Ch. Bowenvale Blue Boy ex Koonoona Coleen) taking WB at San Fernando KC under Judge O. C. Harriman. She was bred by Mrs. Jacqueline Abarta and is owned by 1969 STCA President Frank Abarta and L. E. Gillette. Lower photo at Tucson KC show is of CH. SILKALLURE CANTERBURY BELLE (by Ch. Coolaroo Sir Winston ex Woorina Penny) winning BOB under Judge Edward Pickhart and handled by George Payton. Breeder-owners are Fred H. Stern and Leonard J. Pilley. They also own CH. SILKALLURE WINANDY, pictured above winning BOB at the 1967 Sir Francis Drake KC show under Judge Mrs. Merle Smith and handling of Tom Witcher. Bred by V. and M. Bracco, Winandy was sired by Ch. Silkallure Rexandy ex Bondoon's Silkie Sullivan.

frequently differ in their interpretation of the breed standard, especially as to which virtues are most important and which faults are most serious, so that placements of the same group of dogs may differ from one show to the next. The exhibitor should remember that it is not a matter of life and death whether his dog wins or loses. He should also keep in mind that he brings the same dog out of the ring that he took into the ring. A judge's decision may confirm or contradict your opinion that your Silky Terrier is an excellent specimen, but his placement does not in any way affect the actual quality of your dog.

CH. SIR JOSHUA DE LAFAYETTE C.D.X. (by Kajon Kahlualure Kim ex Stelander Missy II Fawny) was bred by Stella P. Anderson and is owned by Susan and John Henry. He was handled to his conformation and obedience titles by Sue Henry.

In this connection, if your dog does lose in the ring after doing his best to perform as you want him to, do be sure to praise him. Your Silky cares not at all whether he went 1st or 4th in his class—all he cares about is your approval, and he should certainly have that regardless of a judge's decision.

Readers wishing further information about shows and showing are advised to see *How to Show Your Own Dog*, by Virginia Tuck Nichols. Published by T.F.H. Publications.

CHAPTER 9

A Look at Genetics

Genetics is defined as: "(1) The branch of biology dealing with heredity and variation among related organisms, largely in their evolutionary aspects. As an applied science it deals with the fundamentals of plant and animal breeding, especially in the production and development of improved strains, varieties, breeds, etc." and "(2) the genetic make-up and phenomena of an organism, type, or group." (from *Webster's New Collegiate Dictionary*, G. & C. Merriam Co., Publishers).

It is strange that more Silky Terrier breeders (and those in other breeds as well) have not studied this subject for the help available in improving their dogs. When we consider the time, effort, and money spent on breeding and exhibiting, one must wonder why so many have overlooked this splendid source of assistance. Many breeders have told me that they would like to study genetics, but that it is "too difficult" or "too technical" to understand. Because of this, and my own continuing fascination with this most engrossing of all subjects, I will endeavor to present here some of the more basic facts on this subject. This is not intended to be an extensive scientific treatise on the subject, which I am not qualified to write, but rather as a sort of "stepping-stone" to further study. My hope is that the somewhat simplified presentation following will enable readers to proceed to some of the excellent textbooks written by qualified geneticists. While much is not yet known of the method of transmission of specific characteristics in different breeds, enough is known to enable each of us to better understand those forces with which we work. The principles of genetic inheritance do apply to dog breeding, whether or not we are aware that they are in operation.

One of the aspects of dog breeding that fascinates us all is the feeling that we play at least a small part in the creation of better animals. While we do not ourselves create, we do share in the direction developments will take when we select the dog and bitch to be mated together. Along with that share in creation comes the responsibility to do our very best toward the goal we should all share, the creation of the perfect Silky Terrier.

CH. LARRAKIN GORGEOUS GEORGE (by Maryanne Sir Charles ex Larrakin Lovely Lace) was bred by W. S. Guess and is owned by Mrs. Elinor Norton and Mrs. Verna Tucker, who handled him to his title. He is the sire of three champions, with a fourth having almost completed her championship requirements. Among his get is Ch. Fawn Hill the Soroban (ex Larrakin Young Betty), the only Silky ever to win two Silky Terrier Club of America (STCA) Specialty Best of Breed wins.

CHAPTER 10

Gregor Mendel and His Peas

From earliest times, man must have noticed the tendency of related individuals to resemble each other, and for centuries men of scientific minds had speculated as to what it was that caused this resemblance. It remained for an obscure ecclesiastic, patiently working with garden peas, to discover the answer to the puzzle.

Johann Gregor Mendel was born of a peasant family in 1822. He became a monk and later abbot in the Augustinian monastery at Brünn in Moravia (now Czechoslovakia). We can imagine that he was a man possessed of an inquisitive mind; he must surely also have been a patient and methodical man, as he worked with culinary peas there in the monastery garden for eight long years. Observing that there were sharply contrasting characteristics in the species, he set about trying to determine the manner in which these differing characteristics were inherited.

He began his experiments with a pair of pea plants which differed in appearance, one being tall and the other being short (or dwarf). Each of these peas was pure-breeding when mated back to its own kind. By keeping accurate pedigree records, and counting and recording the results, he discovered that there was a regular method of inheritance which could be predicted with mathematical certainty.

In 1866 he read a paper before the Historical Society of Brünn setting forth the theories he had formulated based on the results of his experiments. Although the Society published Mendel's paper in all its detail, their journal was such an obscure one that the report lay unnoticed until 1900. In that year, Dr. L. H. Bailey of Cornell University included a listing of the paper in the bibliography of his research paper on heredity, although it is said that he himself had not read Mendel's report. When Dr. Hugo

DeVries of Holland read Dr. Bailey's paper and bibliography, he did read Mendel's paper, and there he found the answers he had been seeking. Gregor Mendel died at the monastery in 1884, some 16 years before the scientific world became aware of his revolutionary theory.

For many years before Mendel, others had been working on the same problem, but the generally accepted theories of those days had to do with the mixing of blood. The theory of blood blending held that a mixing of inherited characteristics occurred anew with each generation. The process would be comparable to a cook preparing a pudding, in that the separate entities of milk, eggs, sugar, and flavoring would be blended together, but in such a way that they could never be unblended to again become separate entities. It is from these theories that we get the word "bloodlines" so commonly used today, although it is actually incorrect in its connotation of blood-mixing.

Although Mendel's theory was revolutionary for his time, it was the only one found to work in practice and to account for all known facts. He kept accurate pedigree records, and having observed, counted, and recorded the results of his experiments, developed the theory that certain "factors" or "particles," as he called them (later to be known as genes), were inherited in related pairs, one from each parent. The factors (genes) came together in the fertilized egg cell and worked on each other in various ways, but each factor (or gene) remained a separate entity and could be passed on to the next generation as such. Beginning his experiments with a pair of pea plants differing in characteristics, but each pure-breeding when bred back to its own, he worked out the formulas with which the results of matings could be predicted. He further discovered that when the two parents showed different characteristics, the factor inherited from one parent could suppress the action of the factor inherited from the other parent. The factor which suppressed the action of the other, he called *dominant*; the factor which was suppressed (that is, hidden), he called *recessive*.

It is important to remember that the gene is always a separate entity. It is inherited by the individual dog as a separate unit and is passed along to his offspring as a separate unit. Whatever physical appearance may be produced by the pairing of the two genes, one from the sire and one from the dam, there is no mixing or blending of the genes themselves. It may help the new student to visualize the dominant genes as black marbles and the recessive genes as white marbles. Given a large bowl of 100 marbles, half black and half white, and selecting any 50 at random, you would find some black (representing the dominant) and some white (representing the recessive). Repeating this mixing and random selection a number of times, you would find that each 50 selected would contain varying numbers

Pictured are the foundation dog and bitch owned by Mr. and Mrs. Robert Franceschi. On the left is CH. REDWAY FLYING TIMOTHY, C. D., and on the right is REDWAY BLACK-EYED SUSAN. Timothy is by Prairie Roger ex Ch. Redway Splinters and was bred by Mrs. M. E. Smith; Susan is by Ch. Wexford Pogo ex Canberra Cupie and was bred by Karen and Dorothy J. Vanderhoof.

of the black or white marbles, which as dominant and recessive genes would produce different characteristics in different dogs, but the individual marbles would not change in size, shape, or color.

Before going further into Mendel's theory of inheritance, we will explain and use some of the symbols customarily used in genetics. The first pair of peas that Mendel used are the "First Parental Generation," or $P._1$ for short. We as dog breeders would call these the parents, or sire and dam. The "Second Parental Generation," $P._2$, is what we would call the grandparents; the third, or $P._3$, is to us the great-grandparents, and so on. The offspring of the first pair of parents would be called the "First Filial Generation," or $F._1$ for short; the offspring of the $F._1$ generation would be the "Second Filial Generation," or $F._2$, and so on down through each generation of descendants.

In describing what Mendel called "factors" and we today call genes, a letter is assigned to a gene which produces a particular characteristic, with the gene which is dominant always described by a capital letter. The gene which is recessive is described by the same letter, but in lower-case form. In this way, the genetic make-up of a plant or animal can be described by a series of letters, without having to go into a lengthy description of the characteristic produced by each gene.

Every plant and every animal, including man, has what might be described as two beings. One of these is his physical appearance, that is, how he looks from the outside. This is called his "phenotype." The other being is his genetic make-up, which is the pattern of genes he possesses.

This very promising female puppy, then about eight months of age, was described by the late Frank Longmore of Australia as one of the best he had seen in a long time. She was bred in Australia, but was later imported and is now owned by James T. and Henrietta Moss, Artarmon's Breeding & Boarding Kennels. She became AM. CH. ROCKWOOD VALMA, sire being Swaledale James and dam Milan Miladi.

We call this his "genotype." Only the breeder who realizes that each of his dogs and bitches have this genotype, which will differ in many respects from the actual physical appearance of the individual animal, can breed with maximum skill. Each dog must possess genes for the characteristics he displays outwardly, but he also possesses genes for some characteristics he does not display, since he has inherited one gene from his sire and one from his dam for any given characteristic.

Mr. and Mrs. Donald Receveur photographed with CH. SOBLU MY FANCY (by Ch. Midland's Fancy Frankie ex Ch. Just a Smidgen of Dixie), bred by Bob Davis, and (right) SHOW STOPPER OF DIXIE (by Ch. Redway Buster ex Ch. Aldoon Bonnie Lass), bred by Mrs. Receveur. On the way to her championship, Fancy won WB at the 1969 Eastern Specialty, while Show Stopper was Reserve to her. The Receveurs have retired from breeding; Fancy is now owned by Mrs. Merle E. Smith and Stopper is owned by Mrs. William Lehnig.

Returning to Gregor Mendel's experiments with peas, we find that one of the characteristics in which the first pair of peas (First Parental Generation, or P_1) differed was that one was a tall plant and the other a dwarf (or short) plant. We must remember that each was pure-breeding when mated back to its own kind. In the offspring of the first pair, the First Filial, or F_1 Generation, all of the pea plants were tall, so that the gene which produced tallness was dominant to the gene producing shortness*. Let us call the gene for tallness by the letter "T." In this generation, all offspring had the physical appearance, or phenotype, of the tall parent. The F_1 plants were allowed to become self-fertilized, and in the F_2 generation, the genes had recombined, so that tall and short plants were both present, in the ratio of three tall to one short. Let us call the gene for shortness by the letter "t." The F_2 plants were permitted to become self-fertilized, and it was found that while every plant exhibiting the recessive appearance for shortness bred true, only one of every three exhibiting the dominant appearance for tallness bred true. Two of the three which were tall in phenotype did not breed true, but produced tall and short plants

*That is, lack of tallness.

in the same ratio as had the self-bred $F._1$ individuals, or three tall to one short. Thus it was clear that although the three tall plants produced by $F._1$ appeared the same, their genetic make-up, or genotype, was different. From many generations, Mendel found that there were six possible ways in which a pair of determiners could combine, and that the combinations were mathematically predictable.

FAIR DINKUM CHRISTOPHER (Ch. Koolamina Aussie ex Elysium Matilda) was bred and is owned by Mrs. Lucille Preston.

The tall plants which bred true would be described genetically as "TT," or pure dominant for the gene for tallness; they are described as "homozygous" for the dominant trait. The short plants, which also bred true, would be described as "tt." They are homozygous for the recessive gene for the trait, having received one recessive gene for the characteristic from each parent. The tall plants which did not breed true would be mixed,

CH. GARONA CHARGER is owned by Miss Phyllis Cook, who imported him from his Australian breeder, Mrs. Helen Thornton. His sire is Aus. Ch. Semloh Cassius; dam is Garona Lady Vicki.

or hybrids, so that their genotype would be "Tt," representing one gene for tallness inherited from one parent and one for shortness from the other parent. In such cases, where one dominant and one recessive gene make up the pair, they are described as "heterozygous."

The list below will show the physical appearance, or phenotype, of parents and offspring by the descriptive word, tall or short. The genotype of each parent and offspring will be shown by the genetic designation of TT, Tt, or tt. The genotype of the offspring are shown in the ratio in which they will appear, though it should be noted that the ratios represent the average at which combinations will appear over a large number of matings. Although this shows the predicted ratio from Mendel's experiments with tall and short pea plants, the identical ratio can be applied to any characteristic in a dog which is governed by a single pair of genes. The table is *not applicable* to tallness or shortness in our Silky Terriers, as size in dogs is the result of a number of gene pairs working together.

TT Tall	to	tt Short	(Genotype) (Phenotype)	Tt Tall	Tt Tall	Tt Tall	Tt Tall
Tt Tall	to	Tt Tall	(Genotype) (Phenotype)	TT Tall	Tt Tall	Tt Tall	tt Short
tt Short	to	tt Short	(Genotype) (Phenotype)	tt Short	tt Short	tt Short	tt Short
TT Tall	to	TT Tall	(Genotype) (Phenotype)	TT Tall	TT Tall	TT Tall	TT Tall
TT Tall	to	Tt Tall	(Genotype) (Phenotype)	TT Tall	TT Tall	Tt Tall	Tt Tall
Tt Tall	to	tt Short	(Genotype) (Phenotype)	Tt Tall	Tt Tall	tt Short	tt Short

Since we are primarily concerned with Silky Terriers, let us now apply these ratios to a characteristic seen in our dogs. For purposes of illustration, we will assume that the gene for erect ears is dominant to the gene for non-erect (or pendant) ears, and that ear carriage is controlled by a single pair of genes. Please bear in mind that this is an assumption only, as it is quite possible that ear carriage is controlled by more than one pair of genes or by interaction of genes of the same pair, since we have degrees of the fault of non-erect ears, such as half-up, or tipped-over, ears. A majority of geneticists do assume that erect ears are dominant to the recessive pendant ears.

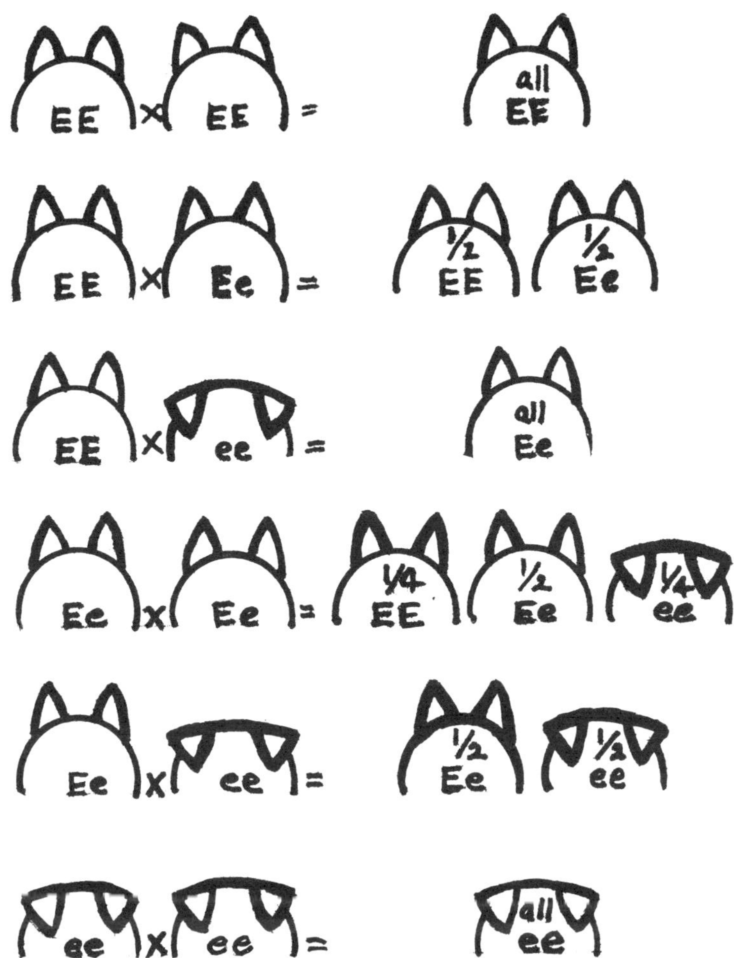

In the above table, the capital letter "E" is used for the dominant gene for erect ears, with the lower-case "e" representing the recessive gene for non-erect, or drop ears. Only in the first, third, and sixth matings will exact expectations be realized in each litter. In the others, the ratios would apply over large numbers of puppies.

Thus we can see from the illustration that the old saying, "Like begets like" holds true only as applied to the genotype of the dog. When applied to the physical appearance, or phenotype, of the dog and bitch to be mated, like will not necessarily beget like. As applied to erect ears, wherein we are assuming that the trait is controlled by a single pair of genes, we find when both parents are genetically homozygous dominant for erect ears, all offspring will show erect ears and will be genetically pure for erect ears. With a dog and bitch, both showing erect ears, but with one having double dominant genes and the other having one dominant and one recessive, all offspring will show erect ears, the characteristic produced by the dominant gene, but half will become carriers of the recessive gene for drop ears. This is the reason we are often warned that recessive genes for undesirable traits are more dangerous than are dominant genes for undesired traits. If the animal has even one dominant gene for the characteristic, he must show it physically, so that dominant genes could be readily bred out by eliminating dogs showing the trait from our breeding programs. With recessive genes, however, several generations of the dogs' ancestors may carry the gene, though it is hidden or masked by the dominant gene. The hidden recessive gene will come to light in the offspring only when the dog carrying the recessive is bred to a bitch which carries the same recessive gene. Conversely, if any dog or bitch shows a characteristic governed by a recessive gene, then he or she *MUST* carry a double dose of the recessive gene, and each parent must have the recessive in at least single dosage.

This mother-daughter duo shows an interesting point on color inheritance. On the right is BONDI'S CAMIRA (Ch. Aldoon Randwick ex Ch. Kanimbla's Mildura Belle), bred by Col. and Mrs. J. J. Pavlas. On the left is her daughter BONDI'S PRINCESS BO PEEP, by Ch. Larrakin Young Jamie. The dam shows black on her face here, which is faulty, though it cleared by the time she was about four years old. Bred to a dog with correct tan face, she produced PRINCESS, who also shows the correct tan face. Both bitches have points toward championship and are owned by Lt. Col. and Mrs. Del Smyth.

Author's Note:
Because color is of such vital importance in this breed—the Silky Terrier that is not clearly blue and tan cannot be a good one—it should be noted that color photographs will not always show a dog's precise coloring. I have personally seen each dog that we show in color, and where color rendition is not true to the actual dog, this has been noted in the picture caption.

CHAPTER 11

Cells, Chromosomes, and Genes

Have you not marveled at that wee creature, the newborn Silky puppy, and regarded with wonder the perfection of even one feature, such as that tiny foot, so intricately formed?

This very promising female puppy, eight weeks old, was bred and is owned by Mrs. Mary T. Estrin, Silti's Kennels. Her Sire is Ch. Silti's Joy Boy and her dam is Ch. Coolaroo Dame Wintiki.

As we come to know something of the manner in which the puppy is created, we must marvel even more. Every unit of the inheritance that makes him what we see was passed along to him in that split second of conception when the sperm met the ovum and he came into being as a single cell. The genes that link him to all of his ancestors, and that he will pass along to his descendants, have come to him from his sire and dam in that fleeting moment of time.

The new being is created when the male sperm joins the female ovum, or egg, and the zygote, or primordial cell, is formed. The cell is the unit of life. It multiplies by dividing—one becomes two, two become four, and so on to become the entire being. It is microscopic and consists of the living substance called protoplasm, surrounded by the cell membrane. The main functional unit of the cell is the nucleus. The nucleus contains the chromosomes, and the genes are carried on the chromosomes.

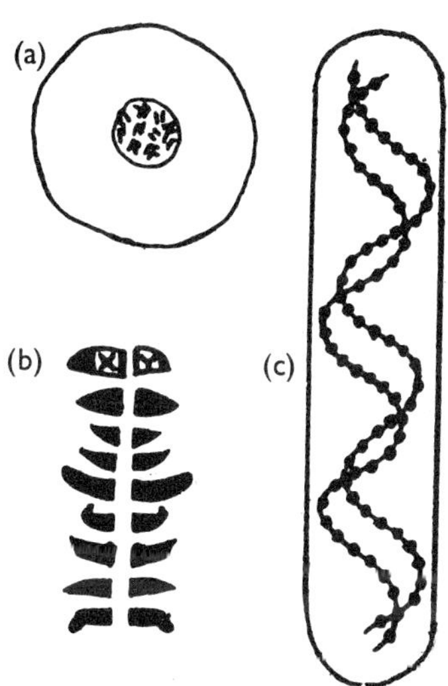

Schematic representations:
(a) A cell—an outer wall enclosing cytoplasm, and a nucleus in which are the chromosomes bearing the genes that determine hereditary characteristics.
(b) Typical pairing of chromosomes, including the female determinant X chromosome and the usually smaller Y chromosome that initiates development of a male.
(c) Conventional delineation of a chromosome with genes strung like beads on the strings of a double helix and one of each paired gene occupying the same position on each string.

The chromosomes are odd-shaped bodies, and the genes are carried on them somewhat like a string of beads (remember the black and white marbles?), with each gene having a specified location on the chromosome. Like the genes, the chromosomes occur in pairs, one member of each pair coming from each parent. Different species have different numbers of chromosomes, but each member of a given species has the same number as others of that species. The *Drosophila* fruit fly, has eight chromosomes, or four pairs; they have been used extensively in genetic research because of their rapid rate of reproduction and their simple chromosome pattern. Maps have been made of the chromosomes of the fruit fly. In humans, the

AUS. and AM. CH. KOONOONA BEAU BRUMMELL (by Aus. Ch. Milan Toby ex Aus. and Am. Ch. Bowenvale Coralee) is one of the few Silky Terriers to have won a Best in Show, All Breeds, in Australia (only three such wins have been verified to date). This momentous win occurred at the Northern Classic KC in Brisbane, Australia in 1966. He was imported by Mr. and Mrs. E. L. Macy and has also finished his American championship. Mrs. Macy (Vickie) has served as an officer in both the STC of Southern California and the present City of Angels Silky Terrier Club. Her kennel prefix is ELMVALE. (Note: this dog has exceptionally rich, clear blue coloration that is regrettably not revealed in the photograph.)

CH. WEXFORD POGO (by Baulkham Royal John ex Elouera Joy) is shown here in the picture used for the cover of the first Silky Terrier book ever published, *How to Raise and Train a Silky Terrier*, by Betty Young, published in 1963 by T.F.H. Publications. Pogo was owned by Mrs. Merle E. Smith and was a consistent winner in the Miscellaneous classes at shows, as well as having become a Top Producer.

number of chromosomes is 46, or 23 pairs. The dog is believed to have 78 chromosomes, or 39 pairs. (Why a particular number in any living thing is unknown.) With one exception, each chromosome is like the other member of its pair, but there is variation in the size and shape of different pairs. The one pair in which the two members differ from each other is the sex chromosome of the male, designated as XY, with the Y chromosome being smaller than the X chromosome. In the female, the sex chromosomes are alike and are designated XX.

After the ovum, or egg, has been fertilized to become the zygote, or rudimentary single cell that will become the puppy, the zygote begins to divide and grow by a process called mitosis until the embryo becomes a puppy. The astounding part of this process is that, as each cell divides, it reproduces itself precisely in the resulting daughter cells, and each cell in the body contains a full set of chromosomes and genes faithfully copied from the original set inherited from the parents. The body of the dog contains billions of cells, so that the duplicating feat of that one original cell staggers the imagination.

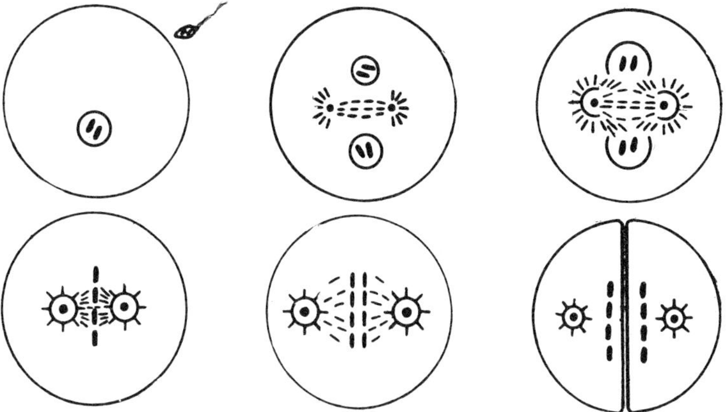

With its complement of chromosomes and a body called the centrosome, the sperm approaches the egg, with the maternal chromosomes in the cytoplasm-surrounded nucleus. Upon entry of the sperm, the fertilized egg becomes a zygote. Then the cell division known as mitosis begins; the centrosome migrates to the center of the cell and extends to form a spindle. Following in the charted sequence, the nuclei are drawn together; the chromosomes line up, then duplicate themselves. Finally a wall forms to divide the cell into a pair of identical daughter cells. These will divide into daughter cells in like manner and such division continues until the body is completely formed, and thereafter during the life of the animal as is required for replacement of cells worn out or destroyed. From the establishment of the chromosomal pattern in the zygote, all cells produced have the identical chromosome formation, however different may be their somatic structure and function in the organs of which they form a part.

The inherited genes not only provide for this remarkable duplication of cells, the pattern of the genes serves as a sort of blueprint which directs the formation of the entire structure. As the embryo grows, the cells are differentiated as to the job each is to have—blood cells, brain cells, bone cells, and all the rest, to function as the blueprint directs, and continue to reproduce themselves as necessary during the life of the individual animal.

There is one exception to the form of cell division just described (mitosis), which is essentially a copying process. This is in the form of cell division which takes place in the sex organs. This method of cell division is called meiosis. Since each member of a species must contain the same number of chromosomes as others of the species, it is clear that if each parent contributed a whole cell, with all of its chromosomes and genes, the puppy would have twice as many chromosomes and genes as he should have. Therefore, the reproductive cells divide to reduce by half the number of chromosomes and genes that will be passed along to the offspring. The chromosome pairs split lengthwise into halves called chromatids. The half-cells formed by chromatic division are called gametes (sperm in the male and ovum in the female). When fertilization occurs, the two half cells are united, so that each puppy will begin as one cell, which carries the half of his genes from his sire and the other half from his dam. Which half of the sire's gene-bearing chromosomes and which half of the dam's gene-bearing chromosomes go into each gamete, later to be joined, is a matter of chance, depending on which sperm fertilizes which of the ova.

The illustrative sketch will give you a rough idea of the process of meiosis. We have used only eight chromosomes here for purposes of simplicity.

The number of puppies in a litter is determined entirely by the dam, depending on the number of ova shed at a particular season. A normally fertile stud will discharge millions of sperm at one mating. Thus it is foolish that some stud owners boast of the large litters sired by their studs, as any fertile stud will produce many, many more sperm than needed to fertilize all the ova shed.

The sex of the puppy is determined by the sire, depending on whether the sperm which penetrates the ovum carries the X gene or the Y gene. The dam passes one of the pair on her sex chromosome to each puppy, and since she has the XX pair, she can only pass along an X. Here again we have a matter of chance, with a male puppy resulting from penetration by the sire's Y-bearing sperm, and a female puppy resulting from penetration by the sire's X-bearing sperm. The following diagram illustrates the process of sex determination.

The sex chromosomes also contain genes aside from those for sex determination, but are not believed to carry as large a number as other chromosomes. It is also assumed that the Y chromosome of the male, which is

CH. NUKARA ANASTACIA OF MIDLAND (by Aus. and Am. Ch. Koonoona Bo Bo ex Artarmon's Nukara Tirrita) has very deep, rich coloring, the dark pigeon blue making a lovely contrast with her rich reddish tan. She is handled by her owner, professional handler Carmen Cananzi. Mrs. Arline Clark, who has served several years on the STCA Board of Directors and is owner of Nukara Kennels in San Francisco, was the breeder.

CH. DAMAE'S CAESAR (by Ch. Sarszegi Buttons ex Ch. Queen's Own Blue Coral) is shown winning the Toy Group under Judge Langdon Skarda, handled by Michele Leathers. He has a number of Group placings, including two firsts, and is owned by his breeder, Earl D. Edge. This Silky has excellent rich silver blue, clear and even through his body coat; he also excels in movement.

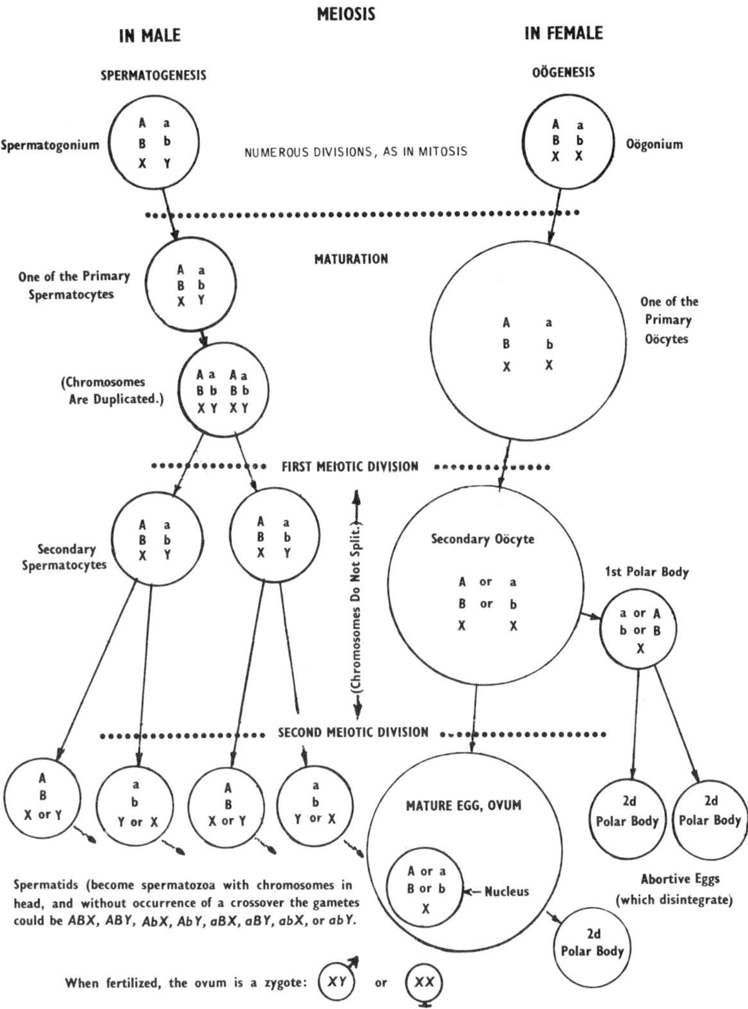

smaller, carries fewer genes than the X of the female. Some genes exert influence upon developments that are called "sex-linked" and produce traits that are linked to the sex of the individual dog or bitch.

It must always be borne in mind that each puppy will receive only half of the genes carried by his sire and only half of the genes carried by his dam. If we know that a particular trait is governed by a single pair of genes and is recessive, then each dog or bitch showing that trait must be pure for the recessive gene. Both members of that particular pair of genes must be recessive in order for the recessive characteristic to show in the phenotype of the animal. However, if a dog or bitch shows a trait which we know to be dominant and also governed by a single gene pair, the only way to determine whether the other gene of that pair is dominant or recessive is through further breeding. If by some magical method, we as dog breeders could direct which of the sire's genes, and which of the dam's genes, would go into each puppy, we might very quickly come up with the perfect Silky Terrier. We cannot do that, of course, but a knowledge of genetics and how it works can help us breed better dogs.

We have discussed primarily characteristics governed by a single pair of genes, although many characteristics are governed by more than one pair, or in ways which we will set forth later. However, a grasp of the principles of this form of inheritance is absolutely essential to those who wish to pursue the study of genetics further.

Before going into the more complex methods of gene operation, we should fix some facts in our minds regarding dominant and recessive genes:

DOMINANT GENES

1. If a dog has even one of the gene pair for a dominant trait, he or she will show that trait in the phenotype.

2. Seventy-five percent of the offspring from breeding animals showing dominant characteristics will also show the dominant characteristic.

3. If a dog or bitch is homozygous dominant for a given trait, viz., having inherited it from both sire and dam, *all* of his or her progeny will show the dominant trait, regardless of the other parent.

4. If a fault is caused by a dominant gene, it can be easily bred out by not using any animal for breeding which shows the dominant fault.

5. Because the dominant gene in single dose causes the animal to show the dominant trait, only breeding tests will enable the breeder to learn whether the other gene of the pair is dominant or recessive.

RECESSIVE GENES

1. If a dog or bitch shows a trait caused by a recessive gene, he or she *must be* homozygous (pure) for the recessive trait, and will pass the recessive gene to all offspring.

2. A recessive gene may be carried but suppressed or hidden by the dominant gene of that pair. Thus it may be carried but hidden for one or many generations, to reappear in the phenotype only when paired by a recessive gene from the other parent.

3. Only twenty-five percent of the offspring will show this recessive characteristic, unless both parents themselves show the recessive trait and are therefore homozygous recessive for that gene pair. In that case, *all* offspring will show the recessive characteristic and will be genetically pure for it.

This four-month-old puppy is owned by Bob and Gwyn Willis of Baltimore. She is LARRAKIN GWYN'S HOLLY (by Ch. Artarmon's Max ex Larrakin Little Sister), bred by Mr. and Mrs. James Young, Jr. Note the very good head, small dark eyes, jet black nose, and V-shaped ears carried vertically. The ears have not been trimmed, and the line of dark tan marks the edges of the ears, with the black-tipped feathering on ears extending $\frac{1}{4}$ to $\frac{1}{2}$ inch beyond. The black on her face will clear and the black of the body coat will turn blue as she matures. This puppy shows about an average amount of black on her face for her age. In type, she is intermediate between the Australian-Terrier-type puppy and the Yorkie-type puppy.

CH. CYPRESS ARISTO (by Ch. Wexford Pogo ex Fair Dinkum Patti of Cypress) was bred by Mrs. Dorothy Hicks (owner) and Georgette Pauwels. The author requested color photo of this dog because he is one of the best-colored Silkys in the country; regrettably the excellence of his blue is not reflected in the picture. He has very dark, deep tan with light fawn topknot, along with very rich pigeon blue which is clear and even through his body coat. Although over seven years old, his blue is still clear, with no bronze or gold hairs in the body coat. Color as good as his is difficult to produce, and is highly prized by knowledgeable breeders. Mrs. Hicks' Cypress Kennels are well known for their Basset Hounds and Toy Poodles as well as Silky Terriers.

4. Because the recessive gene may be hidden or suppressed by the dominant gene of the same pair, recessive faults are more difficult to breed out, as heterozygous gene pairs are more difficult to identify, in the dogs and bitches which carry them.

For most breeds, the characteristics desired in the dogs are governed by dominant genes, while faults are caused by recessive genes. There are, of course, exceptions to this, some in the area of color, others in breeds where features such as undershot bites are desired. Faults of body conformation, in particular, are believed to be caused by the action of recessive genes.

After Gregor Mendel had set forth the method of inheritance from single gene pairs, which he called "The Law of Segregation," he also came up with another theory which he called "The Law of Independent Assortment." In the pea plants with which Mendel worked, he found two sets of characteristics which were controlled by two different pairs of genes. His pea plants produced round seed, which proved to be the dominant, or wrinkled seed, the recessive trait. They also produced yellow or green seed, with the yellow being dominant and the green recessive. He found that the round or wrinkled seed and the yellow or green seed did assort independently so that some of his plants combined the dominant trait from one gene pair with the recessive trait from the other gene pair. This process also worked out in a mathematically predictable ratio. However, there are important exceptions to this "law," so that it is not entirely valid.

After chromosomes were discovered to be vehicles upon which genes were transmitted, it was found that independent assortment applied only when the pairs of genes investigated were carried on different chromosomes. With two or more pairs of genes carried on the same chromosome, there is a tendency for them to assort together, rather than independently. This phenomenon is known as "linkage." When the chromosomes split during meiosis (the sex chromosomes' form of cell division), the resulting half, or chromatid, moves as a unit. This does not always happen, but when it does, the group of genes on that particular half-chromosome inherit together, rather than assorting independently as set forth by Mendel. If such linked inheritance always occurred, the chromosome would be the unit of inheritance instead of the gene. Why it happens in some cases and not in others has not yet been discovered. Experienced breeders have long been aware that in many breeds, certain virtues are almost invariably accompanied by certain faults. Linkage offers a possible explanation for this.

Another process which sometimes occurs during meiosis is known as "crossing-over." This occurs when two of the chromatids come into close contact and a part of one chromatid changes places with the same part of another chromatid. This would, of course, interfere with linkage, and also produce more variation than might otherwise be expected. The following diagram may be helpful in visualizing this process:

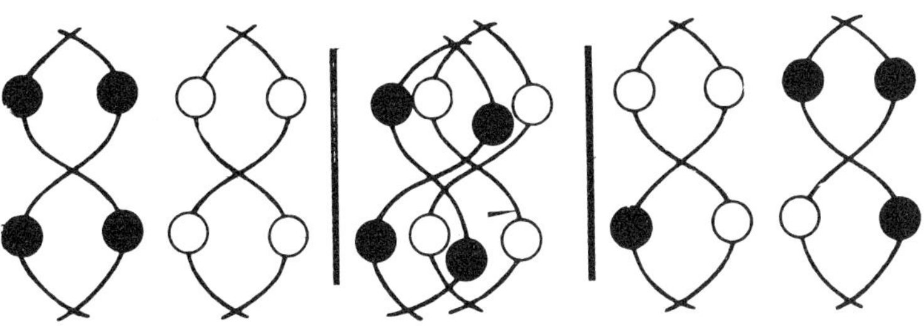

Crossing over involves mutual exchange of genes between homologous chromosomes during the meiotic production of gametes and effects a realignment of parental genes in forming the chromosomal pattern of eggs and sperm produced. Indicated is one manner in which positional changes might be made.

Many of the characteristics of our dogs are inherited through the action of a large number of gene pairs. Height, weight, intelligence, and such qualities, are believed to come from many genes working together. This is called quantitative inheritance. When we observe the transmission of a serious fault like straight shoulders, which is quantitative and acknowledged to be one of the most difficult of all faults to breed out, we might speculate that the combination of genes which produces the fault is in fact a result of linkage. While this is only speculation, such an explanation might provide us with clues as to how such faults could be eliminated, or whether in fact they could only be eliminated by discarding from breeding programs all dogs showing the fault.

There is also a form of genetic action known as "Incomplete Dominance," in which the dominant gene does not fully suppress the action of the recessive gene in the same pair. In these cases, although each gene remains a separate unit, the effect shown in the phenotype is one of blending. It is most often mentioned in connection with color, and may be at least part of the process with which blue coat color is obtained in our Silkys. Shorthorn cattle are usually mentioned as an illustration, as breeding a red parent to a white parent produces a roan, which is a mixture of red and white hairs. The blue color in Andalusian chickens results from black bred to white. This process is frequently illustrated by a flower plant known as the four o'clock. By breeding red-flowering plants for many generations to make them breed true for red, and then crossing them with white-flowering plants, also pure for white color, we get results which appear

From the standpoint of the breeder, this remarkable picture might aptly be titled "This is what it's all about". Alice Hively is shown with four generations of her Silky Terriers. All are of excellent type and very rich tan; regrettably their lovely tans did not reproduce well for the picture. From left to right are: MAD MANOR MATILDA, a Top Producer; her daughter CH. QUEENS OWN SATIN DOLL (by Ch. Redway Buster); her granddaughter Ch. QUEENS OWN FAIR ANGEL (by Ch. Queens Own Black Tracker ex Satin Doll) and her great-granddaughter, QUEENS OWN JEWEL at eight weeks of age. (by Ch. Pine Meadow Prince Sidney ex Fair Angel).

CH. MITZI OF REDMON is pictured winning Best in Match under Judge Edith Izant, handled by Mrs. Dorothy Hicks, at City of Angels Silky Terrier Club match. The entry of 90 was an all-time record number of entries of Silkys in this country. This lovely little bitch has excellent color and also excels in movement. She was bred by Mrs. E. L. Macy, co-owner with Mrs. Hicks. Her sire is Aus. and Am. Ch. Koonoona Beau Brummell; her dam is Koolamina Dinkie Di. Both Mrs Macy and Mrs. Hicks are Officers of the C.O.A. S.T.C. and Mrs. Hicks was one of the early Presidents of the first U.S. Area club, the S.T.C. of Southern California.

quite different from those Mendel found in his pea plants. Instead of the three red and one white we might expect, since red is dominant to white, we would get all pink-flowering plants in the $F._1$ generation. Permitting the pink-flowering plants to become self-fertilizing, however, we get one plant with red flowers, two with pink flowers, and one with white flowers. In other words, the genes themselves have not blended as would appear from the intermediate color; if they had, the parental colors would not reappear. If we use the letter R for the dominant gene for red, and the lower-case r for the recessive gene for white, we find that the genes have assorted just as they did in Mendel's experiments with the tall and short pea plants. For purposes of illustration, we will use only the words for the color of the flowers produced by each plant: red, pink, and white.

Parents	*Generation*	*Offspring*
Red (RR) to White (rr)	F_1	Pink (Rr) Pink (Rr) Pink (Rr) Pink (Rr)
Pink (Rr) to Pink (Rr)	F_2	Red (RR) Pink (Rr) Pink (Rr) White (rr)

Referring to the illustration above and the table on page 126, we see that with the red and white flowers of the four o'clock plants, the pure-breeding red would be genetically RR, while the pure-breeding white plant would be rr. Mating RR to rr will produce all heterozygous Rr gene pairs in the $F._1$ generation, just as happened genetically with the pea plants. In the F_2 generation, the genes would assort in a ratio of RR, Rr, Rr, and rr, one plant producing only red flowers, two plants producing only pink flowers, and one plant producing only white flowers. In this case, we have interaction of the Rr gene pair, or incomplete dominance of R, which produces the intermediate color pink. The red-flowering plants produced in the F_2 generation will breed true, being homozygous dominant for the gene for red. The white flowers also will breed true, since they are homozygous recessive for the gene for white. The pink-flowering plants bred together, however, will again produce in the ratio of one red, two pink, and one white flower. Breeding the red- and white-flowering plants to each other, you will again get pink-flowering plants, and so repeat the entire process.

The ideal breeding animal would be homozygous—pure genetically, for all of his good qualities, so that whatever half of his genes were transmitted to the puppy would be for traits we want in our dogs. Since there are no such perfect breeding animals, it is up to us to try to breed Silky Terriers which are not only good in their physical appearance, or phenotype, but which also contain as many as possible of the genes for desirable characteristics in their genotype. It is admittedly more difficult to ascertain genotype in Toy breeds like our Silkys, since a litter of three or four puppies could hardly be expected to provide even the most knowledgeable breeder with as much genetic information as would a litter of eight or ten puppies. With Silky Terrier studs which are bred to a large number of bitches, the genotype of the studs begins to show itself to the discerning breeder by the time several litters have grown to maturity.

The wise breeder selects sires and dams of his litters on the basis of all the knowledge he can obtain on their respective genotypes. We obtain this knowledge in several ways. First we assess the phenotype of the dog or bitch as to what indicators it gives of genetic make-up. We then evaluate the previous progeny of each, with due consideration for the opposite parent of each offspring. We also apply our knowledge of the ancestors in the two pedigrees, as to what they looked like and what they produced. Because Silky Terriers are a relatively young-in-years breed, we do not have the advantage of as many well-established lines as do some older or numerically larger breeds. Thus it is of the utmost importance that genetic knowledge be obtained and applied to the improvement of our own breeding, and with it, of the breed as a whole.

Current Genetic Research—In every field of science, there seem to be periods when breakthroughs to more knowledge occur in fairly rapid succession. Within the past two decades, discoveries have been made in genetics which have caused such excitement in the scientific world that it has been reflected in the lay press.

You have perhaps read of the substance called DNA (deoxyribonucleic acid) and RNA (ribonucleic acid), which scientists have identified as the material of heredity. Another scientist has put together in his laboratory a solution in which DNA increases by combining the solution's raw materials into new molecules exactly like itself, performing the same fantastic job of self-copying that we described in the form of cell division called mitosis.

A British physicist and an American biologist were awarded the 1962 Nobel Prize in medicine and physiology for constructing a scaled-up model of the structure of the genes and chromosomes. Still others are at work trying to identify what they call the "language" of DNA. Certain "codes" have already been identified, with the sequence of the series of "codes" believed to be the basis for the difference in various species.

It is known that Nature sometimes makes mistakes in some of the genetic processes, but with its complexity, the wonder is not that mistakes are made, but that they are so few. It is felt that "cracking the code" of the language of genetics will eventually lead to the treatment and control, if not elimination, of inherited diseases and defects. It will undoubtedly also yield information that will help us to breed better animals of all kinds, but if breeding better dogs became too simple, perhaps it would lose much of its appeal for all of us!

This five-month-old puppy is owned by Mrs. Mary Uchida. He has excellent color for his age, along with very good head and expression and naturally clean points. He is toward the Australian Terrier in type, as was his dam at the same age; she matured to be excellent Silky type. He was bred by Mr. and Mrs. James Young, Jr. and is by Ch. Artarmon's Max ex Larrakin Lovely Lorelei.

CH. LARRAKIN PRETTY PENNY (by Ch. Artarmon's Max ex Ch. Rebel Little Bo Peep) has unusually rich coloring, both in blue and tan. Unfortunately, the very rich tan on her head and feet did not reproduce for the picture. She also shows exceptionally good head and expression, along with the naturally clean points (ears, feet, muzzle) which are ideal for the breed. Penny was bred and is owned by Mr. and Mrs. James Young, Jr.

CHAPTER 12

The Inheritance of Coat Color

The mode of inheritance of coat color may differ from one breed to another, even with some colors that appear visually to be the same. In many breeds, enough experimental studies have been made to determine the precise manner in which color is inherited, but no such studies have been made of Silky Terriers.

In a breed like Silkys, where color is a fundamental part of breed type, there is naturally much interest in how color is inherited. My search for knowledge on the subject started back in 1960, but it was almost two years before I was able to find published material on a related breed, much less anything specific to Silky Terriers. Many genetics books set forth the mode of color inheritance in Cockers, Dachshunds, Great Danes, and others, even Chows, which are not really numerous, but study of these books produced only negative results with regard to Silky Terriers. Finally, I was able to locate a book—in a local Poodle breeder's attic—which does describe coat color inheritance in the Yorkshire Terrier, a breed closely related to our own. This book is *The Inheritance of Coat Color in Dogs*, by Dr. C. C. Little, published in 1957 by Comstock Publishing Associates, a division of Cornell University Press. The information in Dr. Little's book is based on experimental work done on the subject at the Roscoe B. Jackson Laboratory in Bar Harbor, Maine, with the cooperation of breeders who furnished information from their own records.

My own research includes correspondence with Australian Terrier and Yorkshire Terrier breeders as well as Silky breeders. The late Frank Longmore referred me to an Australian geneticist, Mr. Vern Mathews, who has kindly sent me a great deal of data gathered from breeders in that country, with his interpretation of much of the data based on his genetic studies of color in other breeds.

A quest for knowledge such as this can become exceedingly frustrating, as you begin to feel that you have written thousands of words seeking information to no avail. But, at that stage, some tiny bit of knowledge comes your way which opens another door to possibility, so that you are encouraged to continue. Although a number of years have gone by, I remember clearly my excitement when I first came across the theory of incomplete dominance, illustrated as it generally is by the example of a plant called the "four o'clock." As a small child, my favorite pastime was visiting my grandparents' farm. My favorite flowers in my grandmother's garden were the four o'clocks, because I was told that all the little flowers "went to sleep" at 4 o'clock each afternoon. I was enchanted, and spent many an hour sitting in the garden watching to see each little red, or pink, or white blossom "go to sleep" as the petals of each one folded in toward its center; in the mornings, they opened to greet the sun as it came out. I think I learned to tell time there so that I could get to the garden to watch, but I never dreamed that many years later, as a Silky Terrier breeder, I would again be fascinated by these same flowers, this time because of their color. We will come back to the flowers later in this chapter.

From information gained from Silky, Australian, and Yorkshire Terrier breeders, it appears that some facts on color are established from practical experience. One is that mating of two black (at maturity) and tan specimens always produces black body coats. It also appears that when too many black or very dark blue specimens are mated together in Silkys, there may be a reversion to the short, coarse type of coat seen in Australian Terriers. Another is that continued mating of light silver blue and tan specimens will eventually produce the almost-white body coats, many of which have beige or cream instead of rich tan. Breeders of Yorkshire Terriers seem to have reached agreement of opinion that both those with black body coats and those with lighter blues should be used in breeding programs. The practical information obtained seems to bear out the theory on Yorkie color inheritance set forth in Dr. Little's book.

Many breeders think of the blue and tan in Silkys as being inherited together, but this is not the case, although there may be some genes which have an effect on both colors. It is often true that dark blue Silkys have very dark tan, and that light blue Silkys have light tan, but some with dark blues have light tan, and some with light blues have very dark tan. It makes color inheritance easier to understand if you will think of them as being inherited separately, at least to some extent.

Blues in many breeds are derived from recessive genes, and thus are more easily fixed in the breed. As noted in earlier comments on dominant and recessive genes, a dog or bitch displaying a recessive characteristic governed by a single gene pair *MUST BE* genetically pure for the reces-

MAVROB FAIR JO-DEE C.D. (by Ch. Fair Dinkum Maverick CD ex Koolamina Kristabel). Owner Miss Dee Bierer of Los Angeles wanted a small Silky, and Jo-Dee weighs only 6½ pounds, but she is a big winner in Obedience Trials. She is pictured with the F.G. Franciscus Award for the dog making the highest average score for five times shown with no failures, presented to her by the Hollywood Dog Obedience Club for her score average of 191. This mighty mite and her owner are now working toward advanced Obedience degrees. Miss Bierer also owns a full sister of Jo-Dee with a conformation title, Ch. Mavrob Rosalie. Jo-Dee and Rosalie were bred by Ruth and Dick LaBarre. (Note: Jo-Dee's very rich tan did not reproduce well for the picture.)

CH. WEE BUTTON OF SANFORD (by Ch. Coolaroo Silkallure Rex ex Pixie Roo Coolaroo) was the foundation stud for Mr. and Mrs. James Lawson and their daughter, Linda, now Mrs. Frank Holzer. As a teen-ager, Linda handled Button to his championship in very strong competition. Mrs. Peggy Lawson is President of the City of Angels Silky Terrier Club and has also served in other capacities. Their breeding prefix is ADORALIN. Button was bred by Margaret Peck.

sive trait. For that reason, the blue color can be maintained indefinitely at about the same shade in those breeds. Puppies in these breeds are born blue and the recessive gene is called the gene for dilution (of black) by most geneticists. Dogs showing blues of this type also have nose and eye rims described as "slatey" rather than black, because the dominant expression of this gene pair is necessary for black pigmentation. These blues are also called "Maltese blue dilution" and are often described as having a flat, dull quality. Blue Chows, Great Danes, Greyhounds, and Dobermans are in this group.

In Bedlington, Kerry Blue, and Yorkshire Terriers (and I believe in Silky Terriers as well), the inheritance of coat color is more difficult to

CH. OWENDEN'S BILDAD (by Ch. Clavons Blue Streak ex Ch. Redway Rebel Kathleen) is shown finishing under Judge Dr. H. L. Huggins, handled by co-owner Dave Owen. Bildad was bred and is owned by Mr. and Mrs. David B. Owen.

control. Puppies of these breeds are born black, or black and tan, and attain the blue gradually as the dogs mature. In Silkys, mature color is rarely attained before the age of 18 months, except in some of those undesirable specimens that become almost white and their lack of correct color may be apparent at an earlier age. Many of the darker specimens may remain mostly black until they are 2½ or 3 years old; some of these will finally become blue, but some remain black. Dr. Little ascribes the blue in these breeds to a graying gene which appears to be at least partly dominant and changes a puppy born black in the direction of increasing grayness or paleness. Silky Terriers also carry genes for the tan-point pattern, and perhaps the chinchilla (or paling) gene also, the latter being more active on tan areas of the coat. Dr. Little states that the degree of dominance is controlled by some as yet unknown modifying factor acting on the graying gene. He also states that: "It may be that the more desirable shades of blue are found in Gg animals (that is, those which contain one dominant for graying and one recessive for non-graying in the pair obtained from their parents). If this is the case, black (gg) animals will continue to appear, and they can be crossed with light blues to get intermediate shades of blue coat color by incomplete dominance of G (the graying gene)." He also notes that much more experimentation needs to be done for further conclusions.

Mr. Vern Mathews of Victoria, Australia, reports that in his opinion, there is another graying or paling gene which is of a recessive nature. He states that this is called the gene for silvering and that it has been identified as recessive in Poodles. Mr. Mathews said also that he assumes that this recessive for silvering is active over the entire coat, so that it would affect both blue and tan in Silkys.

As noted in earlier chapters, each gene pair has an assigned place on the chromosome, the gene-carrying vehicle. Dr. Little states that ten locations (called locus, and in the plural loci) on the chromosomes are occupied by genes controlling color in dogs. What follows requires you to recall from previous chapters that gene pairs are described by letters, with the capital letter representing the dominant gene and the lower-case letter representing the recessive gene. Dr. Little describes the probable genetic make-up for Yorkshire Terrier coat color as follows: (Note that he specifies only nine loci here):

a^t B C or c^{ch} D E G m S t

The gene described as a^t is for black or liver with tan points; B produces black; the dominant C is for full pigmentation, while the recessive c^{ch} at that locus produces paling of tan or red areas; D causes intense pigmentation (the recessive d at this locus when received from both parents to become dd produces the blues mentioned earlier in which puppies are

SONNYVALE'S TRIXANNA SUSANNA and her litter of four puppies by Damae's Prince Ivan. These puppies were less than a week old at time of picture. It is always surprising to those unfamiliar with the breed to see a silver blue and tan dam with new puppies, as all Silky puppies are born jet black with tan markings. The tan areas on new puppies are smaller than in mature dogs, and the amount of tan at birth may vary from one bloodline to another. Susanna is owned by Mr. and Mrs. J. L. Matthews.

CH. SMITHFIELD LOVER BOY (by Aus. Ch. Miami Gold Flash ex Prairie Vicky) was bred by the Taylors in Australia. When Jim and Henrietta Moss (Artarmon's Kennels) imported him several years ago, he created a sensation among West Coast breeders because of his outstanding color. He has been instrumental in aiding the Mosses to produce the consistently rich, clear blues and excellent tans for which their breeding is noted. His rich, reddish tan and deep pigeon blue are shown here; note that the blue body coat is deep, rich, and free of any gold or bronze hairs.

born blue); E allows formation of black or brown pigment over the entire body; G is the dominant gene for graying; m is for non-action of M, merling (another blue, but spotted); S is for solid color with no white except small chest or toe markings; t is for the absence of ticking.

At four of the loci concerned with coat color, Dr. Little lists series of alleles, or multiple alleles. An allele, or allelomorph, is the name given to one of a pair of genes which differs from its sister gene. Where multiple alleles exist, there are a number of different genes which may be present at a specific locus, and which effect gradations in a certain characteristic, although no more than two of the series may be present in any one individual, since genes are present only in pairs. Whether we have a case of incomplete dominance in the graying gene, with some other gene pair perhaps causing the difference in degree of graying, or whether a series of multiple alleles is involved, Dr. Little does not state in his book.

In the preceding chapter there was noted the example of the four o'clock plant which has the form of genetic action known as "Incomplete Dominance." The first thing the student of genetics must learn is that genes do not blend, but as he gets farther along, he finds that in some cases, genes *give the appearance* of blending so that the characteristic displayed is intermediate between the characteristics of the two parents. In the four o'clock plant, the pink-flowering plants obtained by breeding the red- and white-flowering plants to each other are more uniform in shade than are the blues obtained in Silkys by breeding a very light blue to black. For that reason, we can assume that the plants lack whatever genetic modifier is present in Silkys (and other breeds which have the graying gene) which causes gradations in shades of blue.

Unless extensive experimental breeding is done on color in our breed, we are not likely to have completely definite knowledge of all the factors that affect coat color. In all long-coated breeds, the method of color inheritance is more difficult to identify than it is in short-coated dogs. There are some tentative conclusions we might reach from practical experience with color problems, along with the application of the genetic knowledge that does exist on coat color.

Obtaining the black with tan points (a^t for this pattern being a recessive gene) has not presented any particular problem, although a few litters have been reported that were solid black. These mature to a solid gray in the ratio that would be expected from a dominant gene on the A locus. I have seen only one mature Silky which appeared to lack the tan-point pattern; this dog was a solid and rather attractive gray color of the same shade over his entire body. In Yorkshire Terriers, puppies are sometimes described as being born solid black, or black with indistinct tan points, but none has been reported that did not mature with the tan-point markings. Silky Terrier puppies have varying amounts of black on their heads at birth, with some showing wide tan areas and others showing very little tan. This does not seem to have any particular significance as it pertains to mature color.

It is agreed by most knowledgeable Silky breeders that light beige or almost-white colors in areas which should be tan are the result of recessive genes. This means to the practical breeder that he can never obtain good tans if both parents have the very light colors instead of rich tan.

The inheritance of the undesirable black masks seen occasionally would appear to be linked somehow with the inheritance of the silver blue topknot. Although black shadings on the backs of ears and blue temple marks are permissible in Silkys, black masks are very serious faults. The actual mode of inheritance is not known, although we might speculate that full masks are the result of recessive genes, judging from the offspring of one black-masked parent and one with the correct tan face. If two black-masked specimens were bred together for several litters and only black-masked puppies were produced, we could be sure of the recessive nature of the gene. However, those breeding from black-masked Silkys are very unlikely to breed to another with the same fault. It should also be mentioned that some Silky puppies which show a partial or full black mask may not retain the mask as they mature. Some will clear fully, while others may clear except for a black line running under the eyes across the face.

It appears from breeding results that some Silkys showing light blues are more dominant for light color than others showing about the same shade of blue. This could possibly result from the action of the recessive gene for silvering at a different locus, as suggested by Mr. Vern Mathews; if so, it would augment the action of the dominant graying gene on the G locus. Or, there could be a series of multiple alleles on the G locus which have not yet been identified. It does appear that Silkys must, as a breed, carry something in their genetic make-up that produces more graying than do Yorkshires as a breed. Many Yorkies mature to be silver blue, but it seems doubtful that many of the almost-white body coats are present in that breed, perhaps because their standard discriminates against lighter blues.

It is well known in every breed that breeding for certain virtues tends to produce certain faults apparently inherited in some manner with the virtues; this may be the result of linkage as described in the preceding chapter. In Silky Terriers, the desirable deep, rich tans may be accompanied by topknots which are also rich tan rather than the silver or fawn specified by the standard. Copper or tan in what should be an all-blue body coat sometimes accompanies very rich tan points. Since rich tan seems to be clearly dominant over pale tans, the extension of copper or

DAMAE'S GO GO GATOR shows the rarely seen silver topknot and a generally excellent head. Note the very rich tan, good small dark eyes (actually darker than shown in the picture), jet black nose, nice V-shaped ears, and the alert "ready to make friends" expression that is so typical of the breed. Note too the attractive blending of blue and tan on the throat, also typical of the breed. He was bred and is owned by Mr. and Mrs. Earl D. Edge of Florida. His sire is Ch. Milan Gay Lad of Iradell, and his dam is Ch. Damae's Angel Face. In Silky Terriers which will have the blue topknot and deep tan at maturity, the puppy black is often a little slower clearing than it is in those that will have the more common fawn topknot.

tan into the body coat may somehow be connected with the fact that sandies or reds in Australian Terriers are dominant to blue and tan. Without more experimentation, this must be only speculation.

The yellowish body coat appears inherited as a recessive characteristic, since it is produced by parents which do not show it, and certain inbreeding results seem to indicate a recessive character. There are two types of recessive genes which could produce this, one the brindling found in many terrier breeds, and the other the wild color, or agouti, seen in Schnauzers and Norwegian Elkhounds. In either the brindle or the agouti, each hair is banded, with black and tan or black and silver alternating on the same hair. The American standard for Australian Terriers calls for "blue-black or silver-black" and describes the silver-black thus: "each hair carries black and silver alternating with black at the tips." One experienced Australian Terrier breeder reported that she felt that in that breed, dogs having the banded type of hairs were more likely to have gold in their body coats. The Australian standard for that breed does not specify any sort of banded hairs. I am sure that all Silky breeders have seen some Silkys with the banded hairs.

There appears to be general agreement among breeders of Silky, Yorkshire, and Australian Terriers that richness of color, both blue and tan, is adversely affected by illness or parasitic infestation in the dog, and some feel that climatic conditions also affect coat color. Many breeders blame poor coat color on too much sun. I am sure that all experienced Silky breeders have noticed at one time or another that one of their dogs appeared washed out in color after severe illness. A Silky Terrier that is dirty will not show clear color, and frequently has yellow in the body coat; this seems to be the type of yellowing seen in humans with gray hair, either because the hair is dirty or because a sort of coating has built up over each hair. Some bitches also show gold in their body coats which seems to result from hormonal action, since it appears in many at the time a litter is weaned. A number of bitches have a fairly consistent pattern of the appearance and then clearing of gold or tan in body coats, with very rich blue apparent at the time of their seasons, gold appearing soon after then but clearing as whelping time approaches, good blue during lactation, and then gold in coat again at about weaning time. There seems to be a tendency for the amount of gold to increase as the bitch grows older, and some bitches have been observed to return to a clear blue after spaying. It is of interest that a Pomeranian breeder reports that her orange Pom bitches show a pattern of paling alternating with rich color which works much like the gold in body coat in Silky bitches.

Analysis of color inheritance is further complicated by the fact that some Silky Terriers may have poor tan as puppies, which darkens and becomes rich when the dogs are about a year old. Blues also may darken, though this happens less frequently than does the darkening of tan. Puppies born with rich tan may also mature with relatively poor tan. Occasionally, some of the Silkys which silver early, generally taken to mean they will be a washed-out blue at maturity, will never show any further lightening and mature with dark blues. Sitting at my feet as I write this is a 4-year-old Silky bitch who has no more silvering now than she did at 8 weeks of age when we obtained her; she is now a very dark blue.

The only certain indicator of good mature tan seen in puppies is the ring of tan or black and tan mixed sometimes around noses. Generally, the wider the band and deeper the color, the darker the mature tan will be. There is no positive indicator of good mature blue, other than observation of mature color in puppies from the same mating, and even this does not always hold true in subsequent litters. As breeders gain experience, and especially as they gain knowledge of the immediate ancestors of their breeding stock, as well as seeing what their own dogs and bitches produce, they will have a better idea on what colors may be expected from a given mating. For example, puppies produced by two dark parents, which have dark ancestors in the first two or three generations behind them, are more likely to mature dark themselves. They may also get some reversion to black and to shorter, coarser coats. Puppies from two light parents, with light-colored ancestors in the first two or three generations, are likely to mature light, often too light to be considered correct blue.

Until we gain absolute knowledge of the genetic basis for color inheritance in Silkys, however, predicting the exact shade of blue at maturity will be impossible. Since our standard permits any shade of blue, this is not as great a problem in selecting for show as it is in selecting for breeding stock.

CHAPTER 13

Methods of Breeding

There are several methods or systems of breeding that are used by dog breeders with varying degrees of success. Some novice breeders get the impression that they must use a particular system, and that doing so is a sure road to successful breeding. This is of course a serious fallacy, as no breeding system can be successful without rigid selection of breeding stock, and knowledge of what genes the individual dogs and bitches are likely to possess and pass along to their offspring. It is the application of a given method of breeding which succeeds or fails, rather than the method itself.

Knowledgeable breeders use whatever method seems indicated by the progress or lack of progress of their breeding programs. They consider the virtues and faults displayed by their breeding stock and by the dogs they have bred, as well as the knowledge they have gained from the results of their previous efforts. The experienced and dedicated breeder is not satisfied to produce a good Silky Terrier occasionally, he or she is interested in upgrading the *average level of quality* of his breeding. This breeder sees quite clearly the worst dog or bitch he has bred, as well as the best. He measures success not in the show ring, but in his objective appraisal of all the Silky Terriers he has bred, with such assistance as he feels he needs from those whose opinions on the breed he considers most reliable.

Factors other than the quality of the dog may so affect show results that they are not a reliable criterion for the true breeder. Show ring wins are gratifying to both breeder and owner, but many are overly influenced by them in decisions on their breeding programs. Those dogs shown constantly, especially by skilled professional handlers, should certainly have more impressive totals of wins than the dog shown occasionally by a relatively unskilled amateur. Despite the win records, the less frequently shown dog may in fact be of better quality and of far more breeding worth, especially for a particular bitch. He is not necessarily so, of course, as many big winners in all breeds have also produced offspring of excellent quality, but intelligent breeders should be aware of and consider all factors involved.

No one has ever produced a perfect dog of any breed. If it were possible to produce a perfect dog, perhaps breeding would lose much of its challenge and thus some of its fascination. And who knows, with breeders being the rugged individualists they are, if a perfect dog were produced, whether or not many of us would agree that this particular dog was indeed perfect!

The three principal systems of breeding are inbreeding, linebreeding, and outcrossing. There are differing opinions on where inbreeding leaves off and linebreeding begins, but here we will discuss them as they are most generally defined.

Inbreeding—This is the mating of dogs and bitches which are very closely related. Such matings as father to daughter, mother to son, half-brother to half-sister, and full brother to full sister are generally considered inbreeding. The mating of full brother and sister is the closest possible mating.

Some geneticists advocate a series of full-brother/full-sister matings for five or six generations to establish what is called "genetic purity" in the breeding stock. The theory is that such close matings for a number of generations would eventually produce animals which would breed true for most of the qualities desired. Rigid culling would be necessary, with only the best specimens retained for further breeding. The experimental inbreeding done by these geneticists, however, is invariably done with breeds more prolific than Silky Terriers, as large litters afford more offspring from which to select, as well as giving more room for expression of inherited traits passed on from the sire and dam. In some instances, the geneticists recommending the series of close matings will also mention that you can expect a decrease in size, vigor, and fertility in the animals used in the course of the succession of close matings. To counteract this, it is suggested that at the end of five or six generations of brother-sister matings, the final products should be outcrossed to gain what is known as "hybrid vigor."

It would appear, however, that the breeder would at this point be back where he started, with an outcross product. Some writers state that with proper selection, vigor and fertility need not be lost, but those who make a series of close matings should understand at the outset that the risks are great in such a program.

In actual practice, the time and money required to accomplish such a program of inbreeding would make it unsuitable for most breeders, even those in the breeds which produce large litters. In Silky Terriers, with small litters and late maturity of coat color, it would be virtually impossible. There is also the possibility that lethal defects would appear which would terminate such a program before completion, since inbreeding fixes faults and defects as well as virtues. In addition, the severe culling and destruction of faulty offspring is difficult for those who love dogs.

Two or three years ago, the National Association of British Veterinarians issued a report stating as their collective opinion that most of the defects and inherited diseases in dogs could be attributed to inbreeding; their statement included as inbreeding some matings that are considered line-breeding in this country. Veterinarians in this country also seem inclined to blame most defects on inbreeding. This attitude is understandable as they are more likely to see the defective puppies produced by inbreeding than those which are normal.

In any case, inbreeding is not for the novice breeder, nor is it advisable for the breeder who lacks the ability to be entirely objective in evaluating his dogs. It should only be employed when the Silky Terriers used are outstanding in quality, and truly outstanding dogs and bitches are few and far between in any breed. Even the experienced and objective breeder should inbreed only when he or she has a great deal of knowledge about the ancestors of the breeding partners.

Inbreeding has been called "a dangerous weapon" and "a double-edged sword," because it does fix faults and defects in a line as readily as virtues. In the hands of the wrong breeder, it can be disastrous.

It is an absolute necessity to inbreed when establishing a new breed, as it is the only way in which breed type can be established. Should you have the opportunity to examine the pedigrees of dogs bred early in the history of Silky Terriers in Australia, you will find that most of them were very closely inbred.

This method of breeding is also useful to the knowledgeable breeder who wishes to ascertain the breeding worth of a particular animal. Let us assume that this breeder has a stud dog which he feels is outstanding in quality and which he hopes to use extensively in his breeding program. By mating the dog back to a number of his daughters, the breeder can identify at least some of the genes carried by the dog—in other words, he will gain knowledge of the genotype of this dog. Should this breeder find that all, or almost all, of the offspring produced from the father-daughter matings are especially good specimens of the breed, he is indeed fortunate. The dog which produces an outstanding level of quality in very close matings is very likely prepotent for his good qualities when bred to less related bitches also, and his get from his daughters should themselves be excellent breeding animals. A more likely result in this case is that a few of the offspring from father-daughter matings will be exceptionally good, but that the average level of quality is not as high as that shown by his offspring from less related bitches. Since most structural faults are considered to be caused by recessive genes, the closely bred specimens will probably show faults that are not shown by the sire, but the genes for these traits are part of his genetic make-up. In that case, the breeder will know that he should avoid using this stud for bitches showing such faults, particularly if they are serious ones, as the combination would produce a high percentage of offspring showing the fault. If the serious fault is recessive and the bitch shows it physically, then she must carry the gene for the fault in double dose, since a recessive characteristic cannot be shown physically except by the dog or bitch which is homozygous recessive for it. If the stud dog produced the recessive fault from his daughters, although he himself did not show it, the breeder would know that he carried the fault recessively although he displayed the dominant trait in his phenotype. Referring to the chart "Mendelian Expectations," it may be seen that the genotype of the dog in this case would have to be heterozygous Ee (one dominant and one recessive gene for the trait). It could, of course, be Aa or Dd, depending on what gene pair was being considered, but he would be heterozygous, or impure, for the trait. If he carried the double dominant for the characteristic, none of his get could show the fault in their phenotype. Further, if he were homozygous dominant (EE) for the virtue on this gene pair, his get would not show the fault outwardly, even when he was bred to a bitch showing the fault (and therefore known to carry it in double dose). Since each offspring would necessarily have inherited the dominant gene from the sire, the dominant condition would show in the phenotype of the offspring. His offspring from that particular bitch would, of course, become carriers of the recessive gene for the fault, since their dam would have only the recessive gene to pass to her offspring. It must be borne in mind here that we speak of a trait governed by a single pair of genes. Many more traits are governed by combinations of two or more pairs of genes than by a single pair. Thus it is more difficult to deduce the genotype of breeding animals by analyzing traits in their offspring than it would be if every character were governed by a single gene pair.

Linebreeding—This is the method most often used by dog breeders in general. It is much the same as inbreeding, but the dogs and bitches to be mated are less closely related. There are differences of opinion on where inbreeding leaves off and linebreeding begins. Matings customarily referred to as linebreeding are grandfather to granddaughter, grandson to grandam, uncle to niece, nephew to aunt, and others less closely related but with one particular ancestor appearing several times in the preceding five generations.

CH. BONDI'S BOBBIN (by Ch. Aldoon Randwick ex Ch. Kanımbla Mildura Belle) is shown finishing her championship requirements under Judge Robert Waters, handled by Mr. Ed Bracy. She was bred by Col. and Mrs. J. J. Pavlas and is owned by Capt. and Mrs. Gary McMullen of Puerto Rico.

Here too, rigid selection must be made in the breeding stock, and the breeder should have knowledge of the Silky Terriers behind his own. It is sad to see the conscientious novice breeder attempting to improve his stock by linebreeding to a dog known to have produced a poor level of quality. Linebreeding to genetically poor Silkys can only produce more poor Silkys. The new breeder fortunate enough to have obtained advice and information from knowledgeable, objective, and experienced breeders is likely to do very well with linebreeding provided that he has sound knowledge of the standard and will apply rigid selection objectively.

It is difficult for the beginner to obtain the sort of information he needs. All bloodlines in any breed have some virtues and some faults, and when the newcomer is advised by one who is not objective, he may gain a very distorted view of different lines. It is well known in the dog fancy that the breeder who has produced two or three litters is more likely to think that he knows all the answers than is the breeder with longer experience. In addition, there are those who are incapable of making an unprejudiced evaluation of their own dogs or of those owned by others, even after many years of experience with a breed. They may, in fact, be incapable of an unprejudiced view of any subject. New breeders who are trying to learn should look as well as listen—the new breeder with the proverbial "eye for a dog" may in fact appraise the individual Silky more realistically than some who have been on the scene for a longer period of time.

The knowledgeable breeder who has been linebreeding for several generations will continue that program if the average level of quality obtained is satisfactory to him. If problems have arisen in linebreeding, with a fault or faults occurring often, this breeder will know that he must act to correct those faults. It is often suggested that the best way to correct the problem is to find a dog from his own line which is strong in the point where his own stock is weak. If this dog or bitch is known not to produce the same fault, when bred to partners which do show it, this would be a good choice. However, any Silky from the same line is very likely to carry the same faults recessively and a judicious outcross is more likely to be successful.

Outcrossing—This is generally considered to be the mating of animals that have no common ancestors within five generations. Used in connection with a linebreeding program, it is assumed that the breeder will return immediately to his own line after using the outcross. Ideally, the prospective outcross dog or bitch would be from a line known to excel in producing the virtue required; he or she should be linebred to the desired line rather than being the product of an outcross mating. The knowledgeable breeder is well aware that when he goes out to another line, he is likely to bring in some faults as well, since all lines have some virtues and some faults. If the potential outcross bloodline has the same faults that he already has, he must find another line to use. The breeder who knows how easy or how difficult certain faults are to eradicate, and who has extensive knowledge of various lines in his breed, should be able to make a judicious selection of the line to be used for the outcross.

After obtaining the virtue he seeks from an outcross mating, the breeder must take steps to set the desired virtue in his own line, hopefully without also setting whatever new faults he may have acquired. Should the level of quality be higher from the outcross line than he has obtained from his original line, he may be wise to incorporate the new line into his own breeding program.

★ ★ ★ ★ ★ ★

Outbreeding is sometimes listed as a method of breeding, but it is more a lack of method, in that unrelated animals are mated in generation after generation. It is generally employed by those who have no clear idea of their objective or of the means necessary to attain it. The general result is unpredictability and lack of uniformity in the offspring. If rigid selection for good qualities is made, a few good Silky Terriers will be produced, but the average level of quality in the dogs produced will be much lower than that obtained by an intelligently planned breeding program.

A phenomenon sometimes mentioned is the "drag of the race." This is a tendency of offspring of any breeding pair to gravitate toward the average level of quality of the breed as a whole. Where only dogs of show and breeding quality within a breed are considered, the average level of quality would be higher. This perhaps explains why, when starting with a mating of a dog and bitch of superior quality, it is difficult to come up with offspring that are as good as or better than their parents. New breeders with a first litter are inclined to think that all of the puppies will mature into great specimens. If that new breeder is objective in his evaluation as the puppies mature, however, he may be disappointed that all of them are not better. If he has done his best to acquire an excellent bitch, considered possible studs carefully and used one that seemed ideal for his bitch, it will be difficult for him to understand why all of the puppies are not better in quality than either parent. This is understandable, since all breeders hope to obtain puppies that will mature with all of the virtues of both parents and none of the faults of either. After a number of years of experience, breeders realize that, regardless of careful planning, a bit of luck is also involved in breeding better dogs. In some matings, we seem to obtain a happy combination of genes that results in the production of truly excellent offspring from a given pair of parents. This is spoken of as a "nick" between the dog and bitch mated, and the breeder fortunate enough to obtain such good results should realize what he has. If he does not realize the importance of such a happy combination of genes having occurred, he may go on to find another stud for his bitch, with the likelihood that such good results will not be forthcoming. When a knowledgeable breeder finds that he gets a particularly good level of quality from a given dog and bitch, he wisely repeats the same mating. If the level of quality obtained is lower than average, of course, he should seek another stud for his bitch.

Breeding as an Art—Breeding dogs is sometimes described as an art. It may or may not be that, depending on the manner in which it is done. The person who breeds a large number of champions in any breed is not necessarily an artist at breeding, he may simply produce large numbers of puppies, some of which are good enough to gain their titles. He may also have more interest and talent than his fellow breeders at getting the products of his breeding into the show ring.

We would define a truly successful breeder as one who has established a *high average level of quality* in his breeding and who is working toward the goal of producing a line of Silky Terriers that are not only of excellent quality themselves, but that will in their turn produce more Silky Terriers of excellent quality. He will learn patience, for it may take many generations to approach his goals. He must learn to be objective about his own dogs and those bred or owned by others. When he can be thrilled at the sight of a really good Silky Terrier, regardless of who owns or who bred the dog, then he can be said to be objective. He will never be fully satisfied with his own breeding, because the true breeder is a perfectionist, and all "perfect dogs" are bred by novices! In order to accomplish his goals, he will know the individual dogs and bitches in his pedigrees, he will be aware of what they have produced, he will study breeding results obtained by others for what bearing they may have on his own breeding program. He will exercise rigid selection in choosing those to be mated. He will correctly analyze what he has already obtained. He will inbreed, linebreed, or outcross as seems best after applying the knowledge he has gained of his breed and his own line, the application of genetic knowledge, and the various breeding methods. Only then can he be said to be a true breeder who is indeed practicing the "art" of breeding dogs.

CHAPTER 14

The Puppy in a New Home

Whether you have purchased a puppy destined for future showing and breeding, or as a pet, the early days in his new home will have important effects on him, especially with regard to his future temperament.

You must remember that your puppy is accustomed to the company and warmth of his brothers and sisters, especially at night, so you should give him extra attention during his first days and nights with you. You can soften the blow of changing homes by giving him extra attention to let him know that he will be loved and secure with his new family. He should not, of course, have so much handling that he will become overly tired.

If you have young children in your family, they should be guided in handling the puppy with gentleness and affection, as the puppy may not be used to children. Never let a child run *at* a puppy, as the puppy will instinctively turn and run from what he sees as a giant rushing toward him. Rather, have the child sit down on the floor and call the puppy to come to him. Should the puppy not go to the child—and most will, as they seem to take readily to youngsters—pick the puppy up and gently place him in the child's arms. You should see to it that the puppy has plenty of rest, as young puppies require a great deal of sleep. With children naturally excited over a new puppy, they tend to handle it too much, with the consequence that the puppy becomes irritable or, in some cases actually ill from overhandling and fatigue. By teaching your children to be considerate and gentle with their puppy, you have not only helped the puppy's adjustment, you have given your children a valuable lesson in kindness and consideration. You may be sure that the child will be amply rewarded by the affection the puppy will lavish on him or her in the years to come.

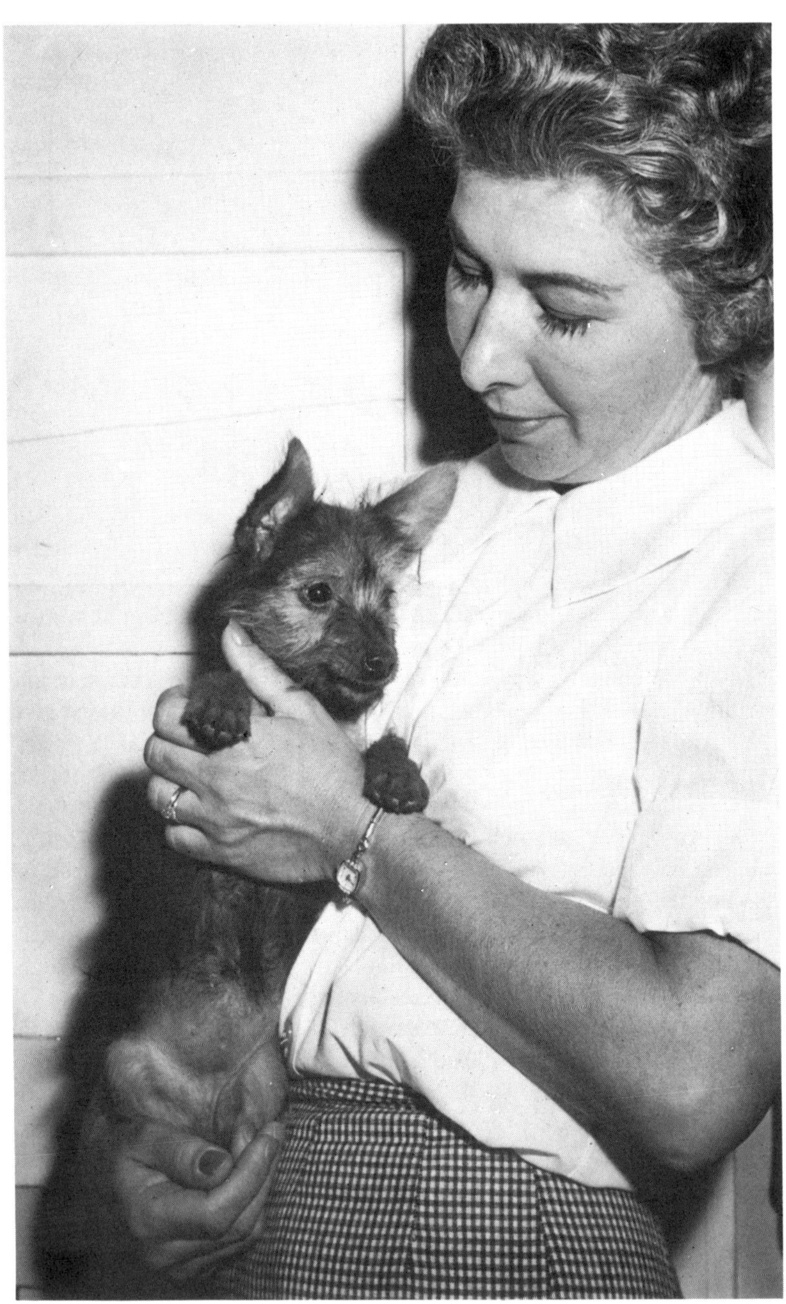

The proper method of holding the puppy, with one hand supporting the chest and the other hand under the hindquarters.

Ask the breeder from whom you buy your puppy to show you and the other members of the family the proper way to pick up and hold a puppy. A Silky Terrier puppy at 9 to 10 weeks of age, when they are usually sold, will weigh 3½ to 5 pounds. Being this small, the puppy must be handled carefully, of course. The usual inclination seems to be to grasp a puppy by his front legs and pick him up this way, but this can be damaging by causing the puppy to become what is called "out at elbow," or even actually strain the elbow and shoulder joints. The puppy should be picked up and held with one hand under his chest and the other hand cupped under his hind parts, taking care that the hand under the chest does not slip up under the puppy's elbows. While teaching your youngsters this method, have them seated on the floor, so that if the puppy should jump or squirm out of their hands, he would not have a fall from a height.

Comparison between puppies of different ages: puppy at left is six weeks old, puppy at right is three months old. The puppy at right is especially good Silky type.

Your puppy's breeder should also give you a list of the food the puppy is accustomed to, preferably several days before the puppy is to be picked up so that you can obtain a supply of the same foods he has been eating. If you wish to change the puppy to a different type of food, the change should be made very gradually. The chapter on feeding will give you more information on specific types of food.

For the first night in his new home, you can almost always prevent the the puppy from crying or whining by putting him in a box or top-opening crate by the side of your bed, or by the bed of one of the older children. Then if he does whimper or cry, you can reach down easily to pet him, and he will be comforted by your nearness. You should put an old bedspread or bathmat in the box or crate for him to curl up on. With a young puppy, it is advisable to have a box large enough to put newspapers in one end and material for his bed in the other, since they usually cannot go through the entire night without the need to relieve themselves. It usually helps, too, if you give him a little warm milk or a dog biscuit as you put him to bed. With the very young pup, it is wise to break the dog biscuit into small pieces for him.

Should the puppy still seem restless or cry, it will often help to put a hot water bottle wrapped in a towel in the bed with him, which will make up for the warmth of his littermates that he misses. (Do not use an electric heating pad with a puppy of this age, as he might chew the cord and electrocute himself.) The ticking of a wind-up alarm clock will also soothe a puppy. After the first night in his new home, and waking to find that the members of his new family are there, ready to love him, there should be no problem with his sleeping through the night. He can usually be moved into his own area to sleep by the second or third night he is with you.

There is one exception to putting the puppy by your bed at night. If the weather is very cold and you customarily sleep with windows open, there would probably be too much draft for the puppy, and some other method should be used.

Before bringing the puppy home, you should select a particular area which is to be his very own. You can purchase a puppy pen for him, or choose a small room in the house in which you can confine him. A spot in the utility room or spare bedroom will do nicely. Be sure there are no appliances plugged in where he could reach the wire—several Silky puppies have electrocuted themselves by chewing on electric cords. Also be sure that he is not in a draft. Furnish his home with a bed, a few toys, and several layers of newspaper. The bed may be anything from a box with an old bedspread or towel in the bottom, to an elaborate metal or wooden bed with a cedar-filled mattress. The wicker beds are very attractive, but they are irresistible chewing material to puppies and do

A Silky puppy's bed is his own special place of refuge, and he comes to love it. A metal or wooden bed is generally better than a bed of wicker construction like the one shown, because Silky puppies find wicker to be irresistible chewing material.

not last very long. The best toys are hard rubber bones or rings, real soup or round-roast bones large enough that the pup cannot swallow them, or rawhide chew sticks or twists. These will give him something to occupy himself with when you aren't fussing with him, as well as serving as teething rings. Puppies will chew on something instinctively, first to help bring in and strengthen their baby teeth and later to help loosen them as the permanent teeth come in. If you furnish him with ample chewing material, he will not be as tempted to chew on your good furniture, rug, or shoes. Never give him an old shoe, belt, or stocking for chewing, as he might then mistake your new shoe, belt, or stocking as chewing material.

Very young puppies should be kept in their own special place many hours daily, for meals, rest periods, and elimination. Having this area will also keep them out of mischief and free of harm when you are away from home. After a time, you will find that the puppy regards his area as a sanctuary, and he will go into it voluntarily when he needs to rest. As he gets older and better with his house manners, he can be allowed out of his area for longer periods of time.

Many puppies are at least partially trained to paper before you buy them, which will make this part of training easier for you. Some may have a bit of a relapse when changing homes, as they will have to learn where you will keep their paper. However, some puppies make the transition surprisingly rapidly, with only a day or two of being unable to locate the assigned spot for their toilet in time. In the area where the puppy will be confined at times, first cover the entire floor of the pen or room with newspapers, except for the space in which you have placed his bed. As his training progresses, gradually move the papers to one corner of the pen. He will usually learn very quickly to look for the paper on which to relieve himself. For the first week or two, take up the most heavily soiled paper, but leave one piece that has been at least slightly damp so that he can pick up the scent. This will aid him in learning to go back to the paper.

Silky puppies are quick learners and adapt readily to paper training.

If the weather is mild, and you prefer to train your puppy to go in the yard, take him out about an hour after each meal and just before bedtime. With a very young puppy, you may have to take him more often. If you wish to transfer him from paper to yard training, it will sometimes help to put a piece of soiled newspaper down in the yard. Most puppies will perform in the yard with no hesitancy, but one of our homebred Silky Terriers was over a year old before she decided it was proper to use the yard. We would let her out in the yard, and she would run and play with the others, but she was careful to wait until she came back into the house to get to her newspapers to relieve herself!

Whichever way you choose to train your puppy, be sure to praise him when he performs properly on either newspaper or the grass, so he will realize that this is what you want him to do. If you have the puppy outside of his own area in your house, watch him for sniffing and circling, as dogs do this just before they eliminate. When you observe this, pick him up immediately and take him to his papers or to the yard. In yard training, it is usually helpful to take pups back to a spot they have used previously so they will pick up the scent.

If you catch the puppy in the act of breaking his training, scold him in a harsh tone of voice, and take him immediately to his paper or the yard. Never scold a puppy *after* he has broken his training, for his memory is short and even a few minutes later, he will not realize what he did that displeased you. The old idea of rubbing a pup's nose into his "mistake" and then punishing him is of no value whatever, and is also unpleasant for both you and the puppy. In the early stages of training, puppies will often go to their paper but get only their front feet on the newspaper, with the "business end" over the bare floor. They should never be scolded for this, however, as they think they are doing what you wish even though the results are not perfect. It is both unwise and unnecessary to punish the puppy physically for breaking his training. Silky Terriers are intelligent and responsive, their greatest desire is to please you, and your disapproval manifested by scolding is all that is necessary, along with your praise when he performs as he should.

The best way to remedy puppy mistakes on your floors, whether carpeted, hardwood, or linoleum or vinyl, is to wipe it up immediately. For hardwood floors, a mixture of vinegar and water can be applied to the spot after the excess has been wiped up. Soap and water will remove spots on linoleum or vinyl as well as on carpets, but it is important to get the carpet as dry as possible before applying soap and water, and also get it as dry as you can after using soap and water. The foam-type cleansers are helpful, since they will not wet the carpet as much as soap and water will, but immediate attention is important in case of urination.

CHAPTER 15

Feeding

When you obtain your Silky puppy, you should get a diet from the person from whom you purchase him or her, as a change of diet will at times cause an upset stomach. If the diet must be changed, make the change gradual. If you are unable to obtain the diet from the puppy's breeder, the schedule given here should prove satisfactory. The schedule is not rigid; if your puppy cleans his plate quickly three times a day and is not getting too fat, you may wish to continue that number of meals beyond the age of three months. If the puppy begins to "pick at" one of his meals, it is usually a sign that this meal can be eliminated. Puppies will rarely go a full day without eating unless they are sick, but if your grown dog refuses food for one day and shows no other signs of illness, don't worry, as he will eat again the next day. If a puppy or adult dog refuses food and shows any sign of illness, however, such as diarrhea, runny nose, listlessness, or fever, you should take him to your veterinarian.

The top grades of commercial dog foods on the market today, dry or canned, are generally excellent, and better balanced nutritionally than any sort of diet from table scraps. The dogfood companies spend a great deal of money in research to produce well-balanaced food, and many dogs are better fed than their human masters, from the nutritional standpoint. If you choose to use the dry foods, such as meal, kibble, and so on, you should add fat to the diet; these products are low in fat content so they will stay fresh longer.

Whatever you feed your Silky, do not let a puppy destined for show become too fat, as excessive weight will cause his feet to break down early. Adult dogs are also healthier without excess fat. The diets of our "Senior Citizens" must be watched carefully, for as they become less active, they tend to put on too much weight.

There are types of canned dog food on the market that confuse some Silky owners. These are the all-beef or all-chicken products. They *DO*

NOT provide a balanced diet when used as the only food for your dog. They are useful to add to some of the dry dog food products for greater protein content and palatability, but an all-protein diet is not good nutrition. When such products are fed exclusively over a period of some months, the Silky inevitably develops health problems connected with nutritional deficiences. If you use canned food for your dog, be sure to get the type that contains a proper balance of ingredients, and not meat alone. Our Silky Terriers seem to do best on the balanced canned food which contains beef or beef by-products; those which contain horsemeat will sometimes cause loose stools.

There are also a number of good food supplements on the market which supply needed vitamins and minerals for your dog. Particularly during puppyhood when bones and teeth are still forming, it is wise to feed one of the supplements daily. Ask your veterinarian for his recommendation as to what brand to use. We find the supplement in tablet form the most satisfactory, and our Silkys regard them as great treats. By using tablets, it is easy to give a measured amount each day. In addition, a dog that is eating poorly would not have adequate intake of the powder or liquid supplement that had been sprinkled over his food, at a time when he might particularly need it. Although the commercial dog foods are well-balanced, with most Silkys being house pets and not getting as much sunshine as they might, I feel it keeps my dogs in top condition to give them general-purpose supplements throughout their lives. This is especially true of dogs and bitches used for breeding, and is also helpful in keeping show dogs in good coat. Some owners do get carried away and add too many supplements, or give overlarge quantities. Seek and follow your veterinarian's advice on this matter.

Many new owners ask whether they should give their Silkys some of the supplements designed to keep dogs in good skin and coat condition. I have not found it necessary to use these except on the rare occasions when one or more of our dogs have had worms of some kind, especially tapeworm, which seems to be especially damaging to the coat and skin. Most breeders have some particular brand of coat conditioner which they feel is the best, but most of these products are quite satisfactory. If any of our dogs are in poor coat condition, we use one of the coat conditioners for three or four months, or as long as necessary for the dog to get back into condition. This is used in addition to the multiple purpose supplement mentioned earlier, but no more than one coat conditioner should be used at a time.

Fresh water should be available at all times for both puppies and adult dogs. Some puppies take great delight in playing in their water bowl, however, which not only gets them wet, it makes a mess for you to clean up. With such a puppy you should offer fresh water three or four times a day and remove the bowl as soon as he has had a good drink. Do be sure to keep the water bowl clean. Some owners, who would not dream of feeding their dog from a dirty dish, will not think about washing the water bowl every day. They probably do not realize that the water bowl can be as much a source of contamination as the food bowl.

Healthy puppies are avid eaters and soon learn where their feeding dish is situated.

If you have an electric dishwasher, food and water dishes should be washed in it, as the higher temperatures possible in such an appliance serve to sterilize the dishes as they are washed. Dishes made of china or stainless steel are best for your dog. Some plastic dishes cannot be washed in an electric dishwasher because they melt, and they are much too attractive to puppies for chewing. The large earthenware bowls are excellent for water, since they can be washed in the dishwasher and are too heavy for the dogs to overturn, as they may do with smaller, lighter-weight water dishes.

Many breeders of larger dogs recommend that their food be placed at a height so they can stand erect while eating, feeling that this helps to develop good necks and head carriage, as well as preventing front legs from going out at the elbow. We have not tried this method here, but it might be worthwhile to the breeder whose Silky puppies were developing poor fronts, or needed better necks and head carriage.

The following feeding schedule is not rigid and may be modified as desired. It is important in puppies that whatever dry food is given them be moistened and permitted to stand at least 20 minutes for the food to absorb the water or broth.

FEEDING SCHEDULE

Age 6 *to* 10 *weeks:* Three meals a day plus warm milk or dog biscuits at bedtime.

Morning Cereal with warm milk (baby food cereals are good), or puppy meal with milk.

Noon Cooked ground meat mixed either with dry dog food or with rice and the liquid in which the meat is cooked, or puppy meal with milk, soup, or broth.

Evening Same as for noon meal.

Bedtime Warm milk, or a dog biscuit broken into small pieces.

Age 10 *weeks to* 3 *months:* Same as above, except that canned dog food may be added gradually to the puppy meal mix. For one meal, you may substitute one of the dry-moist foods.

Age 3 *to* 6 *months:* Two meals per day plus dog biscuit at bedtime. Morning and evening meals as above except for deletion of baby cereal, but liquid in meal/milk mix should be gradually reduced. By this time, the puppy could also have one meal of canned dog food instead of one of the meal/meat mixtures.

Age 6 *months and over:* One or two meals per day, as you prefer. Dry dog food with meat and cooking liquid, dry dog food moistened with hot water and then mixed with canned food, or canned food alone. You may also wish to continue to give the dog biscuit as a reward for settling down promptly at bedtime.

The easiest form of milk to use for a puppy, and the most easily digested, is canned evaporated milk mixed with an equal part of very hot water. This will give the mixture about the right degree of warmth for the puppy without further heating.

The best hamburger for puppies or older dogs is one of the less expensive grades, as these contain more fat which the dogs need. Just be sure that whatever ground meat you buy is fresh. Some breeders prefer to feed raw hamburger, but our puppies and older dogs seem to prefer theirs cooked. For the puppies, I boil the hamburger till it is cooked through but not overcooked. Add the puppy meal or kibble to the liquid while it is still hot. With a full litter of puppies, this can be prepared ahead of time, put into individual containers and frozen until you need it. Proportions for the puppy meal/boiled hamburger mix are approximately three parts puppy meal to one part hamburger.

Be sure that the food you offer your Silky is clean, wholesome, and fresh. A dog can become ill as easily as a human on stale or sour foods.

Give the puppy or older dog about 20 minutes to finish his meal. Remove the food after that time and do not give any more until next regular meal time. In this way, he will learn to eat his food when it is first offered to him. Food left on the floor too long becomes stale and spoiled.

DO NOT FEED your Silky Terrier chicken bones, fish bones, chop bones, or any other bone that splinters easily, as a piece of bone can stick in the throat and choke him. You should also not give him heavily seasoned foods, potatoes or other starchy foods, or raw egg whites.

Although your puppy's or adult dog's basic food will be one of the commercial preparations, if you have only a few dogs and have meat or green-vegetable left-overs, you can add a little of these to the regular dog food. A treat that my own Silkys always enjoy is diced hard-boiled eggs, or scrambled eggs. Never give a dog raw egg white, as it contains a substance that destroys one of their essential nutrients. I also give each of our dogs about half a slice of bacon daily as a treat.

If your Silky Terrier's coat and skin seem dry, as frequently happens in winter when they are indoors in artificial heat most of the time, the addition of bacon grease, cooking oil, or one of the coat conditioners may be helpful in correcting this condition.

It would hardly be possible to over-emphasize the importance of a balanced, high-quality diet for your Silkys. The best-bred dog in the world will not develop properly through puppyhood, or look his best at any time of his life, without proper nutrition.

CHAPTER 16

Housing and Medical Care

The great majority of Silky Terrier breeders in this country do not breed on a large scale, nor do they have kennel facilities as such. Our own Silkys are beloved house pets as well as show and breeding animals. I personally do not feel that Silkys do well as kennel dogs, except in small kennels where the owners have time to give each dog individual attention and affection. With a breed so responsive to people, those dogs kept with little or no handling or affection never develop the intelligence and zest for living that are typically a part of the breed. I have been through small Silky Terrier kennels where the dogs were quite obviously loved and handled as well as being cared for—one I recall, in fact, has a well-deserved reputation for breeding Silkys with particularly good temperament. I have also been through larger establishments where the dogs looked at you, if they looked at all, with dull, lack-luster eyes, with much the same expression you see in people in mental hospitals. There are some large kennels in various breeds whose owners realize the importance of human contact and affection for their dogs, and who have enough employees that each dog does receive attention. There are also, of course, some people who have dogs as house pets who do not show them affection. If these dogs are shown, it is easy to see the difference in responsiveness and self-confidence between them and the Silkys which know they are loved.

A question often asked by new owners is, "Is it true that house pets do not make good show dogs?" The answer must be emphatically that this is untrue, unless you have neglected training the dog and permitted him to become wild and undisciplined. The dog shown by his beloved master, given the proper training, will display the ultimate degree of correct temperament. As new exhibitors gain experience in showing and attend many shows, they may observe that most professional handlers seem to make a particular pet of whichever of their dogs is doing the biggest share of winning. Without affection between the handler and the dog, that rapport displayed in the ideal dog-handler relationship will not be present, be the handler a professional or the owner of the dog.

There are problems in keeping a large number of dogs as house pets, of course, but for most Silky breeders, the love and affection shared with the dogs far outweigh the disadvantages. One of the principal problems in keeping dogs as pets as well as breeding stock is that your original bitches will inevitably grow older and can no longer be bred. If these bitches are pets, you cannot bear to part with them, and at some point, you no longer have "spaces" for additional breeding stock. Some breeders make arrangements to have a few bitches in other people's homes, with a co-ownership breeding plan which is beneficial to both. It is not easy to find just the right person with whom to make such arrangements, and before entering into any agreement, the breeder should check carefully on all the factors involved. There are some who acquire bitches, breed them several times, and then sell them to others; fortunately, there are few of this type in Silky Terriers. After a bitch has given the breeder several litters, and perhaps a champion or two, the breeder should feel that he owes that bitch a great deal, not the least being to make a happy home for her for her declining years. We give our "oldsters" preferred treatment in our home, including some time every day for special attention to them. We take them along occasionally on a show trip, and they do seem to enjoy it. When giving treats of any sort, dogs are served in order of age, with the oldest first and on down the line. This not only pleases the older Silkys, it is good training for the younger ones to be taught that they must wait their turn in line.

For the new breeder who plans to keep Silky Terriers as house pets, we have a few suggestions that may be helpful. First, when you do have several house dogs, discipline is absolutely essential. If you do not manage your dogs, you will find that they are managing you! It is pretty much a necessity also to have individual cages or crates in which they can sleep at night, or in which some can be confined when necessary. We have chromium-plated wire cages, and except for the older Silkys, each is put into his cage for meals. This enables you to check each dog to see that he or she has eaten all his food; it also prevents one from trying to eat another's meal, which may lead to an altercation. If you have a stud dog or dogs, you will need one or more rooms in which to confine bitches in season. Bitches soon to whelp or with small puppies should also have a room to themselves, even when you have only bitches. We use Dutch doors (half doors) for the rooms in our home, with the top half kept open most of the time. This permits air circulation and prevents the confined dog or bitch from feeling isolated, but also provides a barrier to entry and exit when the lower half of the door is closed. Do not under-estimate the jumping and/or climbing ability of your Silky Terriers—we found it necessary to have two of our doors rebuilt when some of our Silkys were able to get over the standard-height lower doors. There are several kinds of puppy gates available, but we have not found any that were sturdy enough to keep the adult Silkys in or out. If you order or make Dutch doors, it is wise to have the lower half of the door cut higher than standard size (which will necessarily make the upper half shorter).

An isolation room is also necessary for any dog or bitch that is ill, not only to provide quiet for the patient, but to prevent as much as possible the spread of disease or dangerous parasites to the other dogs.

You may find that some of your Silky Terriers will fight each other, more likely in males than females, but possible in either sex. If you have this problem, you will need to keep the two fighters in separate rooms to prevent their harming each other.

Exercise

Every dog must have an adequate amount of exercise. With those as small as Silky Terriers, much of their exercising will be done in the house. It is imperative that you have a securely fenced yard, with fencing high enough so that the dogs cannot jump over or climb out of the yard. Regular checks should be made along the fence to be sure there that are no holes large enough to enable the dog to get under the fence. Being terriers, Silkys have a great talent for digging, and may dig out of their yard. We have chain link fencing four feet high; the biggest advantage of chain links is that those dogs which are climbers cannot get a good foothold in this type of fence. With the type of wire fencing having horizontal wires, many Silkys can climb out. The biggest danger to any dog is the automobile, and with our dogs as small and as quick as they are, they must be prevented from reaching a street or road. Never take any Silky Terrier into an unfenced area when he is off lead—no matter how well trained you believe he is, there is always that moment when he spies an irresistible object and makes a dash for it.

If you have two doors leading to fenced yard space, it can be a great help to fence two separate spaces, one from each door. In this way, when a bitch is in season, she can exercise in one yard while the males can be exercised in the other, preferably at a different time. Males kept close enough to bitches in season to pick up the scent are very likely to turn up with prostatitis by the time the season is over. This can be very painful to the dog and usually requires medical treatment to correct it.

The ideal surface for a yard or run is probably washed gravel, or pea gravel as it is sometimes called. Most authorities feel that this type of surface is excellent to keep the dog's feet from breaking down. Most of us who have house dogs must settle for the usual grassy yard. If feet are a particular problem in your Silkys, it might be helpful to have at least a small area which contains the gravel in which they can spend some time each day.

Whatever type yard you have, stools should be picked up and disposed of regularly. There is a set of two tools helpful in this, one being rather like a dustpan with a long handle and the other a fairly straight piece of metal attached to a long handle, the latter to be used to rake the stool into the dustpan-like part. These tools are whimsically called "pooper scoopers" or whatever name their manufacturer has designated, and are also called "dog butlers."

For disposal of dirty newspapers from the house, there are large plastic bags available at grocery stores which are very useful, especially during rainy weather when the soiled papers cannot be burned.

Medical Care

One of the greatest assets a breeder can have is a competent veterinarian with a real interest in that breeder's dogs and his breeding program. We as breeders should know how to observe our Silkys for possible symptoms of illness or disease; we should take them to our veterinarian as soon as symptoms appear, rather than waiting until the dog is very ill. You should know how to take temperatures, as they have so much bearing on possible illness. Normal temperature in the dog, taken with a rectal thermometer, is between 101.0 and 102.0 degrees. A temperature over 102 degrees should always signal an examination by your veterinarian, since most illnesses start with fever. Other symptoms of illness are listlessness, running nose, coughs, refusal of food (with other symptoms), and severe or continuing diarrhea.

No book can teach you how to diagnose and treat your own dogs, but there is much that you can do to keep your dogs in good condition generally. In addition to correct diet as described in the chapter on feeding, you should keep your Silky Terriers free of parasites, both internal and external. We have our house and yard sprayed regularly by commercial exterminators, and feel that the service is more than worth its modest cost. When you consider what a few fleas or ticks can do to the coat of a show dog, it seems only common sense for all of us to keep our Silky Terriers free of them. Silkys do not seem to have fleas as much as some breeds, perhaps because they lack the undercoat in which fleas can hide, but they are extremely sensitive to them when they do have them. We have one bitch with what would be called a "fair skin" in a person—if she gets as much as one flea, she immediately scratches herself raw. The only one of our Silky Terriers to go completely out of coat did so after a neighbor brought in large quantities of fill dirt which was full of fleas, so that some got over into our yard despite our exterminators. Fleas not only cause the Silky to scratch out his coat, they also carry tapeworms, which are difficult to eradicate and which will themselves cause coat loss. Besides regular spraying of house and grounds, it is a good practice to go over your dogs for fleas or ticks whenever you are travelling with them or attending dog shows, as they sometimes pick them up there. Ticks have not been a problem with our Silky Terriers, but they are in some areas. If you do find a tick on one of your Silkys, it should be removed very carefully. If the head of the tick breaks off under the dog's skin, it may cause an infection, and at the least will leave a knot that will itch. Thus it is necessary to put something on the tick so that it will withdraw the head. A small amount of rubbing alcohol may be poured on the tick (put a towel under the dog to catch the excess) and after a few minutes, the tick may be pulled off with tweezers. Should it not come off easily, apply more alcohol and wait a few minutes more. Fingernail polish remover and ether are effective in smaller quantities and may be applied with a piece of saturated cotton. A match from which the flame has just been extinguished or the lighted end of a cigarette may be applied to the tick, if your hand is steady enough to be sure you will not burn the dog. After removing the tick, wash the area with a mildly antiseptic shampoo.

There are regular tick dips which can be applied to dogs with a heavy tick infestation. With the sensitive skin Silkys have, actual dipping is not recommended. Rather, the dip should be applied to the dog with cotton (you will need to wear rubber gloves), left a certain length of time, and then washed off. You can obtain this from your veterinarian, or if you prefer, have him treat your dog for you.

Ear mites are often seen in dogs which are not kept clean, especially if ears are not cleaned out regularly. If your Silky shakes his head frequently and scratches at his ears, look inside the ears for a very dark accumulation of what looks like dried or crumbly ear wax, or have your veterinarian check his ears. If mites are present, he will prescribe treatment.

Flea collars may be used if you follow the directions very carefully. They should be loosely fastened and never allowed to become wet. If you use one, check daily to be sure there is no allergic reaction on the neck. We recently repurchased a bitch which had had a severe allergic reaction to the flea collar. It had been neglected so that her neck had swollen and broken out in ugly sores, a pitiful sight. It took almost four months of daily medication to clear the sores, and she will have scars on her neck for the rest of her life. I do know of Silkys which have worn flea collars, properly applied and checked, for long periods of time with no ill effects. They will have some hair loss from the neck from any type of collar worn constantly. Some medications cannot safely be given to a dog that has been wearing a flea collar and such wear should be called to the attention of your veterinarian before he gives any medicine or a shot.

Worms—There are several varieties of internal parasites which may affect your Silky. Roundworms (usually in puppies), hookworms, whipworms, and tapeworms are the most common. Round, hook, and whipworms are picked up from stools of infested dogs or contaminated ground. They also may be transmitted to puppies before birth by their dam. Tapeworms are transmitted only through fleas. Puppies with roundworms tend to be pot-bellied and have a generally unthrifty look and a scratchy coat. They may also have diarrhea and vomiting. If you have bitches free of worms before breeding, and the puppies are not allowed on an infested surface, they are not likely to have them.

Hookworms—Hookworms are bloodsuckers which attach themselves to the walls of the intestinal tract. Puppies that are heavily infested with them will be anemic, and many die. If you ever see a puppy with very light pink or grayish-white gums, you can pretty well expect a heavy hookworm infestation. They cause poor appetites, weight loss, diarrhea, and eventual death if not eliminated.

Whipworms—They also cause anemia, as well as general debilitation, vomiting, diarrhea, and weight loss. Whipworms are at times very difficult to diagnose, as they may be concentrated in the caecum, a pocket of the intestines, where medication does not always get to them. We once acquired an adult dog, a proven stud, which except for scant coat seemed in good condition. However, he was unable to breed a bitch, although he was tried with several willing bitches over a year's time. His stools were checked by several competent veterinarians on seven or eight occasions during that year before the whipworms were finally discovered. After he had been treated (two treatments were required) and rid of these pests, he became a perfectly normal stud again.

Tapeworms—Tapeworms present an extremely difficult problem in Silky Terriers. Unlike round, hook, and whipworms, they are rarely detected in microscopic stool checks. They can be seen around the anus of a dog or discovered in a stool or his sleeping area, but *ONLY AFTER* the infestation is very heavy. The tape segment when seen in the anal area or in a fresh stool may still be moving, so that you have no doubt what it is. It will be flattish and white, or pinkish-white in color. If the dog is heavily infested, you will observe segments in his bed periodically; when dry, each segment has about the same size and appearance as a grain of brown rice. When semi-dry, they may look like small pieces of shredded skin. At times tapeworms are indicated by the dog "scooting" along the floor or ground on his rear, though this can also be caused by distended or infected anal glands.

In general, by the time a Silky Terrier is so heavily infested that tapeworm segments are seen, he or she will almost certainly have lost much of his or her coat, especially over the rear areas of the body. These worms are transmitted by fleas, and it takes only one flea to infest your Silky. The veterinarian who treated our dogs for many years was considered to be especially competent in treating skin problems, particularly those that had been resistant to treatment. It was his opinion that tapeworms were often an underlying cause, or at least a contributory factor, in many skin ailments. He often told me that the first step in treating stubborn skin problems should be to worm the dog for tapeworms, a practice he had followed with great success. I personally have witnessed a number of Silky Terriers with severe coat loss and/or skin troubles which did regain coat and clear skin after being wormed for tapes. Many veterinarians have long felt that dogs could tolerate a low level of tapeworm infestation without undue health damage, but it does not appear that Silky Terriers are among them, at least those you hope to show. There are many other causes of coat loss, of course—other intestinal parasites, continued fever, inadequate diet, allergies, and thyroid imbalance, to name but a few. However, if your Silky's coat is in poor condition or he has a skin difficulty which has resisted treament, it may be helpful to present this information to your veterinarian for consideration.

Heartworms—These worms, as the name indicates, infest the heart of the dog. They are very difficult but not impossible to treat. Your veterinarian can diagnose them by a simple blood test. They are believed to be transmitted by mosquitoes and have been most prevalent in the southern United States. They seem to have spread to many other areas in the recent past, and are most common in dogs kept in outdoor kennels in areas which have mosquitoes. I have not yet heard of any Silky which had heartworms, and I pray I never do. Dogs kept as house pets, as Silkys generally are, seem less likely to get them. The symptoms are extreme fatigue, gasping, coughing, and sometimes swelling of the feet and legs. It does appear that progress is being made in effective treatment of heartworms.

Anal Glands—As the name implies, these glands are located on each side of the anus. With excitement or for other reasons, they fill with fluid, and when very full, are uncomfortable for the dog. He may drag his rear quarters along the ground, or you may notice an unpleasant odor when they become impacted. Some Silky Terriers never seem to have any accumulation of fluid, while others are very likely to have full glands most of the time. They should be cleaned out periodically to prevent their becoming infected, such infections being rather difficult to clear. The excess fluid may be expressed by using a piece of cotton or several folds of Kleenex and applying pressure, with thumb on one side of the anus and fingers on the other. Most breeders learn to do this for their dogs, but it is a smelly job. If you have never done this, ask your veterinarian to show you how, or have him attend to it for you.

A note of interest to exhibitors is that the condition of anal glands may affect a dog's tail carriage in the ring. If they are full, the dog tends to keep his tail down, and if they are infected and painful, he or she may also be hand-shy of the judge when the hindquarters are examined. When badly infected, the dog obviously feels dreadful generally.

Diarrhea—Dogs may have diarrhea occasionally from a relatively minor digestive upset, even that resulting from a change in diet. However, bloody or black stools, especially when accompanied by listlessness, refusal of food, and fever are likely to mean serious illness. By all means take him to your veterinarian without delay. If the dog has a stool that is only slightly loose, with no other symptoms of illness, adding cooked rice to his diet for a few days will be beneficial.

Tonsillitis and Sore Throat—Inflammation or infection of the throat seems to be the ill to which small dogs are most subject. At times there may be an acute infection, which your veterinarian may be able to clear up quickly. In these cases, the dog may choke and vomit mucous; he has fever; he may scratch at his neck; there may be enlarged glands in the neck, and he may not eat well. The chronic throat infection is often very difficult to clear completely. With a chronic low-grade infection, the dog may not show many symptoms and may even continue to eat, but it is obvious that he does not feel as well as he normally should. Removal of the tonsils is not always the answer, since some dogs continue to have sore throats after a tonsillectomy. In the absence of fever, most veterinarians are reluctant to give antibiotics since dogs, like people, may build up an immunity to them. Keeping food and water dishes very clean is important, and the dogs should not be allowed to sleep in drafts, whether from air conditioners or from open windows. When they come back into the house from a wet yard, feet should be wiped dry. (This also prevents their tracking up your house.) If you have a problem with throats in your Silkys, you and your veterinarian should work together to try to solve it, with medication and with possible remedial measures you could take at home.

Inoculations—All dogs should be immunized for distemper, hepatitis, leptospirosis, and rabies. Until the past two or three years, most puppies were given the so-called "temporary" shots, at weaning time and every 10 days or 2 weeks thereafter until the so-called "permanent" shots were started at about 3 months of age. More recently, most veterinarians have stopped giving the temporary shots (serum), and permanent shots are started at 8 weeks of age. These are given a little differently by different veterinarians, so you should follow his advice. We have the distemper-hepatitis shot given at 8 weeks and repeated at 10 weeks; at 12 weeks, the leptospirosis shot is administered. Rabies vaccine is given at 6 months of age. BOOSTER SHOTS MUST BE GIVEN ANNUALLY OR AS DIRECTED BY YOUR VETERINARIAN TO MAINTAIN THE DOG'S IMMUNITY.

We hope that none of your dogs has the misfortune to contact any of these dread diseases, but the symptoms of each will be noted. Distemper and hepatitis have some symptoms in common—diarrhea, fever, loss of appetite, vomiting, discharges of nose and eyes. In distemper, the diarrhea is black-looking, very loose, and has a very foul odor. In hepatitis, the throat and head seem to swell, with complete closure of the throat sometimes resulting. An early symptom in distemper is that the dog seems to shun light as if it hurt his eyes. Many of these symptoms resemble those of other less-serious diseases, but if any of them appear in an unvaccinated puppy, you should immediately take the puppy to your veterinarian. Both are virus illnesses and may be picked up from other dogs or be airborne. Before I knew the importance of inoculations, I took our very first litter out in the yard when they were 5 weeks old and had not had any shots. A neighbor's child came by and played with one puppy in particular; several days later, this puppy came down with hepatitis or possibly hepatitis and distemper combined. We were fortunate enough to nurse her through it, with daily medication by our veterinarian, but since that time, I do not take puppies out until they have begun their immunizing program. About the time the sick puppy seemed to have passed her crisis, and I slept the first full night since her illness had begun, I awoke to find that the little thing had a blue eye. I was sure that she was blind in that eye for life and could hardly wait for her doctor to reach his clinic to phone him. He assured me that this was a symptom seen in dogs which were recovering from hepatitis, and that the eye would clear, which it did.

Leptospirosis is a bacterial disease which is spread by the urine of rodents (mice, rats, and squirrels) that have the disease or have become carriers, as well as through the urine of other dogs. The two forms are canicola and icterohemorrhagia (jaundice—hemorrhages). In the first, there is erratic fever, listlessness, weight loss, loose stools, jaundice, and stiffness. In the second, vomiting and diarrhea are present, with both usually bloody. In many cases, definite symptoms occur so late in the illness that the dog is lost before diagnosis can be made.

Rabies is contracted from the bite of a rabid animal, either another dog or some other type of animal. It is not prevalent in dogs now, but epidemics of it are reported from time to time in bats or squirrels in certain areas.

These illnesses are all preventable when inoculations are properly given. We described the "permanent" shots earlier as "so-called" because they are not actually permanent throughout the dog's lifetime. Booster shots must be given annually or as directed by your veterinarian. (In case of an epidemic of any of the four diseases in your area, your veterinarian will probably suggest that the booster shot be given in somewhat less than a year.)

Poisoning—If you have reason to believe your dog has been poisoned, prompt measures must be taken. If you can locate the container from which the poisonous substance was obtained, antidotes will be listed on the label. Symptoms of poisoning may vary according to type of poison, but apparent intestinal pain, vomiting, and slimy discharges from the mouth are some of them. There may also be convulsions or coma. If you can identify the type of poison, you should give an emetic to make the dog vomit unless it is an acid or corrosive alkali type of poison. Hydrogen peroxide (3% solution) mixed in an equal amount of water is effective. About 1½ tablespoons would be correct dosage for an adult Silky of ten pounds. Powdered mustard and water is another commonly used emetic, and if you have nothing better available, ordinary table salt may be used. Salt is not mixed with water—about two rounded teaspoons will cause vomiting in a nine or ten pound Silky. After he has stopped vomiting, give him milk to drink, or give it to him like medicine if necessary.

For acid, a solution of baking soda or crushed chalk will neutralize some of it. For alkalis, weak acids like diluted vinegar or diluted lemon juice (two parts water to one part vinegar or lemon juice) can be used.

If you are unable to identify the poison quickly, phone your veterinarian and describe the symptoms to him, then follow his advice.

Never leave insect sprays, rat poison, roach powder, or any poisonous substance where a dog might possibly get to it.

Hemorrhage—Try to staunch the blood with pressure applied to the wound with absorbent cotton pads of a size to cover the wound. If the bleeding is too profuse to be stopped in this manner, apply a tourniquet if bleeding is from a limb, or a pressure bandage on a body wound. If the tourniquet is used (a piece of cloth tightly tied and knotted between the wound and the dog's heart), it should be loosened at 15-minute intervals to prevent gangrene from setting in. Call your veterinarian, or better, have someone else phone him to come while you do what you can do to help the dog until he arrives.

Shock—The eyes appear dazed, with pupils dilated very wide; breathing is shallow, and the dog's body feels cold to the touch. Keep the dog quiet and warm until his doctor can get to him. Shock may occur after surgery, as well as from any sort of severe injury. If the gums are grayish-white or very pale pink, the dog may also be bleeding internally, although shock itself may cause abnormal color of gums.

Allergic reactions to insect stings, medication, or immunizing shots—Silky Terriers seem to have more allergic reactions than some of the larger breeds. One symptom which may occur is swelling of lips, ears, eyelids, and feet, or other parts of the body. Get him to your veterinarian as fast as possible. Antihistamines or cortisone or both can bring immediate relief in many cases, but fast action is imperative. If your veterinarian is not familiar with Silky Terriers, be sure to caution him before he gives shots that some are unduly sensitive to some substances. In our own Silkys, the worst reactions have come from leptospirosis or rabies vaccine among the inoculations, and from sulfa in over-large quantities or iodine in medications.

Giving medicine—Liquid medication is most easily given with a plastic eyedropper (glass ones break if bitten). Put the liquid in the pouch of the lower lip on the side of the dog's mouth, as far back as possible. Empty the eyedropper gradually; if you do it faster than the dog can swallow, it will either be spilled out the side of his mouth or will choke him. Tablets or capsules should be put as far back in the mouth as possible, behind the tongue, working from the side and back of the mouth. Capsules should either be wet with water or covered with butter or margarine to keep them from sticking in the dog's throat.

Periodic checks—Your veterinarian will check your dog out thoroughly when he sees him to give one of his booster shots (always have a stool check made then for worms), or at other times as necessary. You yourself should check each Silky once or twice a week (during grooming sessions is a convenient time). The whites of the eyes are one of the best indicators of health or illness. In the healthy dog, they are clear white; in the sick dog, they may be generally pinkish, or streaked with red veins, or both in combination. You should, of course, learn to observe your Silkys automatically when they show behavior that deviates from normal or seem not to feel as well as usual.

CHAPTER 17

Grooming

One of the questions most often asked is, "How do I keep my Silky Terrier in good coat condition for shows?" The very first requisite for a good coat is general good health. The Silky must be fed a diet of the very best quality; he must be kept free of external parasites; he must be kept free of internal parasites. He must also be groomed regularly and thoroughly. It takes far less time to groom your Silky twice a week than it does to neglect him for several weeks and then spend the amount of time necessary to remove snarls and tangles from his coat.

If you purchased your Silky from a breeder who starts puppy grooming while they are very young, you should have a head start in training him to enjoy grooming sessions. Your grooming should start with your puppy as soon as you obtain him. He should learn to lie quietly on his back in your lap while you comb the coat on his chest and abdomen, and then to stand quietly on the grooming table (or whatever surface you will use) while you do the rest of the coat. Most Silky Terriers enjoy being groomed, since they love having your attention.

You should always be gentle with a Silky puppy.If you accidentally pull at a snarl and hurt the puppy, stop to pet him and let him know you did not mean to hurt him. Otherwise, if you handle your Silky roughly, or scold him for jerking away if you have hurt him, he will come to regard grooming sessions as unpleasant and they will be more difficult for both of you. Being gentle with the puppy does not mean that you should permit him to remain ungroomed because he objects to it at first. As in all dog training, you must be firm and teach the puppy what is required of him. We have had many people bring puppies we bred back to see us, with some of the puppies looking as if they had not been groomed since they left us. These owners usually say that the puppy will not let them groom him, or that the puppy dislikes being groomed. They are invariably amazed when I take this same puppy and proceed to groom him with no objections, or only brief ones, from the puppy. Silky puppies are wrigglers by nature, and when you start training your puppy, you will have to hold him by force if necessary. All Silky Terriers, whether puppies or adults, have a great deal of physical strength for their size, but you can easily hold them long enough to convince them they must be still. At times, when we have acquired 8-week-old puppies that were not accustomed to being groomed, it would be necessary to hold them forcibly, but after one session there is generally no further problem. Even the puppy that is most obstreperous at first is quite likely to fall asleep contentedly while you are still grooming him. A few years ago, we obtained an adult bitch which had tartar on her teeth when she arrived. Since we have quite a number of dogs and bitches, I scale the tartar from their teeth myself rather than taking them to our veterinarian. This bitch was perfectly agreeable about the rest of her grooming, but she was determined that her teeth would not be scraped. After a few poor starts, I finally wrapped a bath towel tightly around her front legs to keep her from pushing my hands away (a slip with a dental scaler can mean a nasty cut in mouth or gums, so a steady hand is needed) while I worked on her teeth. It took three sessions over three days to get her teeth scaled the first time, but ever since, she has been good as gold about it, and seems perfectly relaxed while I work on her mouth—without the towel around her, of course.

Remember always that you should never let your Silky run you—you are the boss, and your Silky will be much happier when he understands this thoroughly.

Equipment—You will need certain supplies to keep your Silky Terrier well groomed. They are: natural-bristle brush, hard-rubber or metal combs, small scissors with blunt ends, toenail clippers, thinning shears, stripping knife (the razor blade type is a good one), and flexible-stick Q-tips for cleaning ears and applying medication. The brush *MUST* be of natural bristle; those made of nylon or metal pins will break off the silky coat. Nylon or plastic combs will also break off the coat, so be sure the combs you buy are either of hard-rubber or metal. If you purchase metal combs, be sure there are no rough edges on any of the teeth. I use the hard-rubber combs in two sizes, a large one about 8 inches long with teeth about 1 inch long, with large teeth at one end and fine teeth at the other; the other comb is small, of the size described as a "pocket comb," and it should also have two sets of teeth. The small combs are useful for head combing, and also for combing through very fine puppy coats to pull out dead hair.

Combing and Brushing—Many puppies have very fine coats, and since they do not shed, you must comb and brush out the dead hairs. First comb through the coat in the direction the hair grows, using the coarse-tooth end of one of the combs. Then comb through the coat again with the fine-tooth end of the small comb, against the direction in which the hair grows. This will remove dead coat and permit healthy growth of new coat. Brushes with very stiff bristles should be used only on adult Silkys, with a brush with less stiffness, though not soft, for puppies. Brushing stimulates the circulation of blood to the skin and helps coat growth. On either puppies or adults, the mostly likely places for snarls are under the forearms and around the base of ears. You can remove these snarls by working them out very gently with a comb and your fingers. When a dog has been allowed to stay snarled or tangled for so long that a mat has formed, soak the mat in baby oil and then work it out with the comb and your fingers. If the coat becomes so matted that tangles must be removed with scissors, cut lengthwise in the same direction as hair growth rather than across the hairs.

Bathing—You should bathe your Silky when he needs it, rather than on any set time schedule. With twice-weekly grooming, he is not likely to need a bath more than about once a month. If you are showing him, however, he should be bathed the day before a show. Any castile or lanolin-base shampoo is satisfactory, and one thorough soaping is usually sufficient. Some of the harsher dog shampoos are too strong for the Silky, with their single coats and relatively sensitive skin. Always use warm water rather than hot, as dogs dislike hot water. If you have a double sink with spray attachment or a laundry tub with spray, these are ideal places to wash the dog, as they are at a height which makes the process easier for you. Be sure you have a grip on the Silky all the time he is being bathed, as occasionally one will decide to jump out of the sink or tub. Be sure to rinse all shampoo out throughly. A creme rinse will make the coat more manageable. With a coat that tends to be coarse, use a heavy solution of creme rinse (that is, one with less water than usual mixed with it). With a very soft coat, less of the creme rinse should be used. After rinsing out all shampoo, apply the creme rinse and work it into the coat throughly with your fingers. Follow the directions on the bottle; most of these products should be rinsed out. Dry the Silky with old bath towels—two are usually necessary for each dog. Older towels are better than new ones because they have less lint on them, some of which will come off on the dog. When you have towel-dried the dog till he is free of excess water but still damp, finish drying with the comb, or comb and brush. You should have washed the comb and brush before bathing the dog, so they will be clean and ready to use. By using the comb to finish drying, any tendency to curl or wave in the coat can be minimized.

Before you start combing the Silky dry, the coat should be parted. The part should extend from the nose back over the head and to the base of the tail, or to the end of the tail if you prefer. Whether you start the part in the middle or at either end is up to you, but in order to get the part straight, you must have the dog in a standing position. If you have a grooming table with neck loop (and if you have several Silky Terriers such equipment is very worthwhile), it will make a straight part easier to obtain. On the head, the hair on the muzzle in front of the eyes should be combed to each side. From the center of the eyes to the base of the ears, part at the middle and comb to sides in front of the ears. The hair behind the base of the ears should be combed back and to the sides with the coat on the back of the neck. Young puppies need not be parted until they are about 6 months old, unless they have quite a lot of coat, in which case it is desirable to start training the coat to part. In puppies and young dogs,

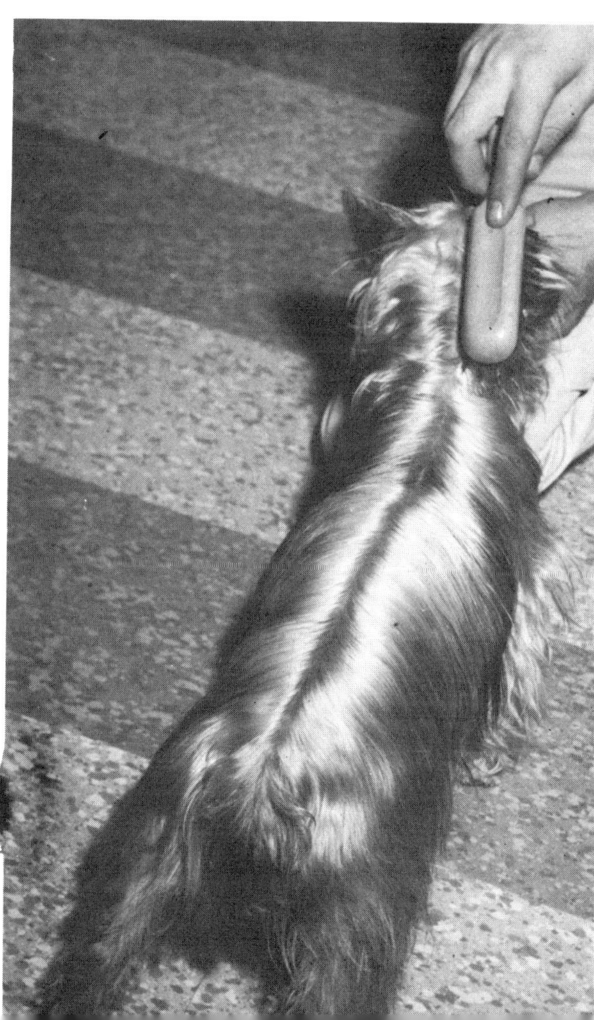

Parting the coat, with the dog in the correct standing position. A comb is used initially to make the part, then the brush may be used to smooth the coat to each side.

as well as some older ones, there is not enough length to the hair on the head and back of the neck for it to stay combed very long at first. With time the hair will grow longer, which helps it stay down of its own weight, and with persistence, you will eventually get it trained. The common complaint of the new owner who is learning to groom his Silky is that they shake as soon as the head has been done, which messes it up again. This is true, and there is not much we can do about it except to comb the head again. Some Silkys will give up shaking the head if you re-do it three or four times, but others will always shake. With more hair length and longer training, it will tend to fall back into place.

Some puppies have considerable wave in their topknots, some being almost crinkled with small waves, even when the rest of the coat is perfectly straight. If your puppy has this problem, obtain and use some of the setting gels, applying it about once a week and combing the hair to each side until it is dry and straight. The wave in the topknot will often grow straight with no attention as the hairs get longer, but if you show your puppy, you may wish to train the wave out as soon as possible.

The hair on the tail is sometimes difficult to manage, having a tendency to curl at the base. In these cases, part the hair on the tail and comb it down to each side with the tail held horizontally. If this is not enough to remove the curl or wave, use some of the setting gel on the tail as well as the topknot.

Be sure to keep your Silky in a warm place until he is completely dry, so that he will not take a cold or sore throat from being chilled while damp.

After you have finished bathing and combing your Silky, make a fuss over him, telling him how beautiful he looks, he is a good boy, and so on, and then give him a dog biscuit or other treat. Over a period of several years, we had four Silky Terriers, so that I could bathe all of them in one day. I doubt they ever got to like being in water, but they enjoyed so much being fussed over and told how lovely they looked that the three who had not been bathed would line up to watch me bathe the first one, as if waiting impatiently for it to be their turn. As I finished washing and combing each of them, that particular dog or bitch got the first biscuit, with the other three also given a biscuit just after the one which had been washed. I was never sure these four did not count to be sure they got four dog biscuits each on bathing day.

The use of electric hair dryers is not advisable. The Silky usually dislikes them because of the noise; they may dry the coat, and the coat is more likely to wave when dried in this manner than it is when combed dry.

There is a type of foam shampoo available at pet shops which is useful in some circumstances. If your dog has been ill, if the weather is particularly cold, or if only one area on the dog needs bathing, they are very practical. We always take a can of this shampoo with us when traveling to dog shows, in case one of the Silkys gets dirt on one area of his or her coat. I find this easier to manage than trying to bathe one of them in the bathtub or shallow lavatory basin in motel rooms.

Trimming—Ideally, the Silky Terrier is naturally clean-pointed—that is, he has no long hair on ears, muzzle, and feet—and with these, little or no trimming is necessary. In actual fact, only about one-fourth of the current breed population possess this virtue, so most owners will need to trim their Silkys.

It is a good idea to start trimming with the feet, if you have not had previous experience, as your Silky will probably be less sensitive there than around his ears and muzzle. Using the blunt-pointed scissors (those I use are slightly curved), trim the long hair between the pads of the feet. It is especially important to keep this hair out from between the footpads, as it will cause the feet to spread when left there; the dog will also have cleaner feet if you keep this hair trimmed. You should proceed slowly to avoid a possible slip into cutting one of the footpads with the scissors. Hold the dog on your lap while you do this trimming. Then stand your Silky on the grooming table or other flat surface at a convenient height, and trim around the outline of each foot, so that the foot has the correct round appearance. The hairs on top of the foot and up to the first joints on each leg should be shortened to $\frac{1}{4}$ to $\frac{1}{2}$ inch in length. Never trim so close that the knuckles of the toes are visible, or down to the skin. The razor blade Dresser is a good tool for this job, or you may again use the blunt-pointed scissors. The first joints up on the front legs are called the wrists or knees, and those on the rear legs are called the hocks. Trim up *to* these joints, but not *over* them. After trimming this portion of each leg, comb the coat that is higher on the leg to see that it is not too long. It should never be so long that it reaches the floor, and some prefer to shorten it to a point just below those first joints. With an adult Silky with profuse coat, use your thinning shears to even this part of the coat to a point just below the knees and hocks.

The long hair on the ears should be plucked by hand. Using your thumb and forefinger, pluck all hair extending beyond the outline of the ear. On the inside edges of the ears, you should go down to the base of each ear. On the outside edges of the ears, there is a little fold or pocket just above the outside ear base. Do not trim the outline of the ear below the mid-point of this pocket. In the beginning, it is better to take off too little hair than too much. Then pluck excess hair from the center back of the ear. Do not try to pluck more than a few hairs at once. You can obtain some precipitated chalk at your drug store (this is nothing more than ground-up chalk) with which to coat your fingers to give you a better grip. The finished look of the back of the ear should be that of velvet, with all hairs to be $\frac{1}{4}$ to $\frac{1}{2}$ inch in length. Then excess hair should be removed from the inside of the ear. This is most easily accomplished by using eyebrow tweezers. The excess hair inside the ear may range from very little to a great deal, and keeping it out of the ear is necessary to keep the ears clean. Ears that are choked up with ear wax and excessive hair are fertile grounds for infection and also have an unpleasant odor. After trimming the hair inside the ear, clean the inside parts of the ear with the flexible-stick cotton swabs. Do not use swabs with wooden sticks, since the dog could jerk and break it, with the result that it might be stuck into the ear. Never clean deeper into the ear than the portion you can see clearly. Each time you groom your Silky and clean his ears, you should check for possible abrasions inside the ear. If your dog has a great deal of hair growth inside his ears, do not try to do the whole job at one time, but over several sessions. If your Silky has a profuse growth of hair on the outsides of his ears, you can also trim them with the blunt-end scissors. If you use this method, cut only a few hairs at a time, using a sort of sliding motion, so that you will not leave jagged edges of hair where the cuts are made. Those who are proficient with plucking can take off excess hair with remarkable speed, but it takes some experience to become this proficient.

There are frequently very fine hairs growing at the inside corners of each eye. They should be pulled out by hand, as they can cause irritation by scratching the eyeballs. If the topknot is so profuse that it hangs over the dog's eyes, you can either train it to stay combed to the sides, or shorten a strip of the hairs just over the eyes, which then forms a sort of "bangs" which will help hold the topknot out of the eyes. The eyes must always be visible.

The muzzle hair should not be trimmed unless it forms a long fall. If it is so long that it forms a sort of beard, then shorten it with thinning shears to a 2- or 3-inch length and comb back into the other hair on the neck. Ordinarily the "feeler" whiskers of the Silky need not be trimmed, but occasionally a dog will have such coarse whiskers that they must be shortened to get the hair on the muzzle to lie flat when you comb it. In these cases, you simply cut them fairly close to the skin with scissors. (These feeler whiskers are the scattering of stiff hairs which all dogs have on each front side of the muzzle; cats have them also.)

Toenails should be kept trimmed at all times, starting with young puppies, as overlong nails cause spreading of the feet. The nails should be kept short enough to clear the floor when the dog is standing. For puppies, the blunt-end type of fingernail clippers or baby scissors are most satisfactory. For adult Silkys, use the standard type of clippers made for dogs. Always trim just a little at a time so you will not cut into the quick and cause it to bleed. Since Silkys have black or dark brown toenails, it is no easy

CH. REDWAY SPLINTERS, bred, owned, and handled to her championship by Mrs. Merie E. Smith. This Silky bitch is naturally very clean-pointed. She is by Ch. Wexford Pogo ex Brenhill Splinters.

CH. D'UNDER LILIBET O' TEA TIME (by Redway Lord Teasel ex D'Under Lilibet O' Blue) is shown as he finished for his title under Judge Alva Rosenberg. He is handled by 1965 STCA Board Member Al Vaughn. This Silky is owned by Howard A. Jensen and Paul G. Hefner.

task to know how far back to trim, and if you are at all nervous about doing it, have your veterinarian trim the nails for you. If you should draw blood while trimming, wet a cotton swab with iodine or merthiolate and hold it against the end of the nail until bleeding stops. Styptic powder may also be used to stop this bleeding. Some groomers make it a practice to cut the nails back quite far so that all nails bleed when cut, but this not only may give your Silky sore feet, if persisted in, it can make the dog very nervous. There are also electric nail grinders on the market, and if you have very many dogs, you should investigate them. We use one of these with our dogs, but they grind the nail so quickly that it is a two-person operation, one to hold the dog and the other to do the grinding. Ours also has a high-frequency motor, and those dogs which are particularly sensitive to sound dislike even hearing the motor run. They do save a great deal of time.

The tail should have about $1\frac{1}{2}$ inches of feathering, measuring with the tail held horizontally. If your Silky has feathering longer than this, shorten it with the thinning shears. First comb the feathering down on each side of the tail, then hold the shears so that the pointed ends are away from the dog and your trimming will begin at the base of the tail. Some Silky Terriers have very bushy tails, and these may be thinned, but tails should never be stripped of all feathering as they are in some other terrier breeds.

The teeth should be checked regularly, at least once a week, for tartar accumulation. Tartar is a yellowish-brown discoloration which begins with the gum line and if not removed, eventually covers the whole tooth. If you see this, have your veterinarian scale the teeth.

In puppies, you should also check regularly to see that the baby teeth come out as they should. The permanent teeth begin coming in at 4 to 6 months of age, and in some cases, the baby teeth are not shed properly. If a permanent tooth is as much as half in, and the corresponding baby tooth is still there, first try loosening the baby tooth with your fingers. If it is not loose enough to come out that way, you should have your veterinarian extract it. This problem occurs most often with the canine teeth (the so-called "fangs") at the front corners of the mouth, and if the baby teeth are not removed, they may cause poor alignment of the permanent teeth.

CHAPTER 18

The Stud Dog

Many breeders do not keep stud dogs themselves, preferring to send their bitches to other breeders' studs for service. Whether or not to keep a stud dog is for each individual breeder to decide, depending on his or her circumstances and inclinations. Either course of action has both advantages and disadvantages, some of which are listed below.

Using Studs Owned by Other Breeders.—*Advantages:* (a) You would have a wider choice of studs; (b) hopefully, you would have seen at least some of the offspring of the selected stud before deciding to use him; and (c) there should be an economic advantage, since the cost of stud fees and shipping your bitch would probably be less than the cost of maintaining and exhibiting your own male. There are exceptions to the latter, depending on shipping charges from your location to the stud, and on how large a fee is charged by that particular stud owner for his services.

Disadvantages: (a) Unless the stud you wished to use was available near you, it would be necessary to ship your bitch, which is a problem in certain areas; (b) there is slightly less chance that a bitch shipped for service will conceive than if she is bred at home; (c) there is a tendency to select the stud on the basis of show-ring success, which is often a very poor practice; and (d) you would know less about all offspring produced by the selected stud than you would about all get of your own stud. Unless you are dealing with a very objective and candid stud owner, he or she is unlikely to inform you about the stud's poor offspring, though you will hear of his better get which have been successful in the show ring.

Owning Your Own Stud—*Advantages:* (a) You would know more the actual virtues and faults of your own stud; (b) you would know about all of his offspring, good or bad; (c) you can make test matings which will greatly increase your knowledge of the genotype of your stud (viz., what he is likely to produce); and (d) breedings to your own bitches are more easily accomplished.

Disadvantages: (a) You would probably have to buy your stud as a puppy and wait for him to mature, since good mature studs are rarely for sale; (b) when your bitch is not to be bred, you would have to keep her away from the stud, which requires great vigilance if both are house pets; (c) if you own more than one stud, they may fight; and (d) you would not have as wide a selection of studs available.

The best solution to this problem is probably to start with two or three bitches and send them to studs owned by others for their first litters. In this way, you would obtain some knowledge of what each bitch would produce and of what particular bloodlines would produce with your bitch, whether good or bad. In this manner, you could proceed more intelligently in choosing a male Silky Terrier for future use at stud. Some breeders will prefer to keep one of the male puppies from these first litters to use later. In selecting the stud to be used for the first litters, the best policy is to choose one which has produced good offspring from bitches from bloodlines similar to those of your own bitch.

The age at which a Silky male should first be used at stud will vary to some extent with the individual dog, as some mature sexually later than others. A litter sired by a dog under 7 months old at time of service will not be registered by the American Kennel Club. If you have a male 9 or 10 months old which shows great interest in breeding a bitch, no harm will be done in trying him, *PROVIDED* the bitch is a steady and willing breeder. A young stud should never be used with a difficult bitch, either one which is not a willing breeder or one that for some physical reason is difficult to breed. You should exercise caution to be sure the dog is not hurt or frightened at this first service, as a traumatic experience at his first breeding may make him an indifferent stud throughout the rest of his life.

If you choose to own your own stud, he will need the same sort of general care that any show dog should receive. His diet should be high in quality and he should be given a good general-purpose vitamin supplement. He must also have plenty of exercise, and should not be permitted to become fat.

There is one relatively minor physical difficulty that occurs occasionally in most males, whatever their breed. This is called balanitis, which is an inflammation or infection of the sheath. The penis of the dog, when he is not actively engaged in breeding a bitch, is covered and protected by the sheath, which is made up of skin and tissue. Since the sheath is both moist and warm, it provides a likely place for infection. Owners of stud dogs should check the sheath periodically. If there seems to be any difficulty there, it can generally be corrected by douching the sheath with a mild antiseptic solution daily for 5 or 6 days. If there is severe infection, of course, it is a matter for your veterinarian. Dogs normally have some discharge from the sheath, which they will keep clean by licking. Before a mating, it is wise to douche the sheath with the same mild antiseptic solution. It is also a good idea to wash the vulva of the bitch and the area around it with a surgical-type soap; a strongly medicated soap should not be used as it could cause irritation of the skin and vulva.

The dog and bitch to be mated should be taken to a room where they will not be distracted by the other dogs. Put a collar on the bitch, as you will need to hold her during the mating. At first, let them play for a few minutes. If the bitch is being bred for the first time, she may need to be coaxed to accept the stud, and an experienced stud dog seems to realize this. After he has teased and played with her for a while and she is ready to stand, as indicated by her back legs being braced and her tail turned to one side, you should hold her head while the dog mounts to breed her. The dog begins the breeding by making a pumping motion, and when his penis fully penetrates the vagina, a large bulb at the base of the penis swells and results in the dog and bitch being locked together while he ejaculates semen. This is called the "tie"; it may last anywhere from five minutes to one hour, but the average is about twenty minutes. The reason for holding the bitch is that many of them will try to jerk away as the tie is consummated, and they may injure the stud or themselves by doing so. Some bitches will try to lie down after the tie, and you must prevent their doing this. Fortunately Silky bitches are small enough that you can hold them up if necessary. Some studs will turn themselves around as soon as they have ejaculated, while others will stay mounted for some minutes. The dog will throw one hind leg over the back of the bitch and turn so that they are back to back and he can put all four feet on the floor. Bitches usually become quiet after the first few minutes of the tie, but it is advisable to hold them for the duration of the tie.

At times a bitch cannot be tied for one reason or another. Occasionally, they will become pregnant without a tie, especially if the male has had a good penetration in the vagina and ejaculated the semen. However, the tie assures the mating if the time is right and both dog and bitch are fertile. We always breed a bitch twice, skipping one day after the first mating, if the bitch is still willing to be bred. The only reason for a second mating is in case the first one was not on the most favorable day of the season, as one mating on the correct day is sufficient to bring about conception. It has been our experience that bitches which first accept the stud as late as their 13th day will usually not permit another mating, but this will vary with the individual bitch.

The dates of the mating and the length of the ties should be recorded, and if the bitch was sent to your dog to be bred, you should furnish a statement to her owner giving this information.

In all cases where the dog and bitch are owned by different people, the amount of the stud fee or other conditions agreed upon should be put in writing and signed by both owners before the bitch is bred, with a copy of the contract retained by each owner. If the breeding is for a puppy, it should be stated clearly that the puppy is to be selected by a certain age. The contract should also state what agreement has been reached in the event the bitch has only one puppy. Most stud owners will agree to accept a cash stud fee if there is only one puppy in the litter and the owner of the bitch wishes to retain it. This is an important consideration with Toy breeds where litters of only one puppy are not unusual. Even before the contract for stud service is signed, the stud's owner and the bitch's owner should furnish written pedigrees of their Silkys to each other. The owner of the bitch should notify the owner of the stud when the litter is whelped, and should send to the stud's owner the Application for Litter Registration with information on the bitch and the puppies filled in. The stud owner should then fill out that portion which deals with the sire of the litter, and either return it to the owner of the bitch or send it along to the American Kennel Club with the proper fee, whichever they have agreed to do.

CHAPTER 19

The Brood Bitch

The Silky Terrier bitch will generally have her first season between the ages of six and ten months. The earliest I have known of was 5½ months, and the latest 13 months. She should never be bred at her first season, as she is little more than a puppy herself. Some attempt to justify such breeding practices by saying she will be a year old before she has puppies, but had she not been relatively slow to mature, her first season would have come earlier. Others try to use the excuse that wild animals breed at the first and every subsequent season, but they overlook the fact that females in the wild state have but one period of estrus a year, compared to two periods in our domesticated bitches. Then, too, most of us would be unwilling to have our beloved Silky Terriers go back to the wilderness rule of "survival of the fittest." It should hardly be necessary to state that just as she should not be bred at her first season, she also should not be bred at every season. Chances for successful whelpings and strong, healthy puppies are best with bitches that are bred for the first time no earlier than the second season, and only at every other season thereafter.

It is also best to plan her first breeding before she is three years old. After that time, she may have lost some of the elasticity of muscle that the younger bitch possesses, and older bitches being bred for the first time seem more likely to have whelping difficulties. In general, Silkys are good natural whelpers, especially in comparison with other Toy breeds.

It should be clearly understood that there are many variations in the period of estrus (more commonly called season, or heat) in different bitches, and with some females, variation from one season to another.

The average season will last 20 to 21 days, though it may be longer or shorter. The vulva will usually swell for several days prior to the commencement of bleeding, but in counting the days of her season, begin with the first day she showed color. The bleeding and accompanying swelling of the vulva will reach a peak at eight to nine days, and with most, bleeding continues, though somewhat diminished in quantity, to about the 11th day. The color will ordinarily change from red to straw color between the 11th and 13th days. At the same time, the vulva has begun to soften, signaling that time for mating is near. As an average, the bitch will first be willing to breed between the 10th and 13th days, but this is by no means the correct time for every bitch.

Novice breeders often have fixed in their minds the erroneous idea that every bitch will be ready to breed on the 10th day, or on the 13th day, or whatever one day they have selected or been told about. This is often incorrect even at different seasons of the same bitch.

There are frequent variations in the duration, as well as the intensity, of individual seasons. Some females will show color before there is any swelling of the vulva. Some have very copious amounts of bleeding, while with others the flow is very scant. When there is relatively little discharge, the unobservant owner may not notice the onset of estrus at all, especially as some bitches make every effort to lick themselves clean. In the past few years, we have encountered several Silky bitches which had abbreviated seasons, with total duration being only 11 or 12 days. In these bitches, the time of ovulation is earlier than in those with more normal periods, and they must be bred on the fifth or sixth day in order to conceive. Bitches with these short cycles are quite often missed entirely, as they are almost out of season by the time the owner thinks they should be sent to the stud dog. It is helpful in these cases to have your veterinarian examine a vaginal smear, starting with the third or fourth day. He may wish to check a second smear the next day, or the second day after, as two readings give him a more accurate picture. After checking one or both smears, he can usually tell you the approximate day on which the bitch will ovulate. If you have a bitch which has not conceived from a previous mating, by all means avail yourself of this assistance from your veterinarian.

In recent months a number of breeders and some veterinarians have suggested another method to determine the day of ovulation. This is the test tape used for urine sugar analysis in diabetics or suspected diabetics. Obtaining this tape from a pharmacy, the author tried it experimentally and found that it could not be considered reliable in all cases. Inserted into the vagina of a bitch on her ninth day of season, the strip turned from yellow to dark green, which is said to indicate that ovulation has occurred or is occurring. This particular bitch had refused to breed on her seventh or eighth days, when a veterinarian had predicted she would ovulate from his judgement of a vaginal smear taken earlier. She was tried with two keen and experienced studs, but would not breed on any day, and by the 11th, apparently had gone out of season entirely. We concluded that either she was an unwilling breeder or that she had ovulated earlier, perhaps on the fifth day, since duration of the total season was short.

However, we then tried the tape with a bitch not in season, and found that it again turned from yellow to dark green. Trying it with an older bitch that had been spayed, we again got dark green, though in this case the strip was spotted with green rather than being solidly green. We tried it in the sheath of a male, and no change from yellow occurred; we tried it with plain water, with no change of color. Then we used a combination of honey and water, and the strip turned a solid dark green. There is an expiration date on these tapes, but the honey-water test indicated that the tape was still good. When I reported these results to our veterinarian, he was unable to explain them and asked that I repeat the experiments. This was done, with the same results being obtained. Without some explanation of the puzzling outcome of these tests, we could not consider this a reliable method.

In addition to possible variations in the duration and intensity of the heat period, there are many bitches which do not have seasons every six months, as the new breeder tends to expect. My own experience in this respect is that a season every eight months is about as usual as the more commonly expected six months between cycles. There are also some which have seasons at five-month intervals, and others which have them at irregular intervals. One of the best-producing dams I know of in Silkys had what might be called a regularly irregular cycle, as she had her seasons at intervals of four months, then eight months, then back to four months, and so on. In the majority of cases, however, an individual bitch will have her periods of estrus at approximately the same intervals, and she will usually accept the male about the same day of each cycle. This is something the breeder learns by observation of his own bitches, and it is a wise breeder who keeps careful records of the length of each season, the intervals between, and the day of the season at which the bitch was ready to be bred.

In the normal bitch, the correct time for mating is when she herself indicates that she is willing to stand for the dog. She will signify this willingness by standing with back legs braced out and tail turned to one side. Some bitches will attempt to stand for the dog before the swelling and tenderness have left the vulva, but as soon as the male touches the vulva, such a bitch will yelp and jump away. If this happens two or three times, take her away from the stud till the following day. A bitch will show signs of willingness to breed with other bitches as well as with dogs, which is helpful for breeders who have several bitches but no stud.

Some bitches are never willing to stand long enough for the dog to breed her, and bitches of this type must be held forcibly if they are to be bred at all. Fortunately, this usually occurs only with a maiden bitch, and after her first breeding, she may be willing to cooperate with the stud.

Occasionally, a virgin bitch may be quite willing to stand, but the stud is unable to make a penetration into her vagina. These bitches should be checked by a veterinarian for possible stricture, which is a web of tough flesh across the vaginal opening. If present, it can be broken by the veterinarian so that the bitch can be bred without further difficulty.

The condition fortunately is rare, but there are a few bitches with such immature reproductive organs that they can never be bred, or if bred will not conceive. Such bitches are occasionally impregnated by artificial insemination, but the risk of losing the bitch in pregnancy or whelping is greatly increased over normal.

Artificial insemination is employed extensively in cattle breeding, but it is not often used in dogs. Medical opinions differ considerably on this subject, with some veterinarians reporting very poor results and others stating that they have very good results. Consult your own veterinarian and follow his advice on this matter.

If you are to ship your bitch to a stud, you should telephone the stud's owner when your bitch comes in season, so that you can decide when to ship her. She should be sent two or three days before she is ready to stand. The female whose previous cycles have been the average with 21 days' duration should be shipped by the 9th day at the latest, so that she can rest a day or two before being bred. Bitches which have had the abbreviated cycles discussed earlier will occasionally go on to have more normal seasons. Most of these, however, will continue to have the short cycles, and they should be shipped the third or fourth day after they show color. Most stud owners would prefer to keep the bitch a few extra days to insure a successful mating.

The just-right stud for your bitch should have been selected long before she comes in season. The owner who starts looking for a stud after his bitch is in season is not likely to obtain the services of a good stud. Conscientious stud owners do not agree to use their dogs with bitches of unknown quality and/or bloodlines. While there are some people in every breed who are interested solely in the amount of the stud fee, the phrase "At stud to *approved* bitches" is taken very seriously by owners of the best Silky Terrier studs.

Arrangements for the service should have been made, pedigrees and pictures exchanged if distance prevents the owners from seeing the stud and bitch to be bred. The amount of fee and other details should also have been decided, as was discussed in the chapter, "The Stud Dog."

Your bitch must be in excellent health before she is bred. If she is not, you should defer breeding until you have her in top condition. All good breeders try to keep their Silkys free of external and internal parasites at all times, but you should have your veterinarian make a stool check just before her season is due, or in any case, immediately after it starts. If worming should be necessary, it is better to have it done before the bitch is bred. Some veterinarians will administer treatment for worms as late as three weeks past the date of breeding, but most prefer to give necessary medication before she is bred. If she has not had a recent "booster" inoculation for distemper, hepatitis, leptospirosis, and rabies, these also should be administered before she is bred. This will not only give her added protection, she will pass more immunity along to her puppies. If she is to be shipped from one state to another, the airline will require a health certificate made out by your veterinarian, and that she has had a rabies shot within a given length of time, which differs with different states.

Also, it is important that the female to be bred not be fat. Should she be excessively so, she will almost certainly have whelping difficulties, and it would be wiser to reduce her weight before breeding her.

We trust that you have a good veterinarian in whom you have confidence, and importantly, that he knows your bitch. It is hardly fair to a veterinarian to telephone him in the middle of the night for assistance with a whelping or other emergency, when he has never laid eyes on your bitch before. It is best for any physician, canine or human, to know his patient in health before being called on to treat the patient in sickness. If you have neglected this very important matter, do take the bitch to a veterinarian before she is bred.

After she has been bred and returned to you, you must take every precation to prevent another dog from breeding her. The fact that she has been bred will not prevent her being bred again by another dog if she is receptive and he can get to her. Some novice breeders think that the little "doggy britches" designed for bitches in season will prevent their being bred. They will not keep her from being mated—a really eager stud is hardly even slowed by them. Nor will the various deodorant sprays applied to a bitch deter a keen stud. They may make his nose feel a little peculiar, but they will not keep him from breeding her, especially as they are washed off every time she urinates. Chlorophyll tablets are sometimes used, but here again, when the bitch is ready to be bred, a good stud will still pick up the scent and breed her. It is your responsibility to see that she is securely confined where no dog can get to her until her season is well over.

False pregnancy—This phenomenon occurs frequently in bitches regardless of breed if not bred at a season. It can be alarming to the new breeder, but unless present in an extreme degree, usually presents no problem. The most likely cause of difficulty in these cases is the overabundance of milk, which can cause caked breasts which are very painful. Also, a caked breast that receives a blow of some kind may abscess, and unless caught very early, may necessitate removal of that breast. Pet bitches with extreme symptoms are usually given hormone shots, but it is risky to give hormones to a bitch you hope to breed. If it becomes necessary to see your veterinarian for a bitch with this condition, be sure to let him know that you do expect to breed her.

Where these false pregnancies exist, the bitch will begin to show symptoms of pregnancy about 7 or 8 weeks after the time of a season when she would have been bred. There will be milk in the breasts which increases in quantity at the time she would have whelped and for varying periods thereafter. Some bitches go through a period of making their nests, and some actually seem to have labor pains. Many bitches have a particular toy that they will "mother" at the time they would have had puppies. Some authorities feel that bitches which do not show at least some of these symptoms are not fertile, at least at that particular season. Others consider that a hormonal imbalance is involved. Whatever the cause, the bitches showing false pregnancies are invariably unusually competent and devoted mothers when they do have puppies. From our experience, it would seem that the tendency toward extreme symptoms is inherited. Some bitches which show false pregnancies after early seasons will not show them to such an extent after they have whelped a litter.

If your bitch produces large quantities of milk with a false pregnancy, check the breasts about twice a day to see that none has become caked. You should reduce her food, and give very small amounts of liquids. When caking occurs, the breast will feel hard and feverish to the touch. It may help to apply alternate hot and cold packs to the caked breast, and also to express a little of the milk very gently with your fingers. (First wash your hands with surgical soap.) Be sure not to press on the breast too much, as they bruise very easily when caked. Some veterinarians recommend the use of camphorated oil, but it has a very strong odor which bothers some bitches and is also very oily and will stain your furniture.

CHAPTER 20

Pregnancy and Whelping

The gestation period in dogs is 63 days, or nine weeks, but in Toy-size breeds, females seem more likely to whelp on the 60th or 61st day. Puppies born earlier than the 56th day are not likely to survive. Those born as early as the 56th day can be raised successfully, but you will need to give them a great deal of attention and have otherwise favorable conditions. Bitches carrying larger litters seem more likely to whelp early, while those with only one or two puppies may go full term or a day or two over. If your bitch has not whelped by the 65th day, you should have your veterinarian check her thoroughly.

Early in pregnancy, there is no need to increase the quantity of food, but it must be of top quality. The diet should be high in protein, available from meat, eggs, and so on. Especially in the later weeks, do not give her bulky foods. She should have her usual general-purpose vitamin tablets daily, and some veterinarians recommend increasing the daily quantity during gestation. She should also be given calcium tablets, starting either as soon as she is bred or by the third week. Your veterinarian will recommend whatever brand and dosage he thinks best. Calcium and phosphorous must be given in correct ratio to each other, and although we refer to them as calcium tablets, they contain calcium, phosphorous, and Vitamin D, the latter helping utilize the calcium.

Observe your bitch carefully throughout her pregnancy—her eyes should be clear, her coat shining, and her general health excellent. She should have plenty of exercise, but should not be allowed to run with rough kennelmates, since a collision can damage her puppies or cause her to miscarry. It is standard advice to keep the pregnant bitch from jumping, but unless our bitches are very heavy in whelp, they persist in jumping up on the sofa or a favorite chair. They seem to regulate themselves on when they should stop jumping, and at that point, they come to stand in front of my husband or me with the unspoken request that they be lifted to their favorite spot.

Very little change will be observed in actions or appearance during the first three or four weeks. Ordinarily, the first indication is that she will rest more than normally. Some breeders report that their bitches are picky with their food during early weeks, but our bitches have always eaten well during those weeks, and ravenously during the later weeks. With some, the nipples will look pinker than usual, but this can also occur at about the same time after a season with bitches that were not bred. When she is about three weeks along, you will probably begin to notice a gelatinous type of accumulation in the vulva. Many breeders consider this an infallible indication of pregnancy, and it has been present in our bitches when in whelp, but I do not know positively that it is always present in the pregnant bitch. This gelatin-like substance should be clear—if it is milky looking or contains pus, there may be infection, and you should have your veterinarian check her without delay.

If you see a bloody, or blood-tinged discharge at any time in pregnancy, have this checked immediately.

As we have said earlier, one of the greatest assets you as a serious breeder can have is a good veterinarian who is interested in your dogs and your breeding program. We would hope that your veterinarian is already familiar with your pregnant bitch, but if not, take her to him once or twice during her pregnancy, even though there is no indication of difficulties. Then if she needs help at whelping time, she will accept his handling more readily than if he were a stranger to her. I also make a practice of alerting my veterinarian when one of our bitches shows that whelping is imminent, so that if we need help when he is away from his clinic, he will have notified us where to reach him For the most part, bitches will whelp during the night, as they wait for the house to become quiet before they settle down to the business at hand.

Some breeders, especially during the early years of breeding, are very anxious to know as early as possible whether their bitch is pregnant. In these cases, the bitch may be taken to the veterinarian at $3\frac{1}{2}$ or 4 weeks so that he can palpate her uterus to see if foetuses are present. (Palpation is an examination made by touch of the fingers.) Some veterinarians have more skill in this than others, and regardless of the degree of skill, it is frequently difficult to get the bitch to relax her abdominal wall sufficiently for her to be palpated. Some veterinarians consider it an unwise practice, since probing fingers might conceivably damage a foetus. *NEVER* attempt to check a bitch in this manner yourself.

If your bitch is pregnant, there will be a gradual broadening over the hips as pregnancy progresses. Between the 5th and 6th weeks, you should see a general enlargement through the abdomen, quite noticeable with a large litter but sometimes barely discernible with a small one.

At $4\frac{1}{2}$ to 5 weeks after breeding, you should increase the quantity of her food, splitting it into two meals daily rather than one. Very bulky foods should not be given this late in pregnancy. Most bitches will eat ravenously by this time, and if given too much at one meal, they will make themselves uncomfortable by over-eating.

At $7\frac{1}{2}$ or 8 weeks you should clean the female's breasts with oil. Many adult bitches have soft blackheads around their nipples, and at times around the vulva as well. By soaking with oil, you can then wipe the blackheads off with a Q-tip or soft towel. All long hair near the nipples should be cut short, but be careful not to cut her tender skin. Long hair on the vulva should also be trimmed off. It is not necessary to cut the other long hair on her rear, as it is rarely thick enough to interfere with whelping. Trim her toenails and clean her teeth. Bathe her at this time too, unless she is so heavy in whelp that you are afraid to handle her. (A bitch showing signs of getting this large should have been bathed sooner, as soon as you realized that she would.) It is necessary to wash the oil off the nipples and vulva, using a good medicated shampoo or surgical soap, even if you do not give her a full bath at this time.

When she is eight weeks pregnant, she should be introduced to her whelping box, which you have prepared and put where you can be near her, and also where she can be away from other dogs or young children. Her temperature should be taken twice daily, beginning on the 56th day, in the morning and at night. She will have a drop in temperature which precedes labor by 12 to 24 hours, so that you have some notice that puppies are coming soon. Normal temperature is considered to be from 101.0 to 102.0 degrees but I frequently find that our bitches show only 100.6 to 100.8 degrees during this last week, provided they are quiet and there is no particular excitement at the time. The temperature will drop to 99.0 degrees or lower before labor pains begin. This is thought to be nature's way of preparing the whelps to come out into the world, which is much less warm than the bitch's body. Keep a written record of temperature and time taken daily. If this particular bitch has had previous litters, pull your written records of them for reference. While there may be variations from one litter to the next in individual bitches, they will often follow a similar pattern of behaviour each time.

The whelping box we use, and which has proven very satisfactory, is made of wood. It is 30 inches by 30 inches, with 8 inch sides. (If you are in a very cold climate, the sides could be made higher.) On one side, there

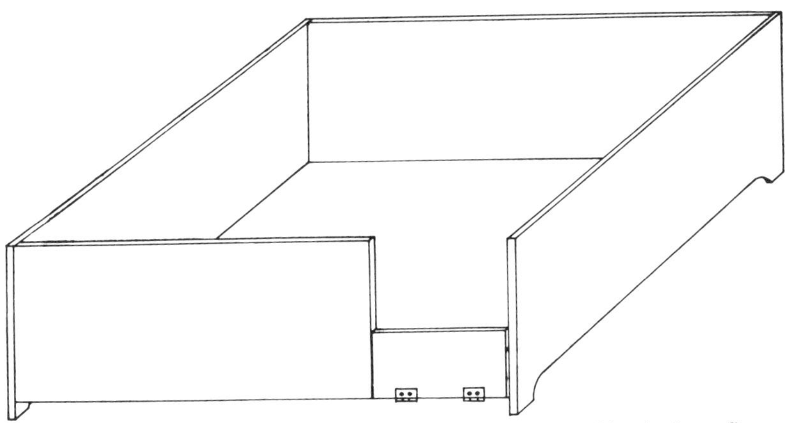

Illustrated is one manner of constructing a whelping box. Height from floor to avoid drafts may be as desired and determined when forming the sides, but angle of puppy barrier-gate when lowered for a ramp should be considered also. A hole bored through the side and into this gate will provide for securing it with a rod or large nail while it is to serve as a barrier to confine very young puppies. Among optional additions are screw-on rubber tips for the legs.

is an opening 9 inches wide. Across the bottom of this opening, there is a wooden bar measuring 3 inches by 9 inches, which is fastened to the floor of the box by screws. This bar is kept fastened in place until puppies are 3 weeks old, which gives the bitch easy access to the box but prevents the puppies from rolling out. A final component of the box is a piece of plywood cut just slightly smaller than the 30- by 30-inch size of the box; the use for this will be explained later.

Put some soft towels in the bottom of the box for the bitch to sleep on. Later on, when she begins nesting, a few face towels and washcloths are added. You will need a good supply of clean towels and washrags. A number of towels will become saturated during whelping and should be replaced with dry ones when they do. Old towels are best, since they are softer and have been de-linted by many washings.

Gather the equipment needed for whelping, sterilizing as necessary. Besides the whelping box, towels, washrags, and the rectal thermometer which you are using to take the temperature of the bitch (a spare should be kept on hand), you will need the following:

A pair of dull scissors, sterilized and kept in alcohol (dull scissors cause less bleeding than sharp ones)

A pair of surgical clamps (lock forceps), sterilized and kept in alcohol.

Eyedropper, preferably blunt-end type, sterilized in very hot water. Keep a spare on hand too.

Spirits of Ammonia.
Shoebox or other box similar in size.
Clock.
Room Thermometer.
Baby oil.
Cotton.
Iodine.
Puppy nursing bottles and nipples, sterilized in boiling water. The bottles should have markings of quantity at different levels.
Can of liquid puppy formula.
Heating pad. Test this before using, and be very sure that it will hold on a low-heat setting. Keep a spare one on hand also.

The first indication of imminent labor is the making of a nest. Some bitches start nesting several days before they go into labor, others only a few hours before. If you do not give her something with which to make her nest, she will make her own selection, so add the smaller towels and wash-cloths to her box when nesting begins. She will scratch vigorously, toss the small cloths around here and there in the box, and even tear some of the material by biting it, until she has the nest in a condition satisfactory to her. She will continue to arrange and rearrange the nest until she is in fairly hard labor. On the average, a bitch will start nesting vigorously about 24 hours before she is to whelp. She will also move around rest-lessly, drinking water now and then and urinating more frequently than usual. Have fresh water in the room for her, and put newspapers on the floor not too far from her box. Most bitches will refuse food for about 12 hours before whelping. Offer food at the usual meal time, but take it away if your bitch refuses it.

As the time comes closer, the vulva will soften and relax and there will be a sticky discharge, nature's way of lubricating the birth passage. The bitch will tremble as if having a chill, and as labor progresses, will do a lot of panting. She may appear strained or anxious, and if this is her first litter, she may seem apprehensive. After the first litter, most bitches seem quite confident and even pleased with the whole proceeding. The early labor pains are not discernible to you and do not come at regular time intervals. Watch to see when she has the first strong contraction, and make a note of the time. These strong contractions are very evident; you can see them, and feel them with a hand on her abdomen. Also record the intervals at which contractions occur, as they will come closer and closer together. Do not try to make her stay in the whelping box, as the exercise of walking around the room will help her with labor. When the pains become very severe and close together, she will probably stay in the box of her own accord. Some females lie on their sides, bracing themselves with their feet against the side of the whelping box with each strong con-traction, while others will stand and bow up in the middle with each strong pain.

IF SHE HAS NOT DELIVERED A PUPPY AFTER TWO HOURS OF HARD LABOR, CALL YOUR VETERINARIAN IMMEDIATELY.

Each puppy is contained in a membranous sac containing fluid, which cushions the puppy as he comes through the birth canal. Normal presentation is head first, but breech birth (buttocks first) occurs almost as often, and does not often cause difficulty. You will first see the sac, which appears to be a dark bubble at the opening of the vulva, in the midst of a strong contraction. It frequently recedes until after two or three strong contractions have brought it through, or partly through the opening. If you can see that the sac containing the puppy is protruding more with each contraction, then do not interfere. (We should never interfere unnecessarily, but we must be ready to help when we are needed.) With a first litter, some bitches become frightened when the first puppy is only partially expelled; she will then stop "bearing down" with the contractions. You must talk to her soothingly to reassure her, and if enough of the sac and puppy are out, grasp it with one of the clean washrags. Both the sac and the puppy are unbelievably slippery and almost impossible to grasp with the bare hands. You should pull gently, and *ONLY* during a strong contraction, then stop pulling when the contraction stops, pulling gently again with the next one.

At times the sac will break before the puppy comes out. If the head emerges first, this should cause no problem. If the feet or buttocks appear first, with no sac, you must work fast to help the bitch expel the puppy's head, since otherwise he may suffocate. Grasp the puppy with the washcloth, and pull gently with each contraction. There is generally no difficulty in getting the puppy out.

When the puppy comes out with the sac intact, it must be broken immediately at the head to start his breathing. If the bitch does not do this, you must do it for her. My bitches seem more inclined to start by biting the cord, frequently before the placenta attached to the other end of the cord can be seen, but after the sac is broken, they will turn their attention to the puppy's head. At that time, if the placenta is still in the bitch, use your lock forceps to fasten over the cord. Place it straight across the cord and near the bitch's body. Before locking the forceps, watch the pulse in the cord as it runs between the puppy's body and the placenta. The forceps *SHOULD NOT BE LOCKED* on the cord except when the blood is toward the puppy. Also, it should be placed across the cord in such a way that the pointed end cannot be pulled back up into the bitch's vulva. You can then lay the forceps down, as they will stay locked and prevent the placenta from going back up into the bitch. Then flatten the cord with thumb and forefinger just below the forceps to push the blood toward the puppy; cut with the dull scissors between your fingers and the forceps, at least 1 inch from the puppy's abdomen. Put iodine on the end of the cord, either by dipping it into a saucer of iodine or by applying liberally from an iodine-soaked cotton pad. Put the iodine on the end of the cord only, and do not let it get on his abdomen, as it will burn the tender skin.

If the puppy does not start breathing as soon as his head is exposed, help the bitch stimulate his breathing by drying and rubbing the puppy with one of the small towels or washrags, rubbing toward the head. Clear off the head first, and if necessary, check the mouth and throat to see if mucous has been expelled. If any mucous is present, use the eyedropper to draw it out. If you and the bitch can induce the puppy to take a good breath, he will obtain enough oxygen to start normal breathing. A pad of cotton saturated with spirits of ammonia may be held in front of the puppy's nose; this will frequently stimulate breathing, but do not overdo it, as the ammonia fumes can burn the nose and mouth.

If the puppy still is not breathing, give artificial respiration, but be very careful with it. The puppy's lungs are tiny, and could be ruptured by too much air too quickly. Take a very deep breath, and then, covering the puppy's muzzle with your own mouth, breathe very gently into his mouth. Then press very gently with thumb and forefinger on the puppy's chest to help him breathe out. This may be repeated if necessary, but ordinarily is not.

As soon as the puppy is thoroughly dry and breathing well, squeeze a drop or two of milk from one of the dam's breasts and put the puppy to the breast. He will usually suck vigorously and can be left there until the bitch starts having more hard contractions. At that time, transfer the puppy to the small box containing a heating pad set on low heat and covered with a towel. After she has had the second puppy, both that one and the first puppy may be allowed to nurse until she indicates she is having more severe pains and strong contractions.

Every puppy must have some of the first milk, the colostrum, as this contains the antibodies which give the puppies the immunities to disease passed on by their dam.

Most bitches will eat the placentas, which seems to have some purpose. Some say it aids milk production, others that it helps the uterus contract. Whatever the purpose, it never seems to do any harm. After a number of years of breeding, all of us come to have great respect for the instinctive wisdom of our bitches.

After all puppies have been born and have nursed for a while, you should take the dam out to relieve herself, putting the puppies in the box with the heating pad. Always check to be sure the heat is not too high before putting a puppy on the pad, as puppy skins are tender and burn easily. The bitch will not want to leave her puppies for any reason, so you must pick her up bodily and take her to relieve herself. For several days after the puppies are born, she will prefer to have her meals in the box, and they should be given to her there. Water should also be offered.

She should have as much as she wants to eat, three or four meals daily, depending somewhat on the size of her litter. Continue her top-quality diet that is high in protein. Her general vitamin supplement should be continued; her calcium tablets should be continued, but the dosage should be increased as your veterinarian directs.

Most bitches are very protective with their puppies during the first week, at least. They will be upset if any of the other dogs come into the room, and especially upset if you allow strangers to come in. The dam's wishes should be respected, and she and her puppies kept where they will not be bothered. After the first two or three days, the bitch will wish to come out with the other dogs occasionally, but it will probably be several weeks before she will permit them to touch her puppies.

Healthy newborn puppies will nurse vigorously and seem remarkably strong for such tiny creatures. They will crawl from breast to breast, and when you see them nursing with backs arched and tails up in the air, you can be satisfied you have a strong, healthy litter.

Some three or four hours after all puppies are born, when you are satisfied that all have nursed a good deal (the puppies will go to sleep when they are full), you should take your bitch to the veterinarian. It is difficult for the layman to be sure that all puppies have been born, as the still swollen uterus can feel much like another puppy. Your veterinarian will check to be sure there are no more puppies to come, and will usually give the bitch a shot called "post-pit" (posterior pituitary). This is for the purpose of assisting her to expel any fragments of placenta that may remain in the uterus, and to help the uterus return to normal size.

The bitch may have a slight elevation in temperature for a day after whelping, but if the reading is over 102.5 degrees, consult your veterinarian. You should also consult him if the elevation persists beyond 24 hours after birth of the litter.

It is normal for the bitch to have some diarrhea after whelping, and because of the placentas she has eaten, there will be greenish to blackish material in the stools. The diarrhea will normally last only a day or two.

She will also have a dark red vaginal discharge for a week or ten days after whelping. If she discharges bright red blood, it may mean hemorrhage, and if the discharge contains any pus or green material, it could be a retained afterbirth, so observe carefully and report to your veterinarian. If infection is present, it must be treated immediately.

We are fortunate in that most Silky Terrier bitches are good natural whelpers, but in any breed, some complications may occur. One of these is called "uterine inertia," because the uterus has lost its power of contraction. This condition may occur very early in labor or even before labor, when it is believed to be caused by hormone deficiency or imbalance. It may also occur as a result of a lengthy and fruitless period of labor. Whatever the cause, it is a matter for professional treatment. As stated earlier, no bitch should be allowed to have over two hours of hard labor contractions without your calling in your veterinarian. If it should prove necessary for her to have a Caesarean section, it should be done before she reaches a point of exhaustion, thus increasing the risk to her and her puppies. The limit of two hours of hard labor applies either to the birth of the first puppy or of subsequent puppies, as at times a bitch may whelp one or more puppies normally, and then be unable to give birth to the next one without assistance. This usually occurs because a puppy is in a position in the uterus that makes it impossible for the contractions to expel him. The uterus of the bitch is shaped like the letter "Y", with puppies attached to the walls of the horns of the uterus, which would be comparable to the two upper arms of the "Y." In some cases, a puppy may lie across the intersection point of the horns and the body of the uterus, in which case he cannot possibly be whelped normally. If your bitch is in good condition generally, and you have not permitted her to become exhausted in hard labor, the outlook for successful surgery is very good.

There is a preparation called "pituitrin" which is sometimes given to encourage labor, but it must be given by the veterinarian. If given at the wrong stage of labor, it may rupture the uterus and cause the death of the bitch. *NEVER* administer pituitrin yourself, or permit anyone but a skilled veterinarian to do so.

Eclampsia may occur either before or after whelping. It is caused by calcium deficiency in the bitch. Although most books on the subject suggest that it is more likely to occur several weeks after whelping, we have never seen it in our bitches except a few days before or after whelping. The first symptom noticed is usually a staggering gait, extreme anxiety, panting, and shivering. The latter two symptoms also occur during labor, but with eclampsia, the bitch will stretch her hind legs frequently as if they were cramping. At times, the feet will draw under the normal position in such a way that the tops of the feet are down and toenails pointing toward back of body. She will feel very cold to the touch in the early stages, but if not caught early, temperature will go quite high, with convulsions and coma. Many will show a staring expression, and they may fall. *THIS IS AN EMERGENCY!* You must summon your veterinarian immediately so that he can inject calcium into the blood stream. When caught early, recovery is dramatic—you can watch the bitch relax and lose the look of fear in her eyes as the calcium is being injected into a vein. If not observed and treated early, the bitch may die. The bitches most likely to have this difficulty, even though they have been given calcium supplementally, are those which produce large quantities of milk, thus causing a drain on the bitch's system. Some bitches produce large quantities of milk even with a small litter. If you have ever had this frightening experience, you will always be alert for any symptoms which may occur. Keep in mind that the panting, shivering, and anxiety are also shown during labor pains. The staggering gait and stretching of hind legs are not shown during normal labor, nor do bitches fall to the floor during normal whelping. Except in very rare cases when a bitch is unable to assimilate calcium, giving calcium supplementally during pregnancy and throughout the nursing period will prevent eclampsia. A larger quantity of calcium should be given when the bitch is nursing puppies.

We have no wish to frighten breeders, especially new ones, by discussing possible complications. Most whelpings go along quite normally, and many of our bitches are capable of handling the entire process without our help. We should not interfere when we are not needed, but we must be there to help if we are needed. Most importantly, we must know enough to observe and recognize symptoms which do indicate possible difficulties, and we must know when the situation is beyond our capabilities and we must call in our veterinarian.

CHAPTER 21

Care of Young Puppies

Food and warmth are the two most important needs of newborn puppies. In a report of a recent study, it was stated that warmth was even more essential than had been thought previously. The puppies and their dam should be in a warm room, free of drafts, with the temperature kept at a minimum of 75 degrees for the first week. If you do not use the heating pad, 80 degrees is recommended. Put the room thermometer near the puppies and at the same low level; you should check it periodically in case heat in the room needs to be adjusted.

The whelping box was described in the preceding chapter in regard to its use for the bitch. As soon as all puppies have nursed for a while, move them to their smaller box containing the heating pad while you prepare the whelping box for them. The soiled towels in the box should be removed, of course. You will now utilize the square piece of plywood cut slightly smaller than the whelping box. Using two clean soft bath towels, fold one over the board one way (which will cover two of the edges of the board), and then fold the other over the board so that it will cover the other two sides of the board. Fasten ends of the towels together with strong safety pins, so that the towels are tight across the board with no slack. Place the towel-covered board in the whelping box, with the pinned side down. The dam will jump back into the box the minute you finish it, anxious for her puppies, which can now be put back with her. Slip the heating pad under the top towel in one corner of the box; be sure that as little as possible of the cord to the pad is inside the box, since a puppy might entangle himself in excess cord. If you wish, you may tape the cord to the side of the box with masking tape. The control switch should be outside of the box. The towels pulled tight give the puppies a good surface on which to move, and are easily removed for washing, which should be done daily. The puppies will not need to have the heating pad turned on when the dam is with them; the first few days, you will use it only when you take the bitch out to relieve herself. It is surprising how quickly the tiny puppies will crawl over to lie on the heating pad when the dam is not with them. If they get too warm, they will crawl off of it again.

Most Silky Terrier bitches will have adequate milk supply for the puppies from the first day onward, but occasionally it is the second or third day before the supply is completely sufficient. Puppies that are receiving adequate amounts of milk will spend their days eating and sleeping. If they fret and seem to go from breast to breast very quickly, you may need to supplement the dam's milk. Another sign of inadequate milk supply is continuous nursing. There is also an occasional puppy that is too small and weak to nurse; by hand-feeding for two or three days, you can help such puppies to become strong enough to nurse the dam.

You should also make it a practice to weigh each puppy soon after birth, and then daily thereafter, recording the weights for each. Baby scales are excellent for this purpose. Average birth size is usually 4 to 5 ounces, and there should be a gain of at least one-half ounce daily. A gain of 2 ounces in three days is better. If the puppies are not gaining, they may not be getting enough milk. If all puppies in the litter are strong enough to nurse, it is best to supplement the larger, stronger ones, so that the smaller ones can nurse the dam. In any event, each puppy should nurse the bitch at least part of the first day, as the colostrum, which is the first milk, contains the immunities to various diseases the dam passes along in this manner. (If your bitch has had a Caesarean section, be sure to ask your veterinarian how soon it is safe for the puppies to nurse from her; this will depend on the type of anesthetic used.) With a puppy that is too weak to suck, you can squeeze out some of the colostrum with your fingers and attempt to get some into him that way.

At the time you weigh newborn puppies, you should also check each puppy for distinguishing marks. Many Silky puppies have white spots at birth, which may alarm the new breeder. These are most likely to be on the chest or on the feet, with perhaps a tiny white spot on the chin. They will usually disappear as the puppies mature. Many Yorkshire Terrier breeders say that white chest or chin spots indicate good mature color in their breed. From the birth records I have and knowledge of Silkys of our breeding at maturity, I do not find any correlation between the white spots and mature color. These markings will help you to tell one puppy from another, however. When very young, each puppy is so much like others in the litter that it is often hard to differentiate.

Feeding the dam three or four meals daily while nursing will help her maintain a good milk supply, and supplemental general-pupose vitamins and increased dosage of calcium tablets will help her stay in good condition. It is always distressing to see a bitch that has been allowed to become thin and gaunt while nursing puppies, as this simply is not necessary. Good nutrition will also prevent loss of coat after a litter, at least in most cases.

If you find that you must supplement food for one or more puppies, watching the puppies for a while will show you which puppy is most vigorous and aggressive. This will be the best one to supplement, so that the smaller puppies can nurse the dam. We seem to have one fellow in every litter that I think of as "the submariner," since he or she will crawl along very rapidly under the other puppies' feet and knock the smaller ones away from the breast. If you have a puppy like this, select him for supplementing. You will have to watch him even if you do not supplement any puppies, to be sure that he does not prevent the small or less aggressive ones from nursing when they should.

As noted in the preceding chapter, the puppy-nursing bottles and nipples, and an eyedropper, should all be sterilized before using. The best possible formula to use is the liquid supplement for puppies. This has come on the market within the past few years, and it is a wonderful product. It can be warmed and then fed just as it comes from the can. Some breeders have recommended use of the canned liquid formulas for human babies, but we almost lost a puppy from gastritis when we used the human product.

The stronger puppies usually nurse quite well from puppy nursing bottles. Half an ounce per feeding is adequate, and some can only take about one-fourth ounce at a feeding. With puppies that are too weak to suck, an eyedropper must be used, with the formula given by placing one drop at a time on the puppy's tongue. You should hold the puppy upright in one hand as you feed with a dropper. Caution is necessary here, as the puppy can choke if too much is given at once. A drop or two of honey and warm water mixture at intervals may help a weak puppy nurse.

In the recent past, a number of breeders and some veterinarians have been recommending tube feeding of puppies. You can try this for puppies less than a week old if your veterinarian considers this method worthwhile and instructs you on proper procedure.

When all puppies are nursing the dam and gaining normally and seem contented, another thing you need to check regularly is the possibility of caked breasts. Some bitches have too much milk for the size of their litter (though it usually regulates itself after a time). In other cases, it seems that the puppies are more likely to use certain breasts and not others, and the unused breasts may cake. Check for this at least twice a day, as breasts may cake very quickly. By moving puppies to the fullest breasts, you may prevent it entirely. When caked, the breasts are very hot and hard to the touch, and reddish; they are extremely painful to the bitch. If a breast has caked, sponge it off with a washcloth wrung out in cool water, and then press very gently with your fingers to express some of the milk. Do not press hard, as a caked breast bruises very easily. Puppies will avoid nursing from caked breasts, but if you can get a little of the excess milk out so they are softer, the puppies will use them. Put the largest, most vigorous puppy to the breast; if the caking has been reduced enough that he will nurse, he will empty it very quickly.

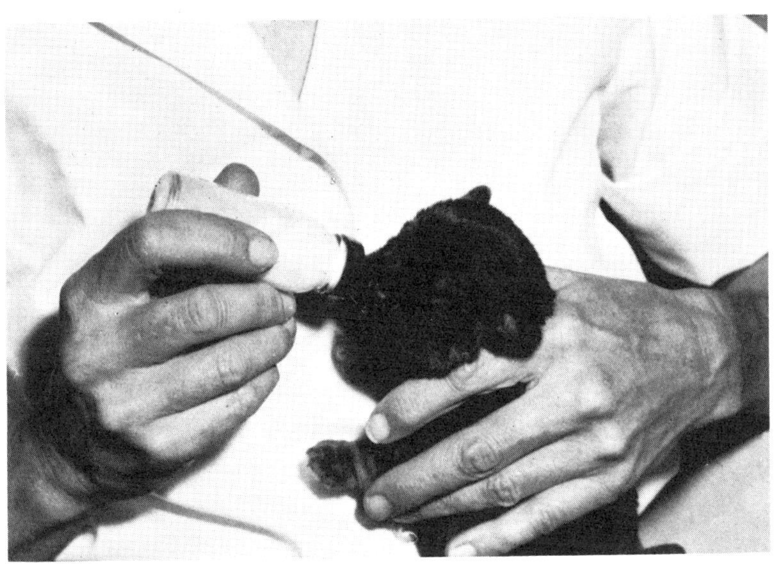

Feeding a Silky puppy from a bottle. Note that the puppy is held in an upright position.

If you have orphaned puppies, or if the dam is too ill to care for them, you must not only feed them, you must stimulate them to eliminate as the dam does. Put some baby oil on a piece of cotton, and gently stroke the urinary opening with the cotton. There is rarely any difficulty in getting a puppy to urinate. Then stroke the anus with circular movements of the cotton. At birth, the rectum contains a sort of waxy plug which looks like a tiny string of beads, and this should come out within at most 24 hours of birth. Once this plug has come out, there is not likely to be any further difficulty with elimination. When the dam is well and functioning normally, she will see that the puppies eliminate; she also eats their movements for the first three or four weeks.

When the puppies are three days old, their toenails should be trimmed. At birth, each toenail is tipped with what looks like a tiny bead, which comes off very easily. Use small blunt-nosed scissors, and be careful not to cut the nail too far back, as they bleed very easily at this age. The nails should be kept trimmed throughout lactation so they will not scratch the dam's breasts.

After the first three or four days, you will notice that there are bruises on the breasts; these are caused by puppies trying to grasp a nipple and missing the mark, as it takes them a few seconds to realize there is no milk there. I know of no way to avoid this.

At the age of four days, tails should be docked and dewclaws removed provided the puppies are normal and vigorous. All puppies have dewclaws on both front legs, but may or may not have them on rear legs. Be sure to check this very carefully, as one missed at this time must be taken off later when it will be harder on the puppy. If your veterinarian has not yet docked tails on Silky puppies, he will expect you to tell him exactly where he should dock them. On the underside and at the base of the tail, there is a more or less triangular marking of tan, with the rest of the tail being black. The marking is in the shape of a "V," except that the end of it is more rounded off than pointed. The tail should be cut *IN THE BLACK AREA* about $\frac{1}{8}$ inch from the end of the tan mark, measuring tan mark at skin. *DO NOT* dock into the tan, but away from the tan and into the black. Joints are not generally well enough defined at 4 days to be easily felt, but if docking is done as late as 1 week, the dock at that point from the tan pattern will also generally be between the third and fourth joints. At one time, we experimented with waiting until puppies were a week old to dock their tails, but they were much more susceptible to shock at that age, so we went back to docking on the fourth day.

Some types of stitches used on tails must be removed a week or 10 days later, while others are absorbed. Your veterinarian will advise you which he has used. Inspect each puppy's tail and the sites of dewclaw removal at least once daily for a week to be sure they are healing properly. Ordinarily they give no trouble, but if the stiches are pulled out, the puppy could hemorrhage if not treated. Some bitches will attempt to pull out the stitches, and I know of at least one Silky puppy which did bleed to death.

Four-day-old puppies must be kept warm when going to and from your veterinarian's clinic; at this age chilling is dangerous and must be avoided. Some bitches become very upset when their puppies have their tails docked, but they are also very upset if you take the puppies and leave mother at home. Your judgment of your own bitch will guide you. We have found that taking the dam with us, but keeping her some distance away from the puppies while the surgery is performed, works best with our bitches. Also, by taking the dam and the puppies in a box together, she will keep the puppies warm.

Eyes will open at 10 to 14 days. When first open, they will appear bluish and hazy, but will begin to darken and clear almost immediately. Occasionally a puppy will show a slight infection in one or both eyes. A gentle sponging with boric acid solution may correct this, or your veterinarian will prescribe an antibiotic ointment to be used in the eye. After the eyes are open, it will still be a few days before the puppies are able to focus them.

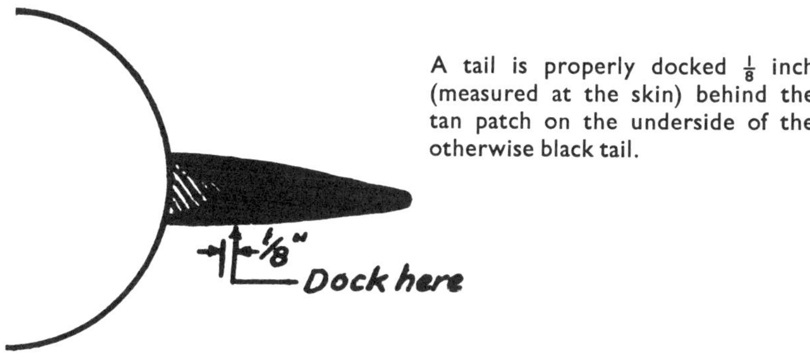

A tail is properly docked $\frac{1}{8}$ inch (measured at the skin) behind the tan patch on the underside of the otherwise black tail.

At the age of 3 to $3\frac{1}{2}$ weeks, the puppies begin to get up on their hind legs and walk. Fatter puppies are likely to be slower in walking. At this time, too, they will begin to play with each other, and by 4 weeks, you should hear them bark and growl. Nothing is more comical than the sight of two puppies, just beginning to walk, charging at each other across their box; generally, they miss each other entirely, but it does not seem to bother them!

As the puppies begin to walk, they will need more space than that afforded by the whelping box. At this time, the wooden bar across the side opening should be removed—easily accomplished by removing the screws with which it is fastened to the floor of the box. The whelping box is then put inside a large puppy pen which measures 3 by 6 feet. It is raised off the floor about 3 inches to prevent drafts, and has aluminum mesh sides about 18 inches high. The door to the pen is made of a solid piece of wood and opens down from the top; thus it serves as a ramp for the puppies to walk into and out of the pen when they are older. The floor of the pen is covered with newspapers, with the whelping box at one end to serve as their bed. The towel-covered board is kept in the whelping box, as is the heating pad as long as necessary. The puppies will learn very quickly to move out to the newspapers to relieve themselves and then return to their box. This is the beginning of their house training.

At three to four weeks of age, the puppies should be offered food in addition to the milk from their dam. They seem to take most readily to a mix of puppy meal and milk, fairly soft in consistency. At first, this should be warmed for them, as they will show little or no interest in cold food. Canned milk mixed with water (half milk and half water) is very satisfactory. To encourage their interest in the food, put a little of it on your finger and offer some to each puppy. They will vary in the age at which they will eat readily, but generally must be four weeks old. After that time, try to feed them from a dish before letting the dam into the pen to nurse, as they still prefer her milk. They will gradually begin to eat enough food from their dish so that the dam will need to nurse them only at night, which will help cut down her milk production. Her food should also be decreased gradually, beginning when the puppies are four weeks old. Our puppies are rarely totally weaned before they are six weeks old. When weaned, they should be fed four times a day, with other foods being introduced from time to time. The consistency of the meal-milk mixture should be made less soft, and meat and/or canned dog food can be added to the mixture as they get older. As time goes by, they should be changed to the older-puppy diet as set forth in the chapter on feeding. Also, as the liquid in the meal mixture is reduced, they should be offered water several times a day. Do not leave the water bowl in the pen with them, as they will play in it or turn it over and get themselves wet.

Inoculations and stool checks for worms should be accomplished.

CHAPTER 22

Selecting Puppies for Show

There are some who say that they can select show-quality puppies from their appearance in the nest; others that the puppy at the age of 8 weeks shows in miniature exactly what he will be at maturity; still others say that by waiting until the puppy is 6 months old, they will know definitely what that puppy will be as a mature Silky Terrier.

In any breed, objective and knowledgeable breeders will say that completely certain predictions of mature quality cannot be made. In a breed such as Silkys, with mature color so late in appearing, the most knowledgeable breeder can only come up with an "educated guess," so to speak. Puppies from different bloodlines develop at different rates, so that the person working with one line will not necessarily know what to expect from another line. For example, during our early years of breeding, we could pretty well depend on puppies being within one-half inch of mature height when they were five months old. Since that time, we have acquired other dogs and bitches which continued to grow after they were a year old. In some lines, ears may be fully up as early as five weeks; in others $4\frac{1}{2}$ to $5\frac{1}{2}$ months is not unusual. In some cases, ears must be given special treatment to become erect as required by the standard. This is discussed further within the chapter.

The new breeder cannot be told how to select; this is something he will learn from experience with his own dogs and bitches. He will need to acquire as much knowledge as possible of the breed, his bloodlines, and of the genotype of his breeding animals. It will aid him tremendously to keep written records from the first litter onward. Height and weight at different ages should be noted, what sort of color and markings are apparent, the age at which ears were fully up, and so on, should be included. As puppies from earlier breedings mature, he will gain knowledge of what may be expected from puppies he breeds later.

Correct breed type, movement, and balance must be learned through experience and observation of as many Silky Terriers as possible. By making a chart from the breed standard, with certain sections for various provisions, the new breeder will be able to compare different litters of puppies as he breeds them.

The breeder working with a bloodline known to produce some Yorkie-type heads (which appear to be inherited recessively and quantitatively), for instance, should note heads carefully in puppies. Those with wide-set eyes and deep stops, especially if muzzles are comparatively short, are likely to mature with Yorkshire-type heads. With bloodlines known to produce under- and/or over-size, the breeder should check heights and weights carefully. Extreme variation in size at birth or in the first two or three weeks will generally indicate either some oversize or some undersize, or both from that litter. Some lines tend to produce oversize dogs and undersize bitches, and these litters show greater early variations than those from lines where size is more stabilized. In lines where size is relatively stable, the differences in heights and weights will begin to be apparent from about seven weeks on. Also, some bitches tend to produce puppies that are fat at birth, while others have thin puppies, though the over-all bone structure and size may be approximately equal, and mature size is likely to be about the same.

In general, all breeders should look for typey heads with small V-shaped ears set high (a puppy with large, low-set ears is likely to have pendant ears at maturity). Avoid puppies with light eyes at 8–10 weeks; they will usually go even lighter, and in some puppies, eyes dark at this age may be light at maturity. Prominent eyes will in most cases grow worse with maturity. A puppy with overly long muzzle will likely be Aussie-headed at maturity, as muzzles usually lengthen with acquisition of permanent teeth. Bites must be correct scissors, with upper teeth fitting just over lower teeth. Some puppies with correct bites when young will have poor bites when permanent teeth come in, either being overshot or undershot. A few puppies with bites only slightly off with baby teeth may have correct bite when permanent teeth come in, but a bad puppy bite usually indicates a bad bite at maturity. Look for good length of neck, a necessity for lovely head carriage. A puppy which habitually carries his head down when moving will usually be found to have either a short neck or a bad front assembly, or both. The shoulder blade must be of good length, with about a 90-degree angle of upper arm to shoulder blade, with upper arm and shoulder blade about the same length. Front legs must be set well under the body.

Alertness, Curiosity, intelligence . . . and sometimes mischievousness . . . are all characteristic of the Silky puppy's expression. This puppy shows excellent head type.

Brisket (lower point of chest) should extend down to elbows, ribs should be well-sprung and well-ribbed back; the ribbing which extends back beyond the half-way point of the body usually indicates good mature top line, as does a good tail-set. Puppies with low tail-sets are unlikely to have good toplines. Most puppies will show some degree of cowhocks when first getting up on their feet, but a puppy that is cowhocked at nine or ten weeks is not likely to improve. Body width through the hindquarters should be about the same as body width through the front assembly at 9–10 weeks. Fiddle fronts, with bowed legs and toe-out of front feet, are not likely to improve, though a puppy only slightly off in front and toeing straight ahead will generally improve as he grows taller. Completely straight front legs are desirable, but take care that the puppy with the best front is not also leggy, as legginess tends to increase. As noted in the chapter on coat color, there is no completely reliable indication of good mature blue, but a ring or band of deep tan, or tan and black together, around the puppy's nose is an almost certain indicator of good mature tan.

We have reasonably complete records of height and weight at different ages in about twelve litters, along with those of a male which matured greatly over-size and a female which matured barely over eight inches but under the standard weight. The latter two represent two additional litters. Mature heights and weights shown were measurements made when the dogs and bitches were about two years of age, after which time some weights might have increased, especially in bitches.

HEIGHT AND WEIGHT CHART
LARRAKIN SILKY TERRIERS

	Matured within Standard		***Matured over or under Standard*	
Age	*Males*	*Females*	*Male*	*Female*
Birth	*$4\frac{1}{2}$ to $7\frac{1}{2}$ oz.	*4 to $7\frac{1}{2}$ oz.	Unknown	$2\frac{1}{2}$ oz.
10 weeks	3 lbs. 8 oz. to 4 lbs. 6 oz. $5\frac{1}{2}''$ to 7″	2 lbs. 14 oz. to 3 lbs. 12 oz. 5″ to $6\frac{1}{2}''$	Unknown Unknown	2 lbs. 6 oz. 6″ at shoulder

Our puppies are usually sold at 10 weeks, so that fewer individual heights and weights are available at the later ages.

3 months	4 lbs. 5 oz. to 6 lbs. 4 oz. 7″ to $7\frac{1}{2}''$	4 lbs. 0 oz. to 5 lbs. 4 oz. 6″ to 7″	7 lbs. 0 oz. $8\frac{5}{8}''$ at shoulder	3 lbs. 0 oz. 6″ at shoulder
Maturity	9 to $10\frac{1}{2}$ lbs. 9″ to $10\frac{1}{4}''$	$8\frac{1}{2}$ to 10 lbs. $8\frac{1}{4}''$ to 10″	15 lbs. 12″ at shoulder	$6\frac{1}{2}$ lbs. 8″ at shoulder

*Although range of birth weight in both sexes is approximately the same, most male puppies were in upper half of weights shown, with most females in lower half.
**Both of these puppies were sired by a 9″, 9 lb. dog from a line which tends to produce both over- and under-size. He also produced some puppies which matured well within the standard.

NOTE: The largest puppy whelped weighed 8 oz. at birth, a female, and was born after a very long and difficult labor. She died within 24 hours believed to result from stress experienced through the long period of labor.

Ears—Some Silky Terrier puppies have such heavy ear fringes that the weight of the hairs may keep ears from going up; in others, ears may go up and then tip over again as the hairs grow longer and heavier. If a puppy 2 months old is showing no lift at all to ears, the hair should be taken off. If it is very heavy, scissoring may be more practical than plucking, as ears are tender at this age, and much plucking is required for heavily coated ears.

Those puppies which do not have ears fully up at 4 to $4\frac{1}{2}$ months should be given supplemental calcium (one-half to one tablet daily of the type given pregnant bitches). The permanent teeth are beginning to come in at this age, and there is a heavy drain on the puppy's calcium supply for teeth and ear cartilage at the same time. Hair should be stripped off ears by this time if it has not been done earlier.

If ears are not fully up at about 5 months of age, taping should be considered. If the ears are over half up at this age, they may become erect without assistance, but anything under half will likely need help. There are several methods of taping ears; if you are in doubt, consult your veterinarian as to what he would specify for your puppy. Whatever method is used, be sure to remove all hair on ears before taping. The most commonly used method is to put a roll of cotton or sponge rubber the length of the ear on the inside front of each ear. Put the puppy on his back, with ears positioned as they should be when erect. After placing the cotton or rubber in position, bring the outside edges to the front and even with each other. Then fasten in place with masking tape, at the same time going completely around the ear with the tape. Use enough tape to hold the ears erect. Adhesive tape may be used, but it is more difficult to remove than masking tape and more likely to cause sore spots on the ears. If you cannot get the ears to stand erect after taping, it may help to fasten the tops of the two ears together, using two strips of tape with the adhesive sides together. All taping should be removed every four or five days and left off for several hours. This not only gives the ears time to get air, which helps prevent soreness, but it also enables you to see the progress ears are making. Before re-applying the tape, clean the ears off carefully with a mild shampoo. If any sore spots are apparent, medication should be applied and the tape left off long enough for healing.

CHAPTER 23

Shipping

There is a great deal about shipping puppies or adult dogs that must be learned by experience, since circumstances vary at different airports. The breeder who ships frequently will become familiar with the airlines serving his locality, destinations reached by different lines, and certain rules and regulations set out by individual airlines.

As an example, one airline in our city will not take more than one dog on any plane. Another places an embargo on shipping any live animal during periods of extreme heat during the summer. Some lines offer crates for sale, while others do not. Still another line has a minimum charge for air freight that is double the minimum of the other lines. No longer than five years ago, some airlines would not accept any dogs for shipment. Some of these individual regulations exist because of the type of planes used by that particular line, but whatever the reason, they will affect your shipping.

The two methods of shipping are Air Express and Air Freight. The Railway Express Agency, Air Express Division, offers shipment by Air Express, while each individual airline has an Air Freight Division. Air Express is said to take priority over Air Freight shipments because of the contract between R.E.A. and the airlines but personnel of many lines take a particular interest in dogs shipped through their Air Freight Division. Employees of airlines in various localities will differ also in their concern about animals, and as you gain shipping experience, you will learn which you prefer to use.

Whichever method you select for shipping, a health certificate made out and signed by your veterinarian is required. Rabies inoculation must have been given within a certain period of time, which varies by state, except that if the veterinarian considers the puppy too young for a rabies shot, he writes this on the health certificate. All veterinarians have a reference book outlining rabies requirements in different states, so you may follow advice in this.

The puppy or adult Silky to be shipped for the first time should be accustomed to his or her shipping crate before leaving home. The dog should be kept in the crate for intervals of time during the day, or put in the shipping crate to sleep for a night or two at home. In this way, the crate will seem less strange at departure time.

In preparing a crate for shipment, labels should be affixed showing the shipper's address and telephone number, the consignee's address and telephone number, and the schedule of shipment if a transfer is involved. The labels should note: "In event of delay, please telephone collect." If there is delay, airline or express employees will not always telephone, but there are those who will. A label or labels should also note, "Live animal, please leave air space." If a bitch in season is being shipped, a warning label should state that she should not be removed from the crate. Inside the crate, place several sheets of newspaper, with shredded paper on top of that. With the size crates we use, I also like to place an old towel at one end, after first putting it in with the dog at home at least for a few minutes, so that he or she will pick up a familiar odor for reassurance.

In a relatively small airport like the one in my own city, dogs must be presented at the Air Express or Air Freight office at least one hour ahead of flight time. At very large airports, two hours or more may be required. In some places, advance reservations are required to ship dogs; in others, reservations will not be accepted. Puppies are customarily shipped to new owners with the charges collect. Owners of bitches being shipped for stud service pay the charges; the bitches are customarily shipped home with the charges collect to the owners. My friends who ship larger breeds say that Air Freight is more economical for them, but for small dogs like Silkys, Air Express is usually less expensive. My feeling is that the choice of which way to ship should depend on which seems best for the puppy or adult dog.

Careful planning is an absolute necessity for successful shipping. You should obtain schedules from whatever lines have flights to the dog's destination well in advance of the tentative shipping date. The schedule should be checked again the day before shipping to be sure a change of schedules has not occurred. Transfers should be avoided wherever possible, especially at very large airports.

I never consider shipping a Silky to any destination where more than one transfer is required, and because of bad experiences previously at some transfer points, will not ship if that city is the only one available for the transfer. If a plane change is necessary, adequate time allowance must be made for the transfer, usually at least one hour at a smaller airport, and two hours or more at a very large one. If a destination within 150 or 200 miles of the buyer's home can be reached by a puppy without transfer, request the buyer to drive to that city to pick up his puppy. (Owners of stud dogs who live near a large airport will advise you if they make a practice of meeting bitches at that airport.) A buyer who is not willing to drive a reasonable distance to meet a puppy should not be sold a puppy in the first place.

After a schedule and date are agreed on between the breeder and buyer of a puppy, arrangements should be made as to what long distance telephone calls will be made on the day of shipment. We take our puppies to the airport and stay with them until we know they are safely in the air. This serves two purposes, one of which is that your presence reassures the puppy that he has not been deserted. If he seems particularly upset, you can take him out of his crate and soothe him, and your being there beside his crate will help him overcome his anxiety at the unfamiliar noise. (Jet engines make such a piercing noise that airline employees must wear ear coverings to work around them, and with a dog's keener hearing, they are probably very painful to them.) The second purpose for staying with the puppy is to be sure he makes the scheduled flight. It does not happen often, but occasionally a flight may be so loaded with passengers and their baggage that some of the freight is put off the plane. After the puppy is safely airborne, we telephone the buyer that he is on his way, giving him the airbill number at that time. We also request that person to telephone us when the puppy has arrived safely, or to phone us if he does not arrive on schedule. If you know that the Silky has missed a connection, you can telephone the Air Freight or Air Express office at the point of transfer, to see that the puppy is all right and when he is scheduled to be put on another flight. If a transfer is required, a water bowl should be attached to the crate so that the puppy can be given water at the transfer point. Some crates have food and water hatches so that water can be given without opening the crate door. These are safest for a bitch in season, and in any event, a label on the crate should state that she should not be taken out of the crate.

We use shipping crates that are larger and heavier than our carrying cases for dog shows. They measure 24 by 18 by 16 inches and weigh 18 pounds; they are wooden crates called "small kennels" by the airline from which we bought them. We use these larger crates because I once observed helplessly as my dog in a small crate was tossed around like a basketball at a transfer point while taking him to a show, and the bigger crates are too heavy to be tossed. Others feel that a smaller crate is safer because the Silky is not as likely to be thrown forcibly against the side of the crate should it fall. Still others prefer to use the lightweight aluminum crates. This is a decision which each shipper must make for himself. Never use the cardboard or fiberboard crates for shipping, though they may be advertised as "safe for shipping." One of our bitches returning from a stud service suffered a broken rib, apparently when a heavier piece of baggage fell on the fiberboard carrier she was in.

There is no question about return of the crate when a bitch is shipped for stud service, since she will be returned to her owner in the same crate. With puppies, however, the breeder may either ship in one of his own crates, or the buyer may request that the breeder buy a crate for him from the airline. They are very reasonably priced. If the breeder's crate is to be returned, the most economical method is by interstate bus.

CHAPTER 24

Basic Training

Every dog should be taught certain basic rules of conduct. In addition to housetraining, as described in Chapter 14, he should learn to obey simple commands such as COME, NO, and BE QUIET. It is also important that your Silky learn how to walk on lead properly, whether you are training him for show or for companionable walks with you.

The successful dog trainer must possess the qualities of kindness, firmness, patience, perseverance, and consistency. Whatever word you decide to use to express each of your commands, always use the same word. Give the command sharply and distinctly but not loudly. Your Silky Terrier is by nature a responsive little dog—the quality of responsiveness is called for in the standard for the breed. He will be as intelligent as you want him to be, and will learn just about as much as you want to teach him. Your approval will be the most important thing in your Silky's life, and he will do all in his power to gain it. You must realize, however, that in order for the puppy to obey your commands, it will be necessary that you convey to him what you want him to do. Training is a repetitious process requiring constant use of the same hand and word commands. With a young puppy, training sessions should be no longer than 10 or 15 minutes daily. Longer lessons will tire him and make him balky and unresponsive. Try to get across to the puppy that training time is a "fun time" so that he will regard the procedure with enthusiasm.

It is also helpful in dog training if you will learn to move and speak slowly. If you are a naturally nervous or very quick-moving person, try to slow down when working with your puppy. Speaking softly to a puppy is also a good idea—remember that the puppy's hearing is much keener than ours, and while you should speak sharply in some commands, it is not necessary to shout. You should also be calm in dealing with puppies, since your nervousness will communicate itself to the puppy and make him nervous too.

We start teaching puppies to come as soon as they are old enough to be allowed out in the house for brief periods, usually at four to five weeks of age. As they grow and improve in their "house manners," the periods outside the pen are lengthened. At first, we let them out for a brief time just before meals, and when I have prepared their food, I say, "Babies, COME." As I put the food down in their pen, they all run through the pen door for it. Later on when each has a call name, I say, "Dolly, COME," "Andy, COME," and so on. It takes only a few repetitions of this before they are ready to respond to the COME command whether for food or simply to be petted. (It also helps the puppy to learn his name.) Always reward the puppy if he comes promptly when called. Even if he is a bit slow to come, do not punish him for his slowness. He must learn to feel that coming to you is a happy experience. Never run after any puppy that does not come to you, as this will frighten him. Instead, summon all your patience, sit down on the floor with his reward in your hand, and coax him until he does come to you. If he does not respond to this (they rarely fail to do so after a few minutes), then stand up and walk away from him. Put the reward you had offered away, and then pick him up and put him in the puppy pen without any reward.

When working with a litter of three or four puppies here, there is usually only one pup that fails to come on command and therefore must be returned to the puppy pen without any reward. The other puppies seem to communicate with the recalcitrant in some manner, as if saying that they are good and he was bad, and that particular puppy generally retreats to one corner of the pen alone for a while. Only rarely does that same puppy fail to respond to COME after that one time. This might be attributed to the writer's imagination, except that at other times, when they are returned to the pen singly without any work on commands, they do not show the same behavior pattern.

With the NO command, we also start early, by saying sharply "NO" or "Andy, NO" whenever the puppy is doing something he should not. If he does not respond immediately, we pick him up bodily and put him in a different place. It takes ten days or two weeks for them to learn that "NO" means to cease whatever they are doing. Older puppies also seem to learn this readily, and it is perhaps the most useful command, since immediate obedience can prevent their being hurt by something they were about to do.

With a puppy or puppies that are making too much noise, you should say sharply, "HUSH" or "QUIET," or whatever expression comes naturally to you. I use "KNOCK IT OFF" with our puppies and adult dogs when necessary, and they learn to respond when I am some distance away, even when they cannot see me. One young Silky fancier of my acquaintance uses the term "COOL IT" with her dogs. When such a command is given, young puppies are usually sufficiently distracted from whatever they were doing to obey immediately, but if they are not, simply walk over to the puppy and hold his mouth shut with your hands for a few seconds. In a relatively short time, even three or four littermates will respond to the "QUIET" command quickly. Of course, they do not always stay quiet for long, and they should be permitted to make a certain amount of noise when playing with each other. Nonetheless, when the noise becomes unduly loud, or it is time for them to have a nap, or you want them to calm down for any reason, they must learn to obey your command.

It is my feeling that puppies, like children, are happier for having a certain amount of discipline. Aside from the fact that training makes them nicer members of your household, and more attractive to your friends as well as yourself, the best-adjusted adult dogs are those that have had firm, fair, and consistent discipline from the time they were very small. The spoiled puppy, like the spoiled child, is usually not a happy creature; he is of no pleasure to himself or anyone else.

Our first female Silky Terrier, Ch. Alcarlou Lady Suzanne, was a born mother and a strict disciplinarian, both with her own puppies and those of our other bitches. Suzie taught *us* a great deal about training young puppies! Her method of keeping puppies from being too noisy was to put her muzzle over the puppy's muzzle, gently but firmly enough that the puppy understood her meaning. She also had a particular tone of voice with a balky puppy that had a remarkable effect on them. She used the muzzle-over-muzzle method also to teach puppies not to snap at her and not to snap too hard at each other. She allowed them a certain amount of freedom to play at fighting, but when they got to a particular point of roughness with each other, Suzie stepped in. One of the most amusing sights ever seen was when a five-month-old puppy of hers came back to visit. He had gotten his growth early and by then was slightly larger than Suzie, but when she felt he was being disrespectful, she gave him a proper lecture and had him lie down on the floor on his back so that she could check him over. Our other bitches also discipline their puppies in various ways, but none with the degree of skill that Suzie always displayed. We were fortunate to have her as our first Silky bitch.

The one form of misbehavior that should never be tolerated is snapping and trying to bite seriously. This should be differentiated from the puppy that merely puts his teeth on your hands softly as a form of affection. The puppy which snaps or bites with intent to harm any person, with no provocation, can be dealt with by putting your hands over his muzzle to keep his mouth shut for several minutes. Pulling his chin whiskers two or three time is also effective. If he persists in trying to bite, tap him sharply on top of his muzzle with two fingers. Do not use the tap on his muzzle

AM. and CAN. CH. GO GO'S LOKI OF SELECTA (Redway Selecta Robi ex. Go Go Girl of Dixie) is owned by Jon and Kay Magnussen, Kiku Kennels, and was photographed at one year of age.

except as a last resort, as this action will cause some puppies to become hand-shy and thus will affect their behavior in the show ring. A puppy or adult dog which attempts to bite the judge, of course, is inexcusable, and the judge at his discretion may order him removed from the ring.

In the case of a puppy which snaps because he is being tormented and hurt by children, the fault is with the children and they are the ones who should be corrected. We hope that no Silky Terrier puppy would ever be sold to a family with children of this type, but there are times when visiting children can be a problem. If you cannot keep such youngsters from mistreating your puppy, keep the puppy away from them at all times, as your puppy will be hurt, perhaps physically and certainly emotionally, by this sort of thing. It is also harmful to children if they are allowed to mistreat any animal, since they will grow up with the idea that cruelty to smaller creatures is permissible.

Lead training may be started at any age you wish. I know one breeder, who is now a licensed professional handler, who starts her puppies at the age of three to four weeks, as soon as they are able to move about. This would doubtless be too early for most of us, but it is a good idea to start training your puppy at least by the time he is four months old. For this training, you can use a soft leather collar, not too heavy or stiff, and a lightweight leather lead to go with it. If you prefer, you can use the small nylon show leads, but only when training inside your house or in a fenced yard, as they will occasionally slip out of these leads. To accustom the puppy to the collar and lead, or the show lead, put it on him a few times and let him drag it around. After he is used to the lead, pick it up and pull him gently in the direction you want him to go. He may balk at first, and even try to back out of the lead, but with patience, he will soon learn to come along as you direct. The very first time he does come in the direction you want him to, reward him immediately with praise and a bit of meat or other tidbit which he likes. With an especially balky puppy, I will at times resort to a bit of subterfuge. After several tries, if the pup still does not want to come in the direction I wish, I wait until he has started in whatever direction he himself chooses (keeping the end of the lead in my hand)—then I go along beside him in the direction he has decided on, but praise him and give him a tidbit after going several feet with him. After this, the puppy will generally decide it's a good idea to go your way, since you are going to reward him with that favorite treat when he does! With this one exception to get him started, however, you must make it clear to him that you are in control, and that he must do what you want him to. Train the puppy to walk on your left, the most usual position. Frequent practice sessions will be helpful, and if you make this a pleasant time for your puppy, both of you will enjoy it.

The lead training is basic, whether you plan to show your dog in conformation shows or in obedience trials, or just to have a pleasant pet. After these early lessons, the training will differ according to what you plan for your dog. Some fanciers successfully combine both conformation and obedience showing, but a basic part of obedience training is teaching the dog to sit each time you stop, and sitting will detract from the dog's performance in the conformation ring. It is probably best for the novice trainer to train first for conformation and later for obedience.

CHAPTER 25

Training the Puppy for Conformation

As the puppy begins to get accustomed to walking on lead (on your left side, remember), you should teach him to stand. Some handlers "stack" their dogs on the floor or ground. That is, they kneel down and place the dog in the position they wish him to take. With a dog as small as the Silky Terrier, however, it is infinitely better if you can teach your dog to take proper show stance by himself. The Silky which is built as he should be will naturally assume a terrier stance each time he stops, whether on lead or off, and it is only necessary for you to teach him to hold that stance. This is accomplished by walking along with the puppy on lead, and as you stop, give him the STAND command. In the beginning, he may not want to stay in this position long, but with repetition you can teach him to hold the stance. It might be necessary at first to hold him in position for a few seconds, giving the command "STAND," or "HOLD IT" as you do. Then by praising him and giving him a treat such as a dog biscuit or piece of meat, you teach him to hold the proper position for longer intervals each time. I make it a practice at home never to give our dogs a tidbit of any kind without requiring them to take the stand position. They are also required to wait their turn, with the oldest first, next oldest second, and on down the line. (All of our Silkys are house pets.) The natural tendency for any dog as small as a Silky is to stand on the hind legs for a treat, but however attractive you may find this at home, it will be detrimental to the dog in the show ring. When giving these commands, stretch out the vowel sound longer than you would in ordinary conversation. In this way, "STAND" becomes "ST-A-A-A-N-D"; "HOLD" becomes "H-O-O-O-L-D," and so on. This helps the puppy to distinguish one command from the other. At first, the puppy will not want to hold the standing position, as he would much prefer to get to the treat you have in your hand as quickly as possible. When he breaks the Stand, shake your head in negative manner and at the same time, say "NO, NO." After an interval, a few seconds at first, then longer and longer, give him the treat and say "GOOD BOY" or "GOOD GIRL" or "GOOD DOG," as you wish, to release him from the stand position. Be sure to put the tidbit down at the level of his mouth; never let him stand on his hind legs for it. As soon as he understands that he will not be given the treat unless he has held the position until released, and that he will never be given a treat while standing on his hind legs, he will perform just as you wish.

Another thing I find helpful is to talk softly to the puppy as he moves along. This seems to work especially well when moving them (or gaiting, as it is called) in the ring at shows. I know one excellent handler who says she sings very softly to her dogs as they move. I have been right next to her in the ring and never heard her, but her dogs must, as they all perform beautifully!

The most difficult thing for Silky puppies in conformation showing is usually the table examination. In all Toy breeds, the judge asks the handler to put the dog on a table in the ring so that he or she can conduct a physical examination. Many puppies have never been tabled before except at the vet's, so that they have come to associate tabling with getting shots or something equally unpleasant. If you plan to show your Silky, do by all means buy a grooming table and start working with your puppy on it at the earliest possible age. By starting when he is 8 or 9 weeks old, or as soon as you get him, and making this training pleasant for the puppy, you will have gone a long way toward removing tabling as a stumbling block. Be sure to set his front legs straight and well under the body, as called for in the breed standard. It may help in setting the front legs if you raise his rear off the table slightly as you set the front. Then pull the rear legs back into terrier stance and set them straight, at the same time checking to see that the topline is level. After he has had a number of practice sessions, get a friend to go over the puppy while he is on the table, as if your friend were the judge in a show ring. Judges usually start at the head of the dog, check the bite (and the puppy must learn to let the judge pull his upper lip up so he can see the teeth), then the front legs, shoulders, ribspring, hindquarters, and back legs. He will also check texture of coat by feeling it with his hands. With males, the judge must also feel the testicles, since a dog with one or both testicles missing is disqualified from showing under A.K.C. regulations. Male puppies which are checked while still quite young will learn to accept this examination with no difficulty, whereas a mature dog that has not been checked as a puppy may be very touchy.

It requires considerable patience to train a puppy to keep his tail up while on the table, and many judges will fault him in the show ring if he does not do so. To train for this, stand the puppy on the table for short intervals at first, and hold his tail up while you talk to him soothingly, and pet him very gently. As soon as he gets his tail up voluntarily, reward him with a treat and praise. Increase the length of time you have him stand as lessons progress, and finally, have him hold the position for some time while you give him something especially tasty, such as cooked liver. Give him four or five pieces at about 10-second intervals, or as long as he stands properly. Liver is the most frequently used treat in the show ring; you may buy it and cook it yourself, or buy it in small cans prepared for use in showing. When you buy liver (for training or show) to cook yourself, first boil it till done through, then cut it into small pieces, and bake in the oven long enough for it to be dry to handle. Do not give too much liver in one day, as it sometimes causes upset stomach and diarrhea. It you are going to travel to a series of two or more shows, it is best to buy the canned variety, so that you can open a fresh can for each show. Some exhibitors salt liver heavily for preservation when they bake it, but it does spoil pretty quickly.

In areas where conformation shows are very popular, there are often regular year-round training classes. If they are not available in your area, investigate to see if your local Kennel Club has training classes four or five weeks before their annual or semi-annual show. Many do, with members of the club there to help beginners. These classes are very beneficial for the puppy, as they get him out with other dogs. *DO NOT* take your puppy to any kind of class or show unless he has had his immunizing shots for distemper, hepatitis, and leptospirosis, as well as rabies if old enough. If you are not sure what shots the puppy has had, check with your veterinarian to determine if it is safe to take him out with a group of other dogs.

If there are puppy or all-age match shows held in your area, they will help you as well as your puppy, since you do go through the regular show procedure there, although no points are awarded toward championship The minimum age is usually set at two or three months, so they give your puppy invaluable early experience. The puppy with experience at match shows has a head start toward good showmanship when he gets to the ring at regular shows where points are awarded. At many match shows, you need not mail your puppy's entry beforehand, but can just take him to the show by a specified time and enter him then.

For information on how to enter your puppy at a point-show (he is eligible for entry at the age of 6 months), please refer to the chapter, "Your First Dog Show".

CHAPTER 26

Training for Obedience

If you prefer to work with your Silky in obedience trials, or wish to train him just to be a nicer pet, the early training will still be as outlined in the chapter, "Basic Training." In some of the larger breeds, young puppies may be started with the obedience collar and lead, but with puppies as small as Silkys it is best to introduce these after they are five or six months old.

Formal obedience training should be started when the puppy is about eight months old. Most cities of any size have training classes for this, with very reasonable fees. The classes are generally held once a week for a period of 13 weeks. In larger cities, classes may run year round; in others, there may be only two courses a year. To enroll in one of these courses, get in touch with a well-known breeder in your area for information, or write the American Kennel Club for the address of your local dog training club.

The correct collar for obedience training is called the "choke collar" or "choke chain." This is a collar of metal links or nylon with a ring at each end. It is imperative that this type of collar be put on the puppy in a certain manner, and also that it be considerably longer than necessary just to go around the puppy's neck. The tendency of pet shop employees is to sell the owner a choke collar of very small links for a Silky puppy, but it has been our experience that those with larger links do less damage to the coat on the neck. The nylon choke collars are also said to be less damaging to coat than metal links. *DO NOT ATTEMPT* to put an obedience collar on your puppy unless you understand exactly how it should be done. Preferably, have a person experienced in obedience training show you how to do this. When these collars are put on incorrectly, they can result in real harm to the puppy. Practice with the collar on your own left hand or arm till you feel you have mastered the way it should be done before you try to put it on your Silky.

We will attempt to explain how this is done, but unless you are quite sure you understand the proper procedure, *DO NOT USE* the obedience collar on your puppy.

The first step, with the leash or lead not yet attached to the collar, is to hold one of the rings in your left hand in a horizontal position. With your right hand, hold the ring on the other end of the chain portion the full length of the chain above the ring you have in your left hand. Then with your right hand still holding the ring, lower the chain portion of the collar through the ring in your left hand. Stop lowering when the right-hand ring is about an inch above the left-hand ring. Now slip two outside fingers of your left hand (still holding the ring between left thumb and forefinger) to the left and through the loop formed by the chain as it was lowered through the left-hand ring. After part of your left fingers are through the loop, release the left-hand ring and pull the collar on over your left hand, still holding the other ring securely in your right hand. *NOW TEST* several times, by pulling the right-hand ring up so the collar is tight over your left hand, then loosen it, still holding the ring. If the loop of the chain over your left hand releases itself to become slack (that is, to make a larger loop), you have the collar in correct position. Now gently slip the collar, still holding the right-hand ring, from your left hand over the puppy's head to his neck. You may now attach the lead to the right-hand ring, holding the lead near the ring you have had in your right hand. *TEST AGAIN.* You should be able to pull the lead to tighten the collar, but when you release the tension, the collar must become slack by its own weight. The ring to which the lead is fastened must go *OVER* the puppy's neck, with the other ring slipping along the linkage section over the puppy's neck. If this is reversed, with the lead fastened to the chain which goes *UNDER* the neck, you will quite literally choke the puppy. There is no sadder sight than a puppy or grown dog being dragged along on an obedience collar which is put on improperly.

Such is the importance of proper application of the obedience collar that the first lesson of an obedience course is an explanation of this procedure, along with a movie of obedience-trained dogs. (You do not take your dog to the first lesson; in the usual course of 13 lessons, the Silky will attend class during the last 12.)

The obedience courses are designed to train you to train your dog, and your part of this is vitally important. Just as in basic training, you need to be patient, firm, and consistent. Give commands clearly and firmly, but not in a loud voice. For homework, short daily sessions of 10 or 15 minutes each are better than one or two long ones.

After you have learned to put the collar and lead on the puppy correctly, you should learn the correct way to hold the lead. The dog must always be on your left side in obedience work. You hold the loop on the lead in your right hand (plus any excessive length, which may be folded over several times to shorten it). With your left hand, grasp the lead fairly close to where the collar is attached. Corrections are made with your left hand by giving a short jerk on the lead; just tighten the choke chain momentarily, then release it to be slack again. Never hold the collar tight on the dog's neck more than a moment.

A word of caution must be noted here. When you take your Silky Terrier puppy to his first training class you should avoid permitting any close contact with other dogs, especially of very large breeds, which seem unruly. Because untrained large dogs are more of a problem than untrained small dogs, there will usually be many more big dogs than small ones. If the class is sufficiently large, it may be divided in such a way that smaller breeds are together and larger ones in another class, which is best. If your class is not divided, put your Silky in the line with other small breeds, and see to it that he does not challenge other dogs to fight, as some Silkys will.

As has been noted earlier, your Silky Terrier should have had all of his inoculations for distemper, hepatitis, and leptospirosis before you take him into any group of other dogs; he should also have had his rabies shot by the time he is old enough for obedience classes. Watch to see that he does not walk in stool left by other dogs, large or small, since he can in this way pick up various kinds of worms. Also check him over for fleas as soon as you get home from any gathering of dogs.

The command used to start your dog walking beside you is "HEEL." You always use the dog's name with each action command, so that it would be "Andy, HEEL," or whatever name you have given him. As you give this command, give a short tug on the lead. You always start forward with your left foot, the dog close at your left side. If the puppy lags behind you, give a series of quick tugs on the lead with your left hand. This tightens and then releases the collar. Never tighten the collar too hard, especially in the beginning or with a young puppy, as the neck bones are tiny and you might injure him. Walk briskly and at a steady pace.

An important part of obedience training is to praise the dog each time he executes your commands as he should. Praise should be a vital part of any program of dog training. Your Silky Terrier wants above all to earn your approval, and you must let him know when he has.

The next obedience command is the "SIT." Each time you stop, give the command "Andy, SIT," and if necessary, push his hindquarters down to put him in a sitting position. He will soon learn to sit without a command each time you stop. You may also wish to train him to sit on command when not on lead, which can be accomplished by using the SIT command as you push him to a sitting position. When he is to sit, do not let him lie down or stand; insist that he take the sit position.

Next is the STAY command. You do not use the dog's name with this command, as his name should indicate to him that some action is expected. With him in the sitting position at your left side, give the command "STAY." Use the hand signal for the STAY, which is a downward movement of your hand, palm facing him, and stopping the hand just in front of his face. Gradually work with him on the STAY command until you can walk around, lead still in your hand, to a position facing him. As he progresses, you will move out the full length of the lead from him, still facing him and thus walking backwards. Later on, you will teach him to stay in position when off-lead as well.

Other commands to be learned in obedience training are the DOWN, in which the dog should lie down on the command, "Andy, DOWN." This progresses to the DOWN and STAY together, using the downsweep of your hand for the STAY command after the dog is in the down position. You will also teach him to come to the SIT position at your left side each time you give him the command, "Andy, HEEL."

The STAND command is taught in the same manner as the SIT except that instead of sitting at your left side the dog should stand. Since he has been trained to sit each time you stop, you teach him to stand by the command, "Andy, STAND", and making him understand the difference between this and taking the sitting position. At first, you will have to help by holding him under the hindquarters to keep him for sitting, since this is a change of procedure for him. After he has mastered the STAND, you can combine this also with the STAY command. You should also teach him to obey the STAY command with both your right and your left hands, using the open palm in front of his face with either hand. You will also use some command to release him from the STAY, either "O.K." or "Let's GO" combined with his name. Use whatever word you like, but always use the same one.

REMEMBER ALWAYS the importance of praising your dog when he has obeyed your commands—this is one of the finest things about obedience training, that the dogs are taught by praise and not punishment. Do not give the praise until after you have released him from whatever command you have used, of course.

If your Silky does well with his obedience course, you may wish to enter him in the Obedience Trials held under American Kennel Club regulations. There are three classes in these trials, Novice, Open, and Utility. Degrees which may be earned by your dog are the C.D., or Companion Dog; C.D.X., Companion Dog Excellent; U.D., Utility Dog; and U.D.T., Utility Dog Tracking. If interested in Obedience showing, write the American Kennel Club for their Regulations and Standards for Obedience Trials.

Dogs are scored at Obedience Trials on the basis of their own performance, rather than being rated against each other as they are in the conformation ring. To give you some idea of how the scoring is done, we will list some of them.

In Novice, they are scored as follows:

TEST	MAXIMUM SCORE (for perfect performance)
Heel on lead	35
Stand for Examination	30
Heel free—off lead	45
Recall (come on command)	30
One-minute sit (handler in ring)	30
Three-minute down (handler in ring)	30
Maximum possible score	200

Each dog earns what is called a "leg" toward his C.D. by scoring at least half the possible points for each test and a total of no less than 170 for all exercises. He must have three "legs" for the degree, which means that he must have a qualifying score in three different trials. The perfect score, of course, is 200, and trophies are usually awarded to the "Highest Scoring Dog in Trial," and other categories.

After the C.D. has been earned, the Silky may work toward his C.D.X. degree with the following tests:

TEST	MAXIMUM SCORE (for perfect performance)
Heel free	40
Drop on Recall	30
Retrieve (wooden dumbbell) on flat	25
Retrieve over obstacle (hurdle)	35
Broad jump	20
Three-minute sit (handler out of ring)	25
Five-minute down (handler out of ring)	25
Maximum score	200

The dog must qualify at three trials to earn his C.D.X.

Following this, he can go on to win the U.D., and later, the U.D.T., for tracking. In some ways, Obedience Trials are more rewarding to both dog and owner than conformation showing. While there are a few professional obedience trainers, most Silky Terriers are handled by their owners in obedience, which strengthens the relationship between dog and owner.

Also, since the dog is scored on the basis of his performance rather than his physical appearance as in conformation, every dog entered in any trial might conceivably earn a qualifying score, while in conformation there can be only a limited number of winners. There are several Silky Terriers which have earned championships in conformation and degrees in obedience, which is impressive performance for any dog, whatever his breed.

CHAPTER 27

Top Producing Sires and Dams

The true breeder finds his greatest pride and satisfaction in those of his dogs which pass along their good qualities to succeeding generations. Presented in this chapter are sires of four or more champions, and dams of three or more champions. The information shown for each producer was gathered in September 1969, so that number of champions and total of get shown are to that date, as are the show records reported. Others will qualify as Top Producers, and many of those listed will have additional offspring that will become champions, but the data as shown present an over-all picture of the Silky Terriers and the bloodlines which have shaped the breed during the first decade after A.K.C. recognition.

It is hoped that data presented will provide the novice breeder with a means of readily obtaining knowledge of important producers and bloodlines. It is also felt that experienced breeders will find the information helpful in their continuing study of bloodlines. Those who are statistically inclined will doubtless wish to calculate percentages of champion get to total offspring, evaluate the producing bloodlines in relation to their own, and so on.

The author is indebted to the owners of the Top Producers for furnishing information on their dogs and bitches, and also to Mrs. Merle E. Smith, S.T.C.A. Historian, for her valuable assistance in supplying information which was not available from owners.

Sir Winston was the first Silky to win the Iradell Trophy, awarded on the basis of breed wins, which he did for the half year of 1959 after recognition of the breed by the American Kennel Club.

Mex. Am. Ch. Coolaroo Sir Winston
Sire of 20 Champions, Grandsire of 35 Champions

Owners: Mr. and Mrs. Fred H. Stern, Silkallure Kennels
Breeder: R. J. Cooley

Whelped: 1/31/58
Total Get: 301

Parents	Grandparents	Great-grandparents
Aus. Ch. Bowenvale Murray (Import)	Gwenalre Bobbie	Aus. Ch. Rofter Texas
		Jennie
	Aus. Ch. Riawena Lindi Lou	Gwenalre Bobbie
		Levena Pixy Mason
Aus. Ch. Kelso Lady Susan (Import)	Kelso Beau Ideal	Aus. Ch. Silver Prince of Lithgow
		Aus. Ch. Sparkling Princess Armley
	Mirando of Kelso	Lucky Star of Kelso
		Lady Pam of Hillside

Ch. Redway Buster
Sire of 14 Champions

Owner: Mrs. Beverly Lehnig,
Rebel Kennels
Breeder: Mrs. Merle E. Smith

Whelped: 4/17/62
Total Got: 68

Ch. Wexford Pogo (Imp.)	Baulkham Royal John	Aus. Ch. Ellwyn Gold Prince
		Lady Patsy
	Elouera Joy	Niobe Tim
		Tecoona Tessie
Redway Smith's Gamble	Ch. Wexford Pogo (Imp.)	Baulkham Royal John
		Elouera Joy
	Brenhill Splinters (Imp.)	Prishwood Sir Teddy
		Ellwyn Lady Judy

Casanova was campaigned to a fine record of wins over a 3-year period, handled by E. R. Hastings. He compiled a total of 150 Best of Breed awards, two Toy group wins, and 36 other Group placements. He was Iradell Trophy winner for 1965, 1966, and 1967, and Top Silky Terrier, Phillips System (based on Group wins and placements), in 1967. He is pictured winning the Toy Group at the Pasadena KC show under Judge Mrs. Edith N. Hellerman, handled by Mrs. Hastings. He was the second Silky to win a group in California.

Ch. Silkallure Casanova
Sire of 14 Champions

Owners: Victor & Mona Bracco,
Casa De Casey Kennels
Breeders: Same

Whelped: 1/28/64
Total Get: 111

Parents	Grandparents	Great-grandparents
Mex. Am. Ch. Coolaroo Sir Winston	Aus. Ch. Bowenvale Murray (Imp.)	Gwenalre Bobbie
		Aus. Ch. Riawena Lindi Lou
	Aus. Ch. Kelso Lady Susan (Imp.)	Kelso Beau Ideal
		Miranda of Kelso
Bondoon's Silkie Sullivan	Aus. Ch. Prairie Playboy (Imp.)	Smithfield Max
		Prairie Gypsy
	Peteena Bonnie (Imp.)	Aus. Ch. Aldoon Pete
		Aus. Ch. Ellwyn Lady Susan

Pogo was not defeated by another Silky Terrier for 5 years in Miscellaneous classes, when two of his grandchildren finally went over him. He finished for his championship at the age of 7½ years, after the breed was recognized by A.K.C.

Ch. Wexford Pogo (Import)
Sire of 14 Champions, Grandsire of 49 Champions

Owner:	Mrs. Merle E. Smith, Redway Kennels	*Whelped:* 6/14/52
		Died: 6/9/67
Breeder:	Mrs. M. J. Brennan	*Total Get:* 108

Baulkham Royal John	Aus. Ch. Ellwyn Gold Prince	Pinto
		Ellwyn Gold Lassie
	Lady Patsy	Aus. Ch. Niobe Gloaming Boy
		Aus. Ch. Lady Molly
Elouera Joy	Niobe Tim	Aus. Ch. Newtown Hard to Beat
		Aus. Ch. Miss Lassie
	Tecoona Tessie	Aus. Ch. Niobe Boxer
		Tecoona Patsy

A daughter of Bo Bo, Ch. Midland's Jan's Wendy Anne (ex Ch. Lylac Jan) was the first Silky Terrier to win Best in Show, All Breeds, in the U.S., and Bo Bo himself was the second. He took this award at Macomb County Kennel Club in February 1968 under Judge Gordon Parham, with Mr. Cananzi handling. With a total of 152 BOB wins, he also had 59 Toy Group placings, including 6 Firsts in Group. He is pictured winning under Judge Phil Marsh, Mr. Cananzi handling.

Aus. Am. Ch. Koonoona Bo Bo (Import)

Sire of 10 American-bred Champions and of 2 Imports which became American Champions

Owner: Carmen Cananzi, Midland Kennels
Breeder: Mrs. P. Brown

Whelped: 12/28/61
Total Get: Not known

Bowenvale Midgey	Aus. Ch. Bo Bo	Gwenalre Frisky
		Gwenalre Bimbo
	Ronglyn Nell	Sparkling Royal Duke
		Sparkling Dolly
Aus. Ch. Brenhill Wee Julie	Leighvale Ricky Boy	Leighvale Cheeky Boy
		Leighvale Jess
	Ellwyn Lady Judy	Aus. Ch. Ellwyn Gold Prince
		Princess Judy

Lord Michael was handled by his owner to become the first American-bred Silky Terrier Champion on the East Coast. He was the first American-bred Silky to win BOB at the Westminster show, first American-bred sire of 10 Champions, and is the sire of the only Best-in-Show Brace in the breed.

Ch. Redway Lord Michael
Sire of 11 Champions

Owner: Mrs. Elsa Vinisko, Elmike's Kennels
Breeder: Mrs. M. E. Smith

Whelped: 5/13/57
Total Get: 73

Ch. Wexford Pogo (Imp.)	Baulkham Royal John	Aus. Ch. Ellwyn Gold Prince
		Lady Patsy
	Elouera Joy	Niobe Tim
		Tecoona Tessie
Brenhill Splinters (Imp.)	Prishwood Sir Teddy	Denny Boy
		Tiny Sonji
	Ellwyn Lady Judy	Aus. Ch. Ellwyn Gold Prince
		Princess Judy

Kirby was one of the top winners in the breed, as well as being a Top Producer. During his show career, he had 15 Toy Group placements, including two firsts, and a total of 87 BOB wins. He won the Iradell Trophy in 1963 and 1964, and was second for Phillips System for 1964, missing first by only one point.

Ch. Austral Prince Kirby
Sire of 10 Champions

Owner: Miss Mildred Pequignot, Austral Kennels
Breeder: Same

Whelped: 6/25/59
Total Get: 52

Ch. Sarszegi Buttons	Sarszegi Silver Prince (Imp.)	Roscarberry Bunny Roscarberry Peggy
	Roscarberry Sabrina (Imp.)	Roscarberry Wee Kim Bowenvale Noni
Ch. Rebel Countess Myd	D'Under Count Chequers	Redway Lord Teasel San Gate Lady Crumpets
	Ch. Aldoon Countess Candy (Imp.)	Glenboig Tim Aldoon Lassie

Ch. Clavons Blue Rain
Sire of 10 Champions

Owners: Mr. & Mrs. James Young, Jr.,
Larrakin Kennels (Reg.)
Breeder: Miss Nettie Simmons,
Clavons Kennels (Reg.)

Whelped: 8/26/59
Total Get: 68

Parents	Grandparents	Great-grandparents
Ch. Redway Beau Brummell	Ch. Wexford Pogo (Imp.)	Baulkham Royal John
		Elouera Joy
	Brenhill Splinters (Imp.)	Prishwood Sir Teddy
		Ellwyn Lady Judy
Kanimbla Lady Penelope	Kanimbla Sir Potch	Wee Waa Aussie (Imp.)
		Kanimbla Tinker
	Kanimbla Fatima	Kanimbla Little Boy
		Kanimbla Millicent

Rexandy is shown here with handler Daisy Austad and Judge Miss Iris de la Torre Bueno.

Ch. Silkallure Rexandy
Sire of 9 Champions

Owners: Fred Stern & L. J. Pilley, Silkallure Kennels	*Whelped:* 5/10/64
Breeders: Fred & Susan H. Stern	*Total Get:* 180

Parents	Grandparents	Great-grandparents
Mex. Am. Ch. Coolaroo Sir Winston	Aus. Ch. Bowenvale Murray (Imp.)	Gwenalre Bobbie
		Aus. Ch. Riawena Lindi Lou
	Aus. Ch. Kelso Lady Susan (Imp.)	Kelso Beau Ideal
		Miranda of Kelso
Ch. Silkallure Rexanne	Aus. Ch. Bowenvale Sir Rex (Imp.)	Aus. Ch. Bowenvale Billy
		Bowenvale Beauty
	Ch. Bowenvale Margie (Imp.)	Aus. Ch. Bowenvale Sir Rex
		Mammon Princess Dawn

In addition to the distinction of being a dual champion, with both Obedience and Conformation titles, Maverick scored the very first owner-handled Toy Group placing in California.

Ch. Fair Dinkum Maverick, C.D.
Sire of 8 Champions

Owner:	Richard G. La Barre, Mavrob Kennels	*Whelped:* 1/15/59
		Total Get: 190
Breeders:	Mr. & Mrs. Roy Tindall	

Ch. Koolamina Aussie (Imp.)	Prairie Possom	Prairie Nipper
		Fairy Floss
	Aus. Ch. Kendoral Sybil	Bobby Sparks
		Aus. Ch. Blue La Petite Patti
Elysium Matilda (Imp.)	Greengarth Prince	Stroud John James
		Gymea Silver Dollar
	Aldoon Penny	Aus. Ch. Aldoon Prince
		Ellwyn Marigold

Ch. Koolamina Aussie (Import)
Sire of 5 Champions

Owner: Mrs. Lucille Preston, Fair Dinkum Kennels
Breeder: H. W. Patterson

Whelped: 4/9/55
Died: 2/7/66
Total Get: 58

Parents	Grandparents	Great-grandparents
Prairie Possum	Prairie Nipper	Prairie Peter
		Prairie Lucy
	Fairy Floss	Digger Gold
		Boronia Flossy
Aus. Ch. Kendoral Sybil	Bobby Sparks	Prince Harrie of Low Veine
		Princess Peggy
	Aus. Ch. Blue La Petite Patti	Blue Laddie
		Blue Goldie

This Silky was winner of every Miscellaneous Class in which he was shown. His picture above was used by the American Kennel Club to illustrate the breed when recognition was gained in 1959.

Ch. Delalor Banjo Bluespec of Iradell (Import)

Sire of 4 Champions

Owner: Mrs. N. Clarkson Earl, Jr., Iradell Kennels
Breeder: Mrs. N. Delaney

Whelped: 11/12/54
Died: 1963
Total Get: 36

Comiston Bluespec Nicky	Sparkling Tiny Bluespec	Aus. Ch. Sparkling Armley Bluespec
		Sparkling Bronze Beauty
	Kara Kara Nicolette	Tobias of Deandale
		Elizabeth of Deandale
Delalor Mitzi Maid	Rosanna Monty	Rosanna Spec
		Miss Sydney
	Meden Dale Nola Anne	Kia Ora Tom Thumb
		Maid Marion of Kelso

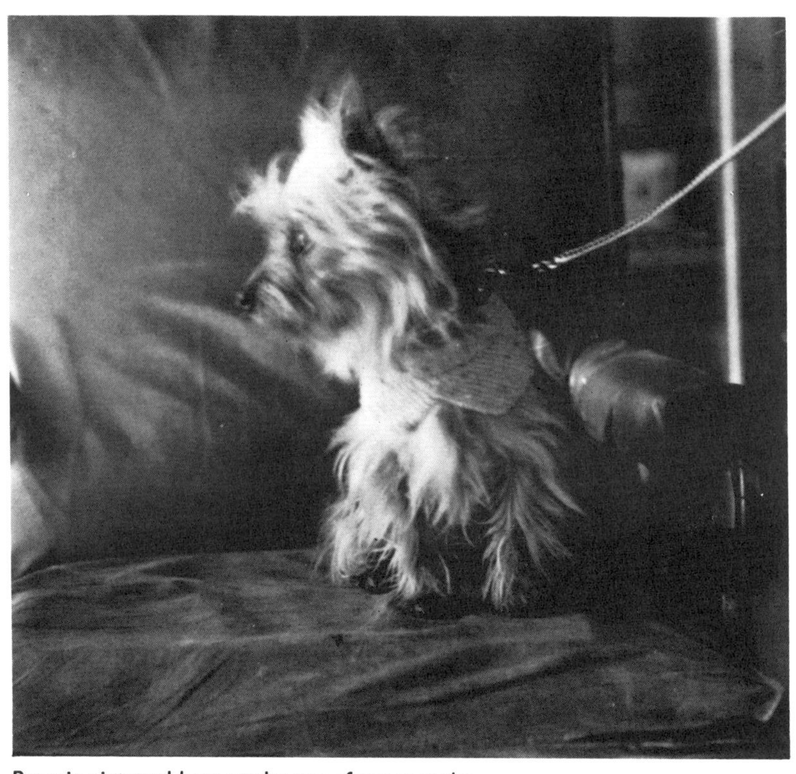

Beau is pictured here at the age of ten months.

Ch. Redway Beau Brummell
Sire of 4 Champions

Owners: Mrs. Phyllis Buchanan and Miss Suzanne Richardson, Buchrich Kennels	*Whelped:* 5/26/55
Breeder: Mrs. Merle E. Smith	*Died:* 5/26/69
	Total Get: 43

Ch. Wexford Pogo (Imp.)	Baulkham Royal John	Aus. Ch. Ellwyn Gold Prince
		Lady Patsy
	Elouera Joy	Niobe Tim
		Tecoona Tessie
Brenhill Splinters (Imp.)	Prishwood Sir Teddy	Denny Boy
		Tiny Sonji
	Ellwyn Lady Judy	Aus. Ch. Ellwyn Gold Prince
		Princess Judy

Can. Am. Ch. Ellwyn Prince Tuffy (Import)
Sire of 8 Champions

Owner: Carmen Cananzi, Midland Kennels
Breeder: R. O'Gregor

Whelped: 5/29/54
Died: 5/3/67
Total Get: Unknown

Ellwyn Golden Don	Little Gem of Jewels	Glitter of Jewels
		Twinkle of Jewels
	Ellwyn Gold Betty	Aus. Ch. Ellwyn Gold Prince
		Ellwyn Gold Winsome
Princess Vicki	Aus. Ch. Prince Peter	Aus. Ch. Newtown Hard to Beat
		Niobe Tess
	Wendy	Peter Pan
		Princess Donna

Ch. Sarszegi Buttons
Sire of 5 Champions

Owner: Miss Mildred Pequignot, Austral Kennels
Breeder: Erica Baan

Whelped: 1/24/57
Total Get: 43

Sarszegi Silver Prince (Imp.)	Roscarberry Bunny	Bambi of Rosanna
		Wee Silver Bell of Lithgow
	Roscarberry Peggy	Roscarberry Wee Kim
		Walywee Peggy
Roscarberry Sabrina (Imp.)	Roscarberry Wee Kim	Bambi of Rosanna
		Wildflower Yvonne
	Bowenvale Noni	Langbrae Jim
		Sparkling Madonna Bluespec

D'Under Count Chequers
Sire of 4 Champions

Owners: Mr. & Mrs. Wm. Lehnig, Rebel Kennels
Breeder: Howard A. Jensen, D'Under Kennels

Whelped: 12/17/55
Died: 9/2/68
Total Get: 14

Redway Lord Teasel	Ch. Wexford Pogo (Imp.)	Baulkham Royal John
		Elouera Joy
	Brenhill Splinters (Imp.)	Prishwood Sir Teddy
		Ellwyn Lady Judy
San Gate Lady Crumpets	Redway Splinters' Boy	Ch. Wexford Pogo (Imp.)
		Brenhill Splinters (Imp.)
	Greenhills Lady Moppet	Venetia Teddy Boy
		Greenhills Matilda

Galvin's Squire Bedivere

Sire of 4 Champions

Owner: Mrs. William Galvin — *Whelped:* 6/19/61
Breeder: Same — *Total Get:* Not reported

Parent	Grandparent	Great-grandparent
Rebel Pal Joey	D'Under Count Chequers	Redway Lord Teasel
		San Gate Lady Crumpets
	Ch. Aldoon Countess Candy (Imp.)	Glenboig Tim
		Aldoon Lassie
Mara's Josephine	D'Under Count Chequers	Redway Lord Teasel
		San Gate Lady Crumpets
	Ella Princess Victoria	Pearl City Duke
		Pearl City Miss Jones II

Maryanne Sir Charles

Sire of 4 Champions

Owners: Mrs. Jim Young & W. D. Campbell
Larrakin Kennels (Reg.) — *Whelped:* 12/7/61
Breeder: Mrs. Waldo E. Seagly — *Total Get:* 15

Parent	Grandparent	Great-grandparent
Ch. Austral Prince Kirby	Ch. Sarszegi Buttons	Sarszegi Silver Prince (Imp.)
		Roscarberry Sabrina (Imp.)
	Ch. Rebel Countess Myd	D'Under Count Chequers
		Ch. Aldoon Countess Candy (Imp.)
Ch. Aldoon Tinkerbelle (Imp.)	Aus. Ch. Aldoon Sivam	Vernena Mickey
		Aldoon Susie
	Aldoon Lassie	Aus. Ch. Aldoon Prince
		Eckral Lady Myrtle

Ch. Rebel Razzle Dazzle

Sire of 4 Champions

Owners: Beverly Lehnig & Betty Receveur,
Rebel Kennels — *Whelped:* 1/25/62
Breeder: W. G. Lehnig — *Total Get:* 19

Parent	Grandparent	Great-grandparent
Aldoon Skipper (Imp.)	Aus. Ch. Aldoon Sivam	Vernena Mickey
		Aldoon Susie
	Aldoon Lassie	Aus. Ch. Aldoon Prince
		Eckral Lady Myrtle
Ch. Aldoon Countess Candy (Imp.)	Glenboig Tim (Imp.)	Aus. Ch. Ellwyn Gold Gem
		Ellwyn Diana
	Aldoon Lassie	Aus. Ch. Aldoon Prince
		Eckral Lady Myrtle

Lady Marrie has the top number of champion offspring of any Silky Terrier bitch in the U.S. She also had a very successful show career, placing in a number of Toy Groups, and winning the Iradell Trophy based on breed wins for the year of 1962. She is pictured above winning BOB under Judge A. J. Brueneman at the Dayton, Ohio show on April 13, 1962. She is handled by Mrs. Sadie Thorn.

Ch. Aldoon Lady Marrie (Import)
Dam of 8 Champions

Owner: Miss Mildred Pequignot, Austral Kennels
Breeder: Mrs. J. Milne

Whelped: 7/20/60
Total Get: 31

Aus. Ch. Aldoon Sivam	Vernena Mickey	Aus. Ch. Tibet Radiant Flash
		Tibet Whispering Hope
	Aldoon Susie	Winsome Beau Ideal
		Aus. Ch. Aldoon Trixie
Aldoon Lassie	Aus. Ch. Aldoon Prince	Aus. Ch. Ellwyn Gold Cobby
		Aldoon Betsy
	Eckral Lady Myrtle	Daniel
		Eckral Lady Bobs

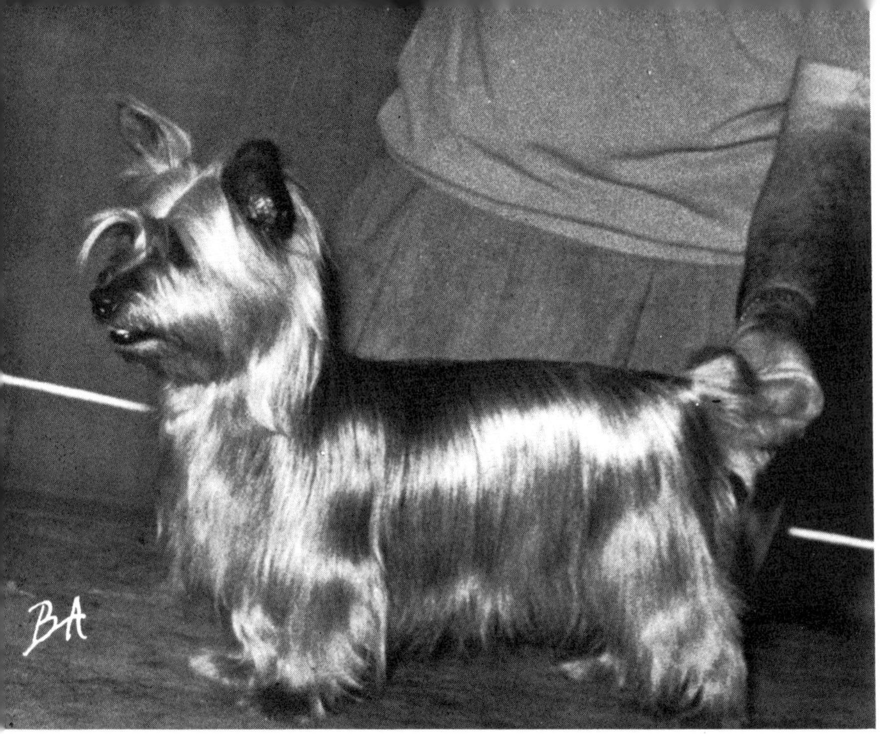

Two of Margie's seven champion offspring are considered Australian-bred, as she was in whelp when imported by the Sterns. She is not only a top producer, she was Best Opposite Sex at the first three STCA Specialties in California in 1961, 1962, and 1963. She was also the first Silky to place in the Toy Group in California.

Ch. Bowenvale Margie (Import)
Dam of 7 Champions

Owners: Mr. and Mrs. Fred H. Stern, Silkallure Kennels
Breeder: Eric Fellows

Whelped: 1/6/60
Total Get: 22

Parents	Grandparents	Great-grandparents
Aus. Ch. Bowenvale Sir Rex	Aus. Ch. Bowenvale Billy	Langbrae Jim
		Aus. Ch. Bowenvale Minnie
	Bowenvale Beauty	Gwenalre Bobbie
		Terry's Gift
Mammon Princess Dawn	Winn Echo Danny	Aus. Ch. Sparkling Armley Jr.
		Roma of Tibet
	Titch Ray	Clar Reynold
		Sparkling Dusky Princess

Jan had a number of BOB wins and several Group placings. She is pictured above in her fine win of Best Opposite Sex at the 1966 STCA Specialty under Judge Forest Hall. Her handler here is one of Mr. Cananzi's daughters.

Ch. Lylac Jan (Import)
Dam of 7 Champions

Owner: Carmen Cananzi, Midland Kennels
Breeder: Mrs. N. E. Glynn

Whelped: 6/29/62
Total Get: —

Leroy Misty	Aus. Ch. Hatfield Master Rex	Aus. Ch. Bowenvale Prince Robbie
		Vanesta Petit Cherie
	Lylac Rhonda	Aus. Ch. Miami Gold Flash
		Prairie Dorothy
Aldoon Wendy Anne	Aus. Ch. Aldoon Prince	Aus. Ch. Ellwyn Gold Cobby
		Aldoon Betty
	Glenboig Jean	Aus. Ch. Ellwyn Gold Gem
		Eckral Lady Jean

Bondoon's Silkie Sullivan
Dam of 6 Champions

Owners: Mr. and Mrs. Victor Bracco, Casa de Casey Kennels
Breeder: Mrs. K. A. Walkey

Whelped: 6/4/60
Total Get: 21

Aus. Ch. Prairie Playboy (Imp.)	Smithfield Max	Prairie Cloud
		Tibet Margo
	Prairie Gipsy	Boronia Rex
		Prairie Neddle
Peteena Bonnie (Imp.)	Aus. Ch. Aldoon Pete	Aus. Ch. Aldoon Prince
		Ellwyn Sally
	Aus. Ch. Ellwyn Lady Susan	Robert Beau
		Araluen Vanda

This lovely bitch is pictured when almost 11 years of age! *Fifteen get have been produced under Mrs. Hively's QUEEN'S OWN banner; Matilda also had one or two litters while owned by Mrs. Marion Shaw.

Mad Manor Matilda
Dam of 6 Champions

Owner: Mrs. Alice B. Hively,
Queen's Own Kennels
Breeders: Mr. and Mrs. J. C. Morrison

Whelped: 10/28/58
Total Get: 15*

Parents	Grandparents	Great-grandparents
Redway Senor Willie	Ch. Wexford Pogo (Imp.)	Baulkham Royal John
		Elouera Joy
	Brenhill Splinters (Imp.)	Prishwood Sir Teddy
		Ellwyn Lady Judy
Mad Manor Cindy	Redway Senor Willie	Ch. Wexford Pogo (Imp.)
		Brenhill Splinters (Imp.)
	Rofter Susie (Imp.)	Rofter Danny Boy
		Deandale Yvonne

Ch. Elmike's Lady Elsa
Dam of 5 Champions

Owner: Mrs. Elsa Vinisko,
Elmike's Kennels
Breeder: Same

Whelped: 6/29/59
Total Get: 20

Ch. Redway Lord Michael	Ch. Wexford Pogo (Imp.)	Baulkham Royal John
		Elouera Joy
	Brenhill Splinters (Imp.)	Prishwood Sir Teddy
		Ellwyn Lady Judy
Tee Pee Little Susie	Stroud Lewis Carroll (Imp.)	Stroud John Henry
		Stroud Kay Leigh Piper
	Stroud Patricia Piper (Imp.)	Aus. Ch. Stroud John Willie
		Stroud Kiera Piper

In addition to qualifying as a Top Producer, Bonnie was also the very first Silky Terrier bitch to win Best of Breed at a national STCA Specialty, which she accomplished in 1967. She was owner-handled to all of her wins.

Ch. Redway Bonnie Lass
Dam of 5 Champions

Owners: Mr. and Mrs. James Young, Jr., Larrakin Kennels (Reg.)
Breeder: Miss Marjorie Smith

Whelped: 2/7/62
Total Get: 12

Ch. Wexford Pogo (Imp.)	Baulkham Royal John	Aus. Ch. Ellwyn Gold Prince
		Lady Patsy
	Elouera Joy	Niobe Tim
		Tecoona Tessie
Redway Rebecca	Redway Senor Willie	Ch. Wexford Pogo (Imp.)
		Brenhill Splinters (Imp.)
	Maurie Lady Lilli	Ch. Wexford Pogo (Imp.)
		Mitry Lady Mandy

This bitch had a very successful show career, with a number of the earlier placings in the Toy Group in the Northeast. Her first litter of three puppies (sired by Ch. Redway Lord Michael) became the first all-champion litter in the breed. A daughter from this litter produced the second all-champion litter of Silky Terriers.

Ch. Shaw's Sapphire
Dam of 5 Champions

Owner: Mrs. Edna Ackerman, Ackline Kennels (Reg.)
Breeder: Marion Shaw

Whelped: 11/14/59
Total Get: 18

Milan Iradell Major (Imp.)	Aus. Ch. Emeraldale Timothy	Emeraldale Danny Aus. Ch. Riverview Megsy
	Milan Margo	Tamworth Drum Major Winn Echo Peggy
Mad Manor Matilda	Redway Senor Willie	Ch. Wexford Pogo (Imp.) Brenhill Splinters (Imp.)
	Mad Manor Cindy	Redway Senor Willie Rofter Susie (Imp.)

*Although Rexanne was whelped in this country, she is considered an Australian-bred Silky, her dam having been imported in whelp.

Ch. Silkallure Rexanne (Import*)
Dam of 5 Champions

Owners: Mr. and Mrs. Fred H. Stern, Silkallure Kennels
Breeder: Eric Fellows

Whelped: 12/26/60
Total Get: 13

Parents	Grandparents	Great-grandparents
Aus. Ch. Bowenvale Sir Rex	Aus. Ch. Bowenvale Billy	Langbrae Jim
		Aus. Ch. Bowenvale Minnie
	Bowenvale Beauty	Gwenalre Bobbie
		Terry's Gift
Ch. Bowenvale Margie (Imp.)	Aus. Ch. Bowenvale Sir Rex	Aus. Ch. Bowenvale Billy
		Bowenvale Beauty
	Mammon Princess Dawn	Winn Echo Danny
		Titch Ray

Suzie was the author's first foundation bitch. She was entirely owner-handled to her championship, which she gained very quickly, never being defeated in her sex. She was named for her breeder, Miss Suzanne Link of New Orleans.

Ch. Alcarlou Lady Suzanne
Dam of 4 Champions

Owners: Mr. and Mrs. James Young, Jr., Larrakin Kennels (Reg.)
Breeder: Miss Suzanne J. Link

Whelped: 6/21/60
Total Get: 14

Parents	Grandparents	Great-grandparents
Mad Manor Tiny Tim	Redway Senor Willie	Ch. Wexford Pogo (Imp.)
		Brenhill Splinters (Imp.)
	Rofter Susie (Imp.)	Rofter Danny Boy
		Deandale Yvonne
Alcarlou Lady Kate	Mad Manor Tiny Tim	Redway Senor Willie
		Rofter Susie (Imp.)
	Kanimbla Lady Jennifer	Kanimbla Sir Potch
		Kanimbla Susan II

This nice imported bitch was owner-handled to a fine win of Best Opposite Sex at the 1965 STCA Specialty under Judge Percy Roberts, held with the Chicago International show. This historic Specialty was the first to be held outside of California.

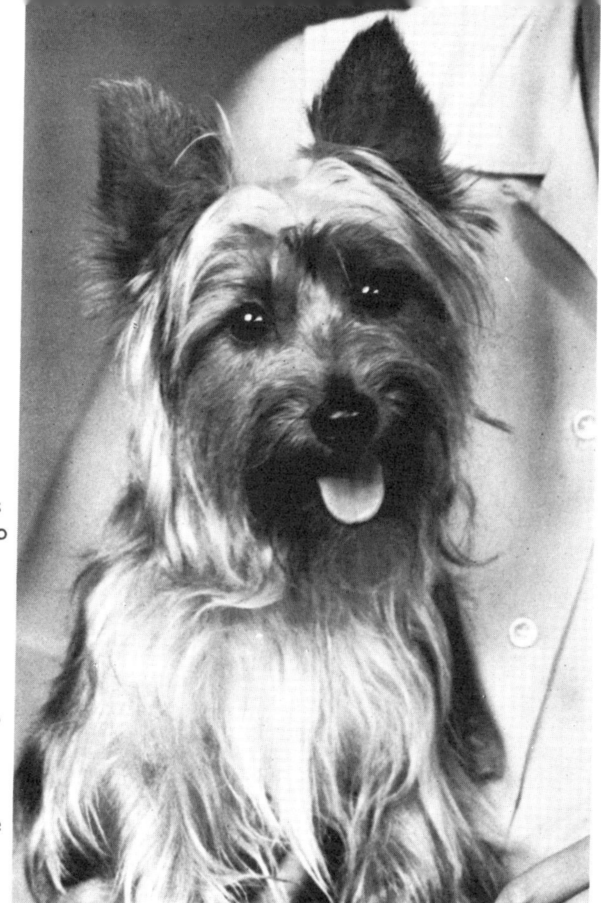

Ch. Aldoon Bonnie Lass (Import)
Dam of 4 Champions

Owner: Mrs. Donald Receveur, Dixie Kennels	*Whelped:* 7/20/60
Breeder: Mrs. J. Milne	*Died:* 7/31/68
	Total Get. 26

Aus. Ch. Aldoon Sivam	Vernena Mickey	Aus. Ch. Tibet Radiant Flash
		Tibet Whispering Hope
	Aldoon Susie	Winsome Beau Ideal
		Aus. Ch. Aldoon Trixie
Aldoon Lassie	Aus. Ch. Aldoon Prince	Aus. Ch. Ellwyn Gold Cobby
		Aldoon Betsy
	Eckral Lady Myrtle	Daniel
		Eckral Lady Bobs

Ch. Queen's Own Blue Coral
Dam of 4 Champions

Owners: Earl D. and Ida M. Edge, Damae Kennels
Breeder: Mrs. Alice B. Hively

Whelped: 1/8/64
Total Get: 13

Galvin's Squire Bedivere	Rebel Pal Joey	D'Under Count Chequers
		Ch. Aldoon Countess Candy (Imp.)
	Mara's Josephine	D'Under Count Chequers
		Ella Princess Victoria
Mad Manor Matilda	Redway Senor Willie	Ch. Wexford Pogo (Imp.)
		Brenhill Splinters (Imp.)
	Mad Manor Cindy	Redway Senor Willie
		Rofter Susie (Imp.)

This bitch had the honor of winning Best of Breed under Judge Percy Roberts at the first Westminster Kennel Club show at which Silkys were shown as a separate breed. She was owner-handled to this fine win by Beverly Lehnig, which is pictured above.

Ch. Aldoon Countess Candy (Import)
Dam of 4 Champions

Owners: Mr. and Mrs. Wm. Lehnig, Rebel Kennels	*Whelped:* 12/11/55
	Died: 6/17/67
Breeder: Mrs. J. Milne	*Total Get:* 19

Glenboig Tim	Aus. Ch. Ellwyn Gold Gem	Kiwi Buddi
		Wee Patsy
	Ellwyn Diana	Winsome Beau Ideal
		Ellwyn Gold Pixie
Aldoon Lassie	Aus. Ch. Aldoon Prince	Aus. Ch. Ellwyn Gold Cobby
		Aldoon Betsy
	Eckral Lady Myrtle	Daniel
		Eckral Lady Bobs

Brenhill Splinters (Import)
Dam of 4 Champions, Granddam of 20 Champions

Owner:	Mrs. Merle E. Smith, Redway Kennels	*Whelped:* 4/21/51
		Died: 6/22/65
Breeder:	Mrs. M. J. Brennan	*Total Get:* 21

Parents	Grandparents	Great-grandparents
Prishwood Sir Teddy	Denny Boy	Araluen Winky
		Aus. Ch. Miss Dolly
	Tiny Sonji	Kenwyn
		Sonji
Ellwyn Lady Judy	Aus. Ch. Ellwyn Gold Prince	Pinto
		Ellwyn Gold Lassie
	Princess Judy	Daniel
		Eckral Lady Jean

Rozalind was owner-handled to Winners Bitch (5 points) at the 1965 STCA Specialty held with Chicago International Kennel Club in 1965, under Judge Percy Roberts.

Ch. Redway Rebel Rozalind
Dam of 4 Champions

Owners: Robert and Edna H. Davis, Soblu Kennels
Breeders: Mrs. Merle E. Smith and Mrs. Wm. Lehnig

Whelped: 1/11/62
Total Get: 12

Aldoon Skipper (Imp.)	Aus. Ch. Aldoon Sivam	Vernena Mickey
		Aldoon Susie
	Aldoon Lassie	Aus. Ch. Aldoon Prince
		Eckral Lady Myrtle
Ch. Milan Redway Rebel (Imp.)	Aus. Ch. Milan Tony	Aus. Ch. Emeraldale Timothy
		Blue Susan
	Milan Julie Anne	Aus. Ch. Emeraldale Timothy
		Milan Lindy Lou

Ch. Kanimbla's Mildura Belle
Dam of 3 Champions

Owners: Colonel Joe and Mary E. Pavlas, Bondi Kennels
Breeders: Mr. and Mrs. Geoffrey Sutcliffe, Kanimbla Kennels

Whelped: 10/10/62
Total Get: Not reported

Zelma Caribou Kelly	Calamondah Sir Sam (Imp.)	Aldington Blue Tim
		Newfarm Blue Judy
	Mabrouka Lady Cleo (Imp.)	Stroud John James
		Miami Trixie
Kanimbla Wee Cootamundra	Kanimbla Sir Potch	Wee Waa Aussie (Imp.)
		Kanimbla Tinker
	Kanimbla Corio Bell	Kanimbla Corio Chief
		Kanimbla Melissa

This lovely little bitch won her first points toward her championship by taking Winners Bitch at the 1962 STCA Specialty under Judge Percy Roberts. She went on to win her points to finish, owner-handled, at the 1963 STCA Specialty under Judge Louis Murr.

Ch. Mavrob Dorable
Dam of 3 Champions

Owners: Mr. and Mrs. R. G. La Barre, Mavrob Kennels
Breeders: Same

Whelped: 10/4/61
Total Get: 2 litters

Ch. Koolamina Aussie (Imp.)	Prairie Possom	Prairie Nipper
		Fairy Floss
	Aus. Ch. Kendoral Sybil	Bobby Sparks
		Aus. Ch. Blue La Petite Patti
Redway Fair Dinkum Rob	Ch. Wexford Pogo (Imp.)	Baulkham Royal John
		Elouera Joy
	Ch. Kendoral Robyn (Imp.)	Kendoral Pancho
		Aus. Ch. Blue La Petite Patti

Butibel is pictured above with ten-month-old puppies from her first litter. All three became Champions. Left to right, they are Butibel with owner Joanne Leonard, Casa de Casey Diamond Jim with Jim Leonard; Casa de Casey My Guy with owner Anne Edgar; and Casa de Casey Waltzing Matilda with Peter Edgar. Sire of the litter was Ch. Silkallure Casanova.

Laurosa Star Butibel (Import)
Dam of 3 Champions

Owners: Mrs. Joanne Leonard
Breeder: L. M. Kane

Whelped: 9/15/65
Total Get: 11

Tamworth Inky	Aus. Ch. Tamworth Indigo	Rofter Beau Dandy
		Trixie Gem of Tamworth
	Tamworth Cindy	Bouden Blue Firefly
		Tamworth Dark Moon
Bayuda Gay Lady	Perrywinkle Nicky	Shelomi Lad
		Cindie Lea
	Yooralla Pinky	Aus. Ch. Milan Tony
		Lauranita Gay Bronwyn

This nice imported bitch is pictured above in a win under Judge J. J. Duncan; she is held by William Lehnig, who handled her in the ring.

Ch. Milan Redway Rebel (Import)
Dam of 3 Champions

Owners: Mrs. Merle E. Smith and Mrs. William Lehnig, Rebel Kennels
Breeders. Mr. and Mrs. A. G. V. Miles

Whelped: 8/18/60
Total Get: 14

Aus. Ch. Milan Tony	Aus. Ch. Emeraldale Timothy	Emeraldale Danny Boy
		Aus. Ch. Riverview Megsy
	Blue Susan	Aus. Ch. Milan Blue Bandit
		Mount Isa Silver Sue
Milan Julie Anne	Aus. Ch. Emeraldale Timothy	Emeraldale Danny Boy
		Aus. Ch. Riverview Megsy
	Milan Lindy Lou	Rosanna Monty
		Silver Susie

Night Mist of the Valley
Dam of 3 Champions

Owner: Miss Grace E. Dietz
Breeders: Lea and Marvin Zamba

Whelped: 11/7/64
Total Get: 13

Ch. Coolaroo Sir Winston	Aus. Ch. Bowenvale Murray (Imp.)	Gwenalre Bobbie Aus. Ch. Riawena Lindi Lou
	Aus. Ch. Kelso Lady Susan (Imp.)	Kelso Beau Ideal Miranda of Kelso
Coolaroo Silver Sheba	Ch. Coolaroo Silkallure Rex (Imp.)	Aus. Ch. Bowenvale Sir Rex Ch. Bowenvale Margie (Imp.)
	Minxie Roo Coolaroo	Aus. Ch. Prairie Playboy (Imp.) Pixie Roo Coolaroo

Bumblebee is pictured winning BOB at Western Reserve Kennel Club show under Judge Lee Murray. She is handled by her owner, Judy Pesa.

Ch. Bumblebee of Iradell (Import)
Dam of 3 Champions

Owner: Mrs. Judith C. Pesa, Mill Creek Kennels
Breeder: Mrs. Consuela V. Earl

Whelped: 2/6/64
Total Get: 12

Aus. Ch. Milan Tony	Aus. Ch. Emeraldale Timothy	Emeraldale Danny Boy
		Aus. Ch. Riverview Megsy
	Blue Susan	Aus. Ch. Milan Blue Bandit
		Mount Isa Silver Sue
Ch. Milan Susanna of Iradell (Imp.)	Milan Peter Pan	Aus. Ch. Milan Tony
		Milan Julie Anne
	Blue Susan	Aus. Ch. Milan Blue Bandit
		Mount Isa Silver Sue

This bitch is the dam of Ch. Hargill's Jolly Jamboree (by Ch. Wilhaven's Wee Sweet William), bred and owned by Miss Harriett Gill; he is the only Silky Terrier with two all-breed Best In Show wins to his credit. She is pictured above in a win under Judge Joseph Faigel, with owner-handler Harriett Gill.

Ch. Rebel Dancing Angel
Dam of 3 Champions

Owner: Miss Harriett Gill, Hargill Kennels
Breeder: Mrs. Wm. Lehnig

Whelped: 6/21/64
Total Get: 11

Parents	Grandparents	Great-grandparents
Ch. Redway Buster	Ch. Wexford Pogo (Imp.)	Baulkham Royal John
		Elouera Joy
	Redway Smith's Gamble	Ch. Wexford Pogo (Imp.)
		Brenhill Splinters (Imp.)
Rebel April Angel	Aldoon Skipper (Imp.)	Aus. Ch. Aldoon Sivam
		Aldoon Lassie
	Millburn Tiger	Ch. Redway Lord Michael
		Millburn May Lady

Rebel April Angel

Dam of 4 Champions

Owner: Mrs. Wm. Lehnig, Rebel Kennels
Breeders: Dr. and Mrs. Milton Comer

Whelped: 4/28/63
Total Get: 15

Parents	Grandparents	Great-grandparents
Aldoon Skipper (Imp.)	Aus. Ch. Aldoon Sivam	Vernena Mickey
		Aldoon Susie
	Aldoon Lassie	Aus. Ch. Aldoon Prince
		Eckral Lady Myrtle
Millburn Tiger	Ch. Redway Lord Michael	Ch. Wexford Pogo (Imp.)
		Brenhill Splinters (Imp.)
	Millburn May Lady	Ch. Redway Beau Brummell
		Peteena Iradell Wattle (Imp.)

Ch. Ackline's Joy of Sapphire

Dam of 3 Champions

Owner: Mrs. Judith C. Pesa, Mill Creek Kennels
Breeder: Mrs. Edna F. Ackerman

Whelped: 1/26/62
Total Get: 3

Parents	Grandparents	Great-grandparents
Ch. Redway Lord Michael	Ch. Wexford Pogo (Imp.)	Baulkham Royal John
		Elouera Joy
	Brenhill Splinters (Imp.)	Prishwood Sir Teddy
		Ellwyn Lady Judy
Ch. Shaw's Sapphire	Milan Iradell Major (Imp.)	Aus. Ch. Emeraldale Timothy
		Milan Margo
	Mad Manor Matilda	Redway Senor Willie
		Mad Manor Cindy

Redway Blue Bet

Dam of 3 Champions

Owner: Miss Nettie H. Simmons, Clavons Kennels (Reg.)
Breeder: Mrs. Merle E. Smith

Whelped: 6/25/59
Total Get: 15

Parents	Grandparents	Great-grandparents
Ch. Wexford Pogo (Imp.)	Baulkham Royal John	Aus. Ch. Ellwyn Gold Prince
		Lady Patsy
	Elouera Joy	Niobe Tim
		Tecoona Tessie
Redway Smith's Gamble	Ch. Wexford Pogo (Imp.)	Baulkham Royal John
		Elouera Joy
	Brenhill Splinters (Imp.)	Prishwood Sir Teddy
		Ellwyn Lady Judy

Glossary

ALLELE, ALLELOMORPH—One of a pair of genes on homologous chromosome, inherited alternately with the other member of the pair.

ALLELE, MULTIPLE—A series of genes at the same locus on the chromosome which cause gradations of expression of certain characteristics; only two members of the series may be present in any one animal.

CELL—The unit of living tissue.

CHROMATID—The half-chromosome resulting from division of chromosomes during sex-cell division.

CHROMOSOME—Microscopic bodies within the cells on which the genes are carried.

DOMINANT—That which suppresses the action of the other member of the pair.

EPISTASIS, EPISTATIC—The masking of the effect of another gene, said of genes not members of the same pair. A kind of dominance which occurs between different gene pairs. Opposite of hypostatis.

GAMETE—The reproductive cells, sperm in the male and ovum in the female.

GENE—The unit of heredity.

GENOTYPE—The genetic make-up of an animal; the pattern of genes carried by each individual.

HETEROZYGOUS—Impure, mixed. Said of the gene pair containing one dominant and one recessive gene.

HOMOLOGOUS—Corresponding in structure, position, and origin.

HOMOZYGOUS—Pure, not mixed. Said of gene pairs containing like genes.

HYPOSTASIS, HYPOSTATIC—The masking of a gene, said of genes which are not members of the same pair. Opposite of Epistasis. A kind of recessive which occurs between different gene pairs.

LINKAGE—The tendency of genes on the same chromosome to inherit as a unit.

LOCUS, LOCI—The location of a gene on its chromosome.

MEIOSIS—The cell division which occurs in the formation of gametes.

MITOSIS—The cell division which occurs in the formation of somatic (body) cells.

PHENOTYPE—Physical appearance. Outward manifestation resulting from genetic make-up.

RECESSIVE—The member of a gene pair whose action is suppressed by the dominant member of the gene pair.

ZYGOTE—The rudimentary cell formed by the union of the male and female gametes.

GENERAL INDEX

INDEX OF DOGS

(Illustrated Silkys appear where page numbers are in boldface; their complete pedigrees, pages 256-293, are not indexed.)